Between Left and Right

I am grateful to Jeffrey J. Anderson, Tina Ruby and Lauren Covert
from Georgetown University's BMW Center for German and
European Studies. I would also like to thank the IASGP Bundestag
election trip—as well as my father for his constant support.
The cover illustration, "Angie" was provided by Christopher Jones,
Signale - Büro für Kommunikation, Berlin, Germany www.signale.com.

● ● ● ● ● ● ● ● ● ● ● ● ● ● ● ●

$\mathcal{B}$ETWEEN LEFT AND RIGHT

• • • • • • • • • • • • • •

The 2009 Bundestag Elections and the Transformation of the Germany Party System

edited by

Eric Langenbacher

Berghahn Books
New York • Oxford

Published in 2010 by
Berghahn Books

www.berghahnbooks.com

©2010 Berghahn Books

Library of Congress Cataloging-in-Publication Data

Between left and right : the 2009 Bundestag elections and the transformation
of the Germany party system / edited by Eric Langenbacher.
   p. cm.
Includes bibliographical references and index.
ISBN 978-0-85745-222-1 (pbk. : alk. paper)
1. Germany. Bundestag--Elections, 2009. 2. Elections--Germany. 3. Political parties--Germany. 4. Germany--Politics and government--1990- I. Langenbacher, Eric.
 JN3971.A95B485 2010
 324.943'0883--dc22

                                                            2010048784

British Library Cataloguing in Publication Data

A catalogue record for this book is available from the British Library

Printed in the United States on acid-free paper

ISBN: 978-0-85745-222-1

$\mathscr{C}$ONTENTS

• • • • • • • • • • • • • •

$\mathscr{I}$NTRODUCTION

$\bullet \bullet \bullet \bullet \bullet \bullet \bullet \bullet \bullet \bullet \bullet \bullet \bullet \bullet$

Eric Langenbacher

"Like a City Council Race in Würzburg"

This volume analyzes the issues at play in and the consequences of the 2009 elections for the German lower house of parliament, the Bundestag. The results of this electoral contest are especially important because in the sixty years of the Federal Republic of Germany, there have never been such dire economic circumstances and thus an urgent need for robust public policy responses.[1] Nevertheless, the 27 September 2009 elections were surprisingly undramatic with the campaign widely considered to be "vapid," "uninspiring," "dull," and boring.[2] *New York Times* columnist Roger Cohen even opined that it was like watching a city council race in Würzburg.[3]

With the exception of a brief incident concerning a minister's use of official cars for private purposes, there were no scandals.[4] At times, it seemed that the most contention was generated by provocative campaign posters–like Christian Democrat Vera Lengsfeld's cleavage-revealing poster with the words "Wir haben mehr zu bieten" (we have more to offer) or a local Green party's "Der einzige Grund, Schwarz zu wählen" (the only reason to vote black [the traditional color of conservatives]) superimposed on an image of a white woman embracing a naked African woman.[5] There were no gaffes, major mistakes, or statements "taken out of context"–similar to the controversial neoliberal economic positions such as the flat tax espoused by Paul Kirchhof that had reduced support for the Christian Democratic Union (CDU) in 2005.[6] There was bickering within the center-right camp as victory looked likely–especially among Bavaria's Christian Social Union (CSU) and Free Democratic Party (FDP) over personnel decisions in a new government, the Liberals' strategy to maximize second votes by encouraging vote splitting, or how appropriate tax cuts were in the middle of a recession–harbingers for post-election tensions, but not worthy of many headlines at the time.

Unlike previous election years, little attention was generated by earlier contests. 2009 was another *Superwahljahr* with elections for six Landtage (Schleswig-Holstein was unexpected), the European Parliament, and the German Presidency—as always, interpreted as bellwethers for the Bundestag. But, there were no major surprises and the outcomes did not affect the federal campaign. CDU-backed President Horst Köhler was re-elected easily for a second term on 23 May. In June, the CDU/CSU won 37.9 percent of the vote for the European Parliament with the Social Democratic Party (SPD) at a dismal 20 percent, but these results are unreliable indicators for national races. Besides, only 43.3 percent of the German electorate actually bothered to vote.[7] More important were the elections in three Länder on 30 August, but even these had only marginal national impact. The CDU lost over 10 percent of the vote in Thuringia and Saarland, but still remained the largest party and senior coalition partner. There were also unique dynamics affecting these two small, unrepresentative Länder (there are more people in Berlin than in these states combined), including the scandal over Thuringian CDU Minister President Dieter Althaus, who was charged with negligent homicide after killing a woman while skiing in January 2009.[8] In Saxony, the Christian Democrats lost less than 1 percent compared to their 2004 score and the Social Democrats even gained 0.6 percent.[9] Perhaps the most drama occurred in Hesse where a second election in twelve months returned Roland Koch and the CDU to power with 37.4 percent of the vote in January. The SPD lost over 13 percent to score a measly 23.7 percent and the Liberals increased their share of the vote to 16.2 percent. Although a realistic premonition of the eventual Bundestag results, the impact of this election was muted due to the specifics of the state's year-long political impasse and the nine months in between the two contests.

Existential issues or major policy differences were remarkably absent from the campaign despite several portentous moments. In early September, for example, the Bundeswehr ordered an airstrike near Kunduz, Afghanistan that unexpectedly killed dozens of civilians.[10] In light of the substantial opposition to the deployment—a June 2009 poll found 49 percent of Germans disapproving (45 percent approving) the mission[11]—such a policy disaster could have dominated the campaign. Instead, all of the parties (except for the Left Party) downplayed the civilian casualties and successfully postponed a reckoning until after the election (which eventually led to governmental instability in the last months of 2009 and to the resignation of several officials, including Franz Josef Jung, who was Defense Minister at the time of the airstrike).[12] Economic issues—precarious public finances, bailouts for banks and industries (e.g., Opel), the necessity of reducing spending, even the FDP-pushed tax cuts—were also de-emphasized. Indeed, many previously divisive policies—nuclear power, energy supplies, subsidies for eastern Germany, the Hartz IV reforms, the European Union, and immigration/ integration—were largely ignored.

The last few days of the campaign were slightly more exciting. There was speculation that the predicted CDU/CSU-FDP majority would result artificially, and, thus with reduced legitimacy, from a technicality of the electoral laws—the overhanging mandates (*Überhangmandate*).[13] The predicted increase to perhaps 30 percent of the electorate that would split their choices between the first, constituency vote and the second, party list vote, as well as the large number of individuals who made their decisions at the last minute (over 50 percent, see David P. Conradt in this volume), generated uncertainty—especially regarding the degree to which the three smaller parties would benefit. Indeed, Angela Merkel was so worried about her hold on the chancellorship being jeopardized by such electoral behavior that she spent considerable time during her last campaign rally pleading for second votes.

But, in the end, the election played out as expected and with absolute efficiency. The first prognoses came in around 6:00 PM (when polls closed) and there were surprisingly few changes to the numbers over the course of the night. By 8:00 PM, the election was called and the losers accepted defeat. At 8:15 PM the major party leaders met on the televised "Berliner Runde," engaged in a quick postmortem, and looked ahead to forming new government and opposition blocs. By 11:00 PM the celebrations (or wakes) were petering out. By the next morning, the posters were coming down and it was almost as if the election had not happened.

The CDU/CSU remained the largest party and Merkel retained her office in a planned coalition with the FDP (overhanging mandates did not affect the majority). The new government received 48.4 percent of the vote (versus 45.6 percent for the three leftist parties) but 53.4 percent (332 out of 622) of the seats. Despite the frenzied speculation about more exotic coalition options—"Jamaica" (CDU/CSU-FDP-Greens) or "traffic light" (SPD-FDP-Greens)—the result was exactly the same "bourgeois" constellation that had governed together from 1949-1957, 1961-66, and 1982-1998. Once again, there was only a partial change in the governing parties—the only complete partisan alteration in power over the sixty years of the Federal Republic happened in 1998—and hence a high degree of policy and personnel continuity. Indeed, seven of sixteen cabinet members have held portfolios in both governments.[14] Unlike 2005 or 2002, the pollsters were much better at predicting the results (even if support for the CDU/CSU and the SPD was overestimated by several percentage points in most prognoses).

Naturally, the final results did generate a few headlines. Although long predicted, the apocalyptic result for the Social Democratic Party at 23 percent of the popular vote and 146 seats (having lost 10 million votes since 1998, depending on how you count, the worst result since 1949, or perhaps 1893) was still shocking.[15] So too was the strong performance of the Left Party, gaining 11.9 percent of the vote (seventy-six seats) even outperforming the Greens, which garnered a respectable 10.7 percent (sixty-eight seats). These outcomes are, of course, related, with many leftist voters disaffected by the SPD's move to the center (especially at the ministerial level) over their eleven years in power. The Social Democrats' exposed left flank was exploited effectively by the Left Party–and to a lesser extent by the Greens. The FDP had its best showing ever at 14.6 percent of the vote (ninety-three seats)–mainly because many southern conservatives gave their second vote to the Liberals. As a result, the FDP had much more influence in the eventual coalition negotiations–receiving five of sixteen cabinet positions (31.25 percent compared to their 28 percent share of the majority's seats). The CDU/CSU did a little worse that predicted–and at just under 33.8 percent of the vote also experienced its worst showing since 1949. This, however, was due largely to the poor result for the CSU in Bavaria–its 42 percent was yet another in a string of recent electoral disappointments.[16] The 2 percent won by the Pirate Party– advocating on-line freedom and less censorship, which resonated especially with younger, male voters–surprised many and may auger the rise of new protest parties. Finally, right radical parties once again did poorly. The NPD with 1.5 percent of the second vote, the Republikaner with 0.4 percent, and the DVU with 0.1 percent fell considerably short of the required 5 percent electoral threshold.

The two *Volksparteien* continued to witness marked declines in support to the extent that many analysts have proclaimed their demise as true catch-all parties. The three smaller parties increased their appeal (combined 37.2 percent of the vote and 237 or 38.1 percent of the seats). The number of effective parties (based on seats) increased to 3.97 (from 2.80 after 2002 and 3.44 after 2005), moving the party system closing to the multiparty type.[17] We may very well be witnessing the emergence of a 5-party system in Germany–with all of the complications that this entails (more unwieldy, less ideologically cohesive, and more unstable coalition governments). Electoral volatility also increased to 12.69 percent (up from 7.97 percent in 2002 and 10.60 in 2005), which is more than the long-term European average of a little less than 9 percent (although volatility increased across the region after the end of the Cold War).[18] Obviously, the legendary, hyper-stable party preferences of the old Federal Republic have given way to a floating electorate–indeed, as few as 25 percent of voters can be considered *Stammwähler* (core voters) today. Electoral turnout declined to a postwar low of 70.8 percent (down from 79.1 in 2002 and 77.7 in 2005). These trends are not troubling in the context of Germany's stable democracy and are certainly quite comparable to other continental political systems, but one would hope that the increases in both the effective number of parties and volatility will settle down and that turnout will increase.

"Merkel is the Message"[19]

Barring some unexpected catastrophe, it was never likely that Merkel was going to lose, given her status as the most prominent and powerful politician in Germany. There are three main reasons for Merkel's stature in 2009. First, she had been extremely visible in foreign affairs, over-shadowing her ministers, especially SPD vice-chancellor and foreign min-ister Frank-Walter Steinmeier, and was widely perceived as having increased Germany's prestige in the international arena. Notable successes were the European Union Presidency in 2007 (which paved the way for the Lisbon Treaty that was ratified in late 2009), the G8 summit held in Heiligendamm in June 2007, and the successful hosting of the World Cup of soccer in summer 2006. She improved relations considerably with the Bush Administration (although there has been a degree of dis-tance with President Barack Obama, despite his high favorability ratings in Germany), maintained a productive cordiality with Russia, fostered closer ties with Poland (even with the prickly Kaczynski twins), and, despite rumors of a mutual personal dislike, has worked intensively with President Nicholas Sarkozy in France. Merkel has struck a balance be-tween the older reflexively multilateral tendencies that muted national interest and a new assertiveness–at times even unilateralism (e.g., May 2010 ban on "naked" short selling of stocks). Conventional wisdom is that over her tenure, especially after the financial crisis hit, power has shifted considerably towards Berlin: "… the eurozone crisis has exposed the cold reality that Germany is the power in Europe that counts the most. Top brass in Brussels, or Paris can talk as much as they like. But until Ms. Merkel agrees, nothing happens."[20] This new leadership role has resonated with German voters, who appear less averse than previ-ously to professions of national pride.[21]

Second, Merkel's economic management had been widely praised. This was already true before the economic crisis–although she had inherited a booming economy (profitable companies, export world champion, low unemployment, decent public finances) generated mainly by the neoliberal reforms (Hartz IV, Agenda 2010) of the out-going Red-Green government and the generally prudent fiscal management of SPD Finance Minister Hans Eichel (1999-2005). Her post-crisis economic management (at least before the election), was even more lauded. The economic situation in 2008-2009 was terrible. Export-dependent Germany had a deeper contraction in output than most others with the exception of those countries that had a property market bubble like Ireland or the UK and/or high levels of external debt like Greece or Spain. GDP contracted by 6.9 percent in the first quarter of 2009 and overall the economy contracted by about 5 percent over the year.[22] Unemployment started to creep up and was just over 8 percent at the time of the election. Looming bankruptcies at big employers like Opel, Hertie, Woolworth, and Arcandor (owner of the Karstadt department store chain)–and problems in many banks such as WestLB, HypoReal, and IKB Deutsche Industriebank (and which led to a big public bailout in December 2008) were real causes of Angst. In fact, it was the most severe economic downturn since World War II.

As a response to these troubles, the stimulus packages passed in late 2008 and early 2009–about 3.4 percent of 2008 GDP, dwarfing French and British efforts[23]–appeared to work. In fact, a July 2009 study from the Boston Consulting Group concluded that the German stimulus was the most successful in international comparison.[24] Particularly the "cash-for-clunkers" (*Abwrackprämie*) program, subsequently much copied in the U.S. and elsewhere, boosted consumption and helped the struggling auto industry. Public subsidies to businesses incentivizing them not to lay off or fire workers, but rather to reduce and ration hours, did much to maintain employment levels. Government guarantees for General Motor's Opel subsidiary–highly controversial and ultimately without effect–did at least buy enough time for the company to recover on its own (also thanks to U.S. taxpayer support for the parent company). Merkel's Grand Coalition staved off the worst and voters were justifiably grateful.

Despite these efforts, the German government was criticized vociferously for not doing more. Influential American economist and columnist Paul Krugman, among others, lambasted the Grand Coalition's overly timid and presumably short-sighted response.[25] The Chancellor's unwillingness to support greater domestic and European Union (EU) stimulus spending or bailout packages for several struggling East European countries such as Hungary earned her the derisive nickname "Madame Non" in France and elsewhere[26]–but praise at home from weary taxpayers. Rhetorically, Merkel was adept at initially blaming the global downturn on the Anglo-American neoliberal model (even though German banks were deeply implicated). This may have tapped latent but widespread anti-Americanism, thereby relegitimizing *Modell Deutschland* or Rhineland capitalism, the core component of German national sentiment.

Luck or at least good timing may also have played a role in her re-election success. By the high summer of 2009, when the election campaign geared up, the economic situation began to improve. The U.S. economy and stock markets stabilized, while China and much of the developing world were back to high growth rates. The unemployment rate did not increase substantially; business confidence, manufacturing and exports started to recover. Even the heavily-hit car makers were returning to full production and the economy started to grow again by the third quarter. The negative consequences of all of the stimulus spending–budgetary, inflationary, and fiscal challenges–were put off successfully until after the election. This is not even to mention the still-festering structural issues that will have to be confronted–labor market rigidities, over-reliance on exports (and the concomitant weakness of domestic consumption), bureaucratic hindrances to starting new firms, seemingly uncontrollable healthcare spending. Nevertheless, these downsides were repressed during the campaign.

Third, even though many analysts (including several of the authors in this volume) believe that the Grand Coalition put off major, needed policy reforms, leading to a worrying backlog, I think that the first Merkel government pushed though more than is often realized–not even discounting for the constant crisis mode that was unavoidable after 2008. At the least, many of the reform initiatives of previous governments were continued with on-going performance improvement–in education and welfare for example.[27] Public finances were put on a sounder footing, especially after the increase in the Value Added Tax in 2007.

Other policy areas witnessed new initiatives–especially efforts to reach out to immigrants (with Merkel's various integration summits).[28] Like most other European countries, there are still major challenges in this area in light of the close to 20 percent of the population that currently has a *Migrationshintergrund* (migration background)[29] and disparities between this segment of the population and others. In terms of parliamentary representation, for example, the sixteenth Bundestag (2005-2009) had eleven members with such a background (1.80 percent of the 612 members), a total that increased to twenty for the current seventeenth Bundestag (3.20 percent of the 622 members). In both cases, the "people's house" comes nowhere near representing the characteristics of almost a fifth of the German population—a segment that is now probably larger than the population of the old East Germany.[30] Politicians like current Green co-leader Cem Özdemir (Turkish ancestry) and Minister of Health Philipp Rösler (born in Vietnam, adopted as an infant) may pave the way for future changes. In any case, the political scene contrasts markedly with the national soccer team (third, again, in the 2010 World Cup) where ten out of twenty-three on the 2010 roster (43.5 percent) had a migration background.[31]

Most importantly, Merkel's influence on the status of women in Germany cannot be underestimated. She is indeed a "Superfrau," the 1985 hit by East German rocker Petra Zieger that was played at the CDU rally on the Saturday before the election.[32] From a policy perspective she and Minister of Families, Senior Citizens and Youth Ursula von der Leyen pushed through a major increase in state payments to families, an increase of childcare places, and more generous parental leave.[33] More generally, her chancellorship long has been interpreted as a considerable advance for German women in politics, and she has indeed been ranked by *Forbes* to be the most powerful woman in the world since 2006.[34] There is already evidence that her example may be helping other women. Andrea Nahles (SPD General Secretary since 2009), Renate Künast (Green Parliamentary Caucus leader), Gesine Lötzsch and Petra Pau (Left Party leaders) are all major political figures today—continuing in the shoes of pioneers like Annemarie Renger (President of the Bundestag 1972-1979 and SPD candidate for the federal presidency in 1979), Petra Kelly (Greens), Rita Süssmuth (CDU President of the Bundestag 1988-1998) and Gesine Schwan (SPD candidate for the federal presidency in 2004 and 2009). In addition to the powerful female ministers at the federal level (six/sixteen in the current cabinet), women have also been making progress at the state level becoming Minister Presidents—Christine Lieberknecht (CDU, Thuringia since 2009), Hannelore Kraft (SPD, North Rhine Westphalia since 2010), on the shoulders of the very first Heide Simonis (SPD Schleswig Holstein, 1993-2005).[35] Germany is one of the best performers on the World Economic Forum's Gender Gap Index—twelfth in 2009, albeit slipping from fifth in 2006.[36] This score is based on the low 32.8 percent share of women Bundestag deputies—a share that has stagnated since 1998 (31.6, 32.5 and 31.8 percent in the last three Bundestag legislative periods).[37]

One might also mention that there have been two homosexual male state chiefs (Ole von Beust in Hamburg from 2001-2010 and Klaus Wowereit in Berlin since 2001), as well as the current Foreign Minister, Vice

Chancellor and FDP leader Guido Westerwelle. Considering also Minister Presidents David McAllister (with a British father in Lower Saxony since 2010) and Stanislaw Tillich (Sorbian ancestry in Saxony since 2008), almost one-third of the minister presidents are not the archetypical straight ethnically German male. Thus, Merkel represents and has presided over the continued transformation of a "new" postmodern, postnational, and more equitable Germany. Her governing record, popularity, and symbolic importance made the election result almost a foregone conclusion and hence the campaign rather inconsequential. Even U.S. President Obama predicted an easy victory for her in July.[38]

Merkel was responsible for the unexciting campaign in other ways. She was never a charismatic campaigner like her predecessor Gerhard Schröder, or even Helmut Kohl in his own avuncular manner. In fact, it is pretty obvious that she dislikes campaigning–her political skills lie elsewhere in her aforementioned managerial prowess and especially in her ability to work effectively (and often ruthlessly) behind the scenes. One should not forget the brilliant machinations that led her to outmaneuver Wolfgang Schäuble (and Kohl) to become CDU party leader in 2000–or her success in sidelining intraparty rivals like Friedrich Merz, Edmund Stoiber, Koch, and most recently, Christian Wulff. By the summer of 2010 the media was even lamenting the lack of party counterweights.[39] Moreover, Merkel effectively managed the campaign, clearly intending to keep controversial issues out of the discussion or putting off unpopular policy decisions until after the election. In an almost presidential style, she was able to appear above the fray, letting ministers do the dirty work, while taking credit for the Grand Coalition's policy successes. Merkel was also able to box in the Social Democrats so that they could not repudiate their own governing record. Such strategic and tactical success speaks to her pronounced skills behind-the-scenes.

Merkel was not the only contributor to the campaign's charisma deficit. There were few other visible faces on the Union side, although von der Leyen and young CSU minister Karl-Theodor zu Guttenberg have generated some enthusiasm.[40] SPD chancellor candidate Frank-Walter Steinmeier–not coincidentally Chief of Schröder's Chancellory (1999-2005)–equally lacked charisma and is, at base, a technocrat. Westerwelle has flashes of charm, but also a testiness that puts many off. For example, just a few days after the election he caused a stir by refusing to answer a BBC reporter's question posed in English.[41] The Green candidates (Renate Künast and Jürgen Trittin) were nondescript and the only real charisma was to be found in the anachronistic Left Party (which campaigned on "tax the rich" and "wealth for everyone") and their leadership duo of Gregor Gysi and Oskar Lafontaine (who resigned all posts three months after the election in any case due to a cancer diagnosis).

The specific structural circumstances of the 2009 political environment also affected the tone of the campaign. Merkel was forced into a grand coalition after the shocking 2005 outcome (unforeseen by pollsters) in which the SPD did much better than predicted because of Merkel's campaign style, her attempt to pursue a stridently neoliberal platform that scared away many voters, middling results for the FDP, and the political genius of Schröder, who ably exploited every misstep. This led to four years of moderate, lowest common denominator policy in many areas. Merkel had to run on this record in 2009 and was not going to go in a militant neoliberal direction after being burned in 2005. The SPD also had to run on this legacy—and had seven previous years of policy making to justify as well. More importantly, it was not always clear that the desired majority for CDU/CSU and FDP would materialize, perhaps necessitating a continuation of the Grand Coalition (which many believed was preferred by Merkel, considered by many to be a social democrat in sheep's clothing).[42] Thus, both *Volksparteien* needed to mute their attacks on the other because they could very well have had to govern together again. Mention should also be made of the camaraderie among Merkel and the SPD ministers—especially Steinmeier and Finance Minister Peer Steinbrück, both of whom Merkel seemed to genuinely like (more so than many in her own party).

The Contributions

This volume[43] delves much deeper than these political dramas "ripped from the headlines." Bringing together academics from the United States, United Kingdom, Canada, and Germany, the authors analyze the structural dynamics and longer-term consequences surrounding this fateful election. Some of the major questions addressed include: how successful was Merkel's leadership of the Grand Coalition and what does her new partnership with the Free Democrats auger? In the face of economic crisis, why did German voters empower a center-right market-liberal coalition and re-elect one of the incumbent parties that had presided over the recession? Why did the SPD, one of the oldest and most distinguished parties in the world self-destruct and what are the chances that it will recover? Going beyond the contemporary situation, however, the chapters analyze the long-term decline of the catch-all parties, structural changes in the party system leading to the emergence of a five-party system, electoral behavior, the evolution of perceptions of gender in campaigns, and the use of new social media in German politics.

Clay Clemens leads off with a retrospective analysis of the Grand Coalition. He argues that contrary to many common expectations for an oversized coalition, Merkel's 2005-2009 CDU/CSU-SPD government produced few major policy changes. Its modest output is generally attributed to polarized competition between two co-equal, longtime rivals that blocked cooperation. Yet, interparty gridlock was less decisive than intra-party paralysis. Indeed, the CDU, CSU, and SPD coalesced when each was plagued by internal divisions over programmatic identity, fueled in turn by interrelated strategic and leadership struggles. The result was caution, confusion, patchwork measures, side payments, and reversals.

Moving to detailed analyses of the election itself, David Conradt notes that while the 2009 election resulted in a familiar governing coalition, the longer-term dealignment of the party system continued. Support for the once-major parties dropped to historic lows as did turnout. This chapter delves into the factors underlying this dealignment process. In addition to familiar demand-side variables—social structure, values, and interests—particular attention is given to the supply side of the dealignment equation: the role of the parties, their leaders, strategies, and policies. The consequences of these changes for the future of the party and political system are then discussed in a comparative context.

Steven Weldon and Andrea Nüsser echo these conclusions. Although characterized by widespread public apathy and record low voter turnout, the 2009 Bundestag election solidified a stable, but fluid five-party system that will likely be a defining feature of German political life for the next generation. The three minor parties each achieved historical bests at the polls with steep losses for the two traditional *Volksparteien.* Drawing mainly on data from the German Longitudinal Electoral Study (GLES), this chapter examines the nature of this new five party system with a closer look at each party's voters in the 2009 election. The analysis shows the breadth and stability of the five-party system—each party draws significant support across all sixteen Länder; and, despite a growing number of swing voters, each party has a core group of committed voters that alone exceeds the 5 percent national electoral threshold. The authors also find evidence that the increased volatility and fluidity of the party system is structured along the left-right ideological spectrum with the parties divided into two major camps and vote-switching much more likely within the respective camps rather than between them.

Next, William E. Paterson and James Sloam focus explicitly on the dramatic collapse of the venerable Social Democratic Party. Indeed, the 2009 electoral debacle led some commentators to speculate about the end of the SPD as a "catch-all party" and–given the recent poor performance of center-left parties across Europe–"the end of social democracy." This chapter contextualizes the result of the 2009 Bundestag election within the settings of German party politics and, more comparatively, of European social democracy. The authors show how the electoral disaster for the SPD can be explained by broad, long-term political developments. Nevertheless, the defeat in 2009 provides an opportunity for renewal at a time when the governing Conservative-Liberal coalition (in disarray for most of the year after the election) must take some tough decisions with regard to the resource crunch in German public finances and on-going instabilities in the Eurozone.

The next three chapters focus more specifically on coalitional dynamics both before and after the 2009 election. Thomas Saalfeld notes that an interesting puzzle arises through a comparison of the 2005-2009 cabinet Merkel I (the "Grand" Coalition) and the Christian Democrat-Liberal coalition cabinet Merkel II formed in 2009. Political commentators and coalition theorists alike would have expected the CDU/CSU-SPD coalition to experience a relatively high, and the CDU/CSU-FDP coalition a relatively low level of overt inter-party conflict. In reality, however, relations in the CDU/CSU-FDP coalition were relatively conflictive, whereas the Grand Coalition seemed to manage disagreements between reluctant partners successfully. This chapter seeks to explain these seemingly paradoxical differences between the two coalitions. It demonstrates that both the positioning of the coalition parties in the policy space and important institutions constraining coalition bargaining after the formation of the cabinet Merkel II (portfolio allocation, role of the CDU/CSU state minister presidents) disadvantaged the FDP in pursuing its key policy goals (especially tax reform). As a result, the Liberals resorted to "noisy" tactics in the public sphere. The Grand Coalition, by contrast, was an alliance of co-equals, which facilitated a more consensual management of inter-party conflict.

Frank Decker and Jared Sonnicksen observe that the election warrants structural consideration for a number of reasons, not the least of which is that the results are indicative of several trends developing since unification and that will continue to play an important, if not ever increasing role in German politics. These developments include the intensifying fragmentation of the German party system and German voters' growing electoral volatility, both of which are hampering the parties' ability to form government coalitions. In this chapter, they distill five fundamental aspects of the election. Building upon this analysis, they explore their meaning as well as potential impact on the German party system and partisan competition, as well as coalition patterns. At the same time, the authors address the overarching question of whether–and if so, to what extent–German politics is experiencing a trend toward bipolarity between a center-right and center-left camp and whether such an antagonistic model will be a passing phase or is indicative of a more established five-party system in Germany.

Charles Lees draws upon the formal coalition literature in political science to demonstrate that party system change over the last thirty years means that the *Volksparteien* enjoy more coalition options and greater ideological leverage within coalitions that form than was the case in the past. The Free Democrats have lost their kingmaker status and the distribution of party weights over recent elections allows no other small party to act in this manner. By contrast, the numerical and ideological resources possessed by the two *Volksparteien* means that they remain the only parties within the German party system that can act as *formateur* in the coalition game and are less vulnerable to threats of a decisive defection by small parties to alternative coalitions than they were in the past.

Louise K. Davidson-Schmich delves into the topic of gender quota compliance. Her chapter examines the candidates for the 2009 Bundestag election and asks three questions. First, did German political parties comply with their voluntarily adopted gender quotas for their electoral lists–both in terms of the numbers of women nominated and their placement on the party list? Second, did parties without gender quotas place female candidates in promising list places? In other words, did quotas exert a "contagion effect" and spur political groups without quotas to promote women's political careers? Third, what propensity did all parties have to nominate female candidates for direct mandate seats? Did the quotas used for the second vote have a spillover effect onto the first vote, improving women's odds of being nominated for constituency seats? She finds that while the German parties generally complied with the gender quotas for their electoral lists, these quotas have had only limited contagion effects on other parties and on the plurality half of the ballot. Gender quotas in their current form have reached their limits in increasing women's representation to the Bundestag. To achieve gender parity, a change in candidate selection procedures, especially for direct mandates, would be required.

Next, Hartwig Pautz analyzes the impact of new technologies on political participation and turnout. He starts his chapter by observing a crisis in Germany's parliamentary democracy: the major parties' membership is in decline and barely existing in East Germany, election turnout is decreasing at all levels, and the reputation of politicians has never been worse. At the same time, however, Germans are more interested in politics than in the 1990s, overwhelmingly support democracy, and are keen on participating particularly in local political decision making. Out of this situation emerged www.abgeordnetenwatch.de–a website that aims to re-establish the link between electors and elected by allowing voters and representatives to communicate via a publicly accessible question-and-answer structure. Pautz addresses the questions of whether such an instrument can revitalize representative democracy and whether it did so in the context of the 2009 federal elections.

The volume concludes with Jan Techau's chapter on foreign policy. He argues that foreign policy issues did not play a decisive role in the general election campaign. While Merkel conducted a decidedly presidential campaign, her main rival, Frank-Walter Steinmeier, found it difficult to break out of his role as Merkel's partner in the Grand Coalition that the two had led for four years. This was especially true with respect to issues on foreign policy, where both candidates had cooperated rather smoothly. Neither the issue of Afghanistan (despite the hotly debated Kunduz airstrike), nor the unresolved issues of the future of the European Union's Lisbon Treaty could antagonize the main political protagonists in Germany. The overwhelming foreign policy consensus among the mainstream political forces remained intact. Nevertheless, the changing international landscape and increased German responsibilities abroad will turn foreign policy into a relevant campaign issue, probably as early as the next election in 2013.

"Iron Lady Angela Merkel Vanishes amid Troubles at Home and Abroad"[44]

During the campaign, the conventional wisdom was that divisive policy decisions, as well as inter and intraparty tensions would emerge only after the election.[45] Rarely has conventional wisdom been so true. If the campaign was likened to a small Bavarian city council race, the post election period is more like politics in Italy, South Carolina, or Chicago.

One of the first major developments was the expected blood-letting within the SPD. In November 2009, the party repudiated the centrists (like Franz Müntefering) who were ascendant since 1998 and selected a new, younger leadership team: Sigmar Gabriel (Lower Saxon Minister President from 1999-2003 and federal Environment Minister from 2005-2009) as

Party Chair, Andrea Nahles (a left-wing leader) as General Secretary, and Steinmeier as leader of the Bundestag caucus.[46] The new leadership troika is stressing a more traditional left-wing course–supporting minimum wages and opposing a return to nuclear power for instance–as well as "new left" forms of deliberative and direct democracy. Moreover, they have relentlessly and effectively attacked the Black-Yellow government–stating that the first hundred days encompassed "clientelistic politics for hoteliers, heirs (*Erben*), tax consultants, speculators, pharmacists (*Apotheker*), the pharmaceutical industry, and the atomic power lobby."[47] Given the instability of the party leadership over the last decade, it will be vital for the party's future success that this team and its more left-wing course remain in power for some time. Interestingly, despite the severity of the 2009 electoral defeat, the SPD appears to have recovered by mid-2010. It did well in the important regional election in populous North Rhine Westphalia in May (eventually leading a minority coalition) and by July 2010 hovered around 28 percent in national polls.[48]

Overall, the left has increased its level of support in the year since the election. There were many voices who thought that the Left Party has reached its zenith in 2009 benefitting temporarily from disaffected Social Democratic voters and channeling the protest vote. In addition, analysts thought that it would be hard-pressed to maintain its cohesiveness and nation-wide appeal, given the tensions between the larger rump PDS, eastern portion of the party (and its rather pragmatic governing style, for example, in Berlin) and western German activist types.[49] The resignation of the charismatic Lafontaine in early 2010 did not auger well. Yet, even more strident than the new SPD, its criticism of the government's planned cuts to social welfare–deemed "social clear-cutting" (*Kahlschlag*)–have resonated.[50] Polls in July 2010 put this party's support at 10 percent. The same surveys show that the Greens have surged to 15-18 percent national support after achieving 12 percent of the vote in North Rhine Westphalia in May and now part of a minority coalition government there.[51] The party is running even with the SPD in Berlin and may win the mayoralty in fall 2011.[52] Voters appear to think that the Greens have stuck with a discernible political profile, to trust the party to implement its agenda, and to like the fact that it has been out of power nationally for five years.[53] Summer 2010 polls show that Red-Green would have a majority of seats if new elections were held and, together with the Left Party command the support of 58 percent of the electorate versus a mere 34 percent for the governing parties.[54]

Self-destructive tensions within the governing camp have continued unabated since the campaign. As discussed above, there are major disagreements among the coalition partners (already visible before their victory)—especially CSU and FDP.[55] But there are also tensions within each party. The FDP over 2010 has been in free fall—summer polls put it around or even below the 5 percent electoral threshold, a ten point decrease from the 2009 election. Lest we forget, that stunning result largely was the result of one-off strategic vote-splitting and hardly represented a ringing endorsement of the party's programmatic views. This decline in support was perhaps an inevitable consequence of the shallowness of the FDP's appeal—for years the party has been all about Westerwelle and really no one else. And, as mentioned above, Westerwelle is prone to periodic "tirades," for example in February 2010 against the "decadent" social state and welfare recipients, and is widely perceived to comport himself as if he were still in the opposition.[56] The Liberals had a weak pool from which to choose ministers—even bringing back Sabine Leutheusser Schnarrenberger as Justice Minister (who held the same portfolio from 1992-1996)—although Rössler was an inspired choice. Moreover, the party has reduced its platform to tax cuts and other neoliberal economic doctrines that seemingly would benefit solely the better-off. The social, left liberal tradition so important during the period of coalition with the SPD (1969-1982) is virtually nonexistent today, thus diminishing the party's potential support.

The CSU has been in crisis for several years now—and seems barely to have stabilized itself. Horst Seehofer is a flawed,[57] transitional figure, but new leadership talent is difficult to perceive. The party has not recovered from its poor performance in the Bavarian state elections in September 2008 in which it received 43 percent, a decline of 17 percent from 2003 when the popular Edmund Stoiber was still in charge.[58] Stoiber stepped down from all posts in January 2007, to be replaced with the lackluster Erwin Huber as Party Chair and Günther Beckstein as Minister President—both replaced by Seehofer in 2008. The instability in the party leadership, the lack of inspiring leaders from a new generation (with the exception of zu Guttenberg), and perhaps intellectual exhaustion from decades of running the Free State have unleashed much dissension within the party. The CSU's internal problems also have generated a new electoral threat, the Freie Wähler, which garnered over 10 percent of the vote in 2008. Like the rest of the country, rich, predominantly Catholic, and conservative Bavaria has evolved socially and culturally over recent years. The CSU has had major problems modernizing itself and its platform based on its "clear Christian-social value orientation" that is "deeply rooted in the population."[59] Hence, many of the tensions at the federal level are exacerbated by the lack of direction and self-confidence with the

Bavarians. By August 2010 for the first time in its history, the party may have sunk below 40 percent support (according to a secret survey), which CSU politicians attributed, of course, to an "unconservative" CDU.[60]

The most drama of all has been within the CDU itself. Virtually all of the party barons who opposed Merkel are now gone. Once again, one must admire her brilliance in wiping out opponents behind the scenes–even if the press has been surprisingly negative about the current lack of rivals and has questioned her right to modernize the party and recruit her own cadre. Günther Oettinger, Minister President in Baden-Württemberg from 2005-2010, became an EU Commissioner in February. North Rhine Westphalian Minister President Jürgen Rüttgers (never a vociferous critic in any case) lost his re-election bid in May 2010 and later stepped down from all political offices. In late May, Koch announced his resignation, taking effect at the end of the summer, to pursue opportunities in the private sector. At the end of June, Wulff (Minister President of Lower Saxony from 2003-2010) was elected to the ceremonial sinecure of the Federal Presidency–and thus sidelined as a political threat. In July, Merkel ally von Beust, who had led an innovative Black-Green coalition in Hamburg announced his impending resignation. These men now join market liberal leader Merz, who gave up his party leadership posts in 2004 and left the Bundestag in 2009 and Matthias Wissmann who entered the private sector in 2007. The only senior CDU bigwig to remain is Schäuble now leading the Finance Ministry. Nevertheless, his effectiveness as a counterweight has diminished due to serious health issues over most of 2010 and, in any case, he has reconciled with Merkel over recent years, largely dissipating the bad blood from her ousting him from the party leadership in 2000.[61]

By common consensus the first half of 2010 was the most difficult of Merkel's tenure as chancellor.[62] During this time, she was in constant internal crisis management mode confronting a series of economic and electoral setbacks. First, the on-going financial and economic problems worsened in the early months of 2010. The Greek sovereign debt crisis threatened to infect other troubled countries (like Spain or Portugal), bring down transnational (many German-based) banks, and negatively impact the value of the EURO which declined by 15 percent compared to the U.S. dollar in the first six months of 2010.[63] These crises and the proposed remedies (intergovernmental bailout, European Central Bank guarantees, empowered economic governance at the EU level) created major tensions domestically and in the coalition which constrained the chancellor's response. Merkel found it difficult to justify a speedy bailout of the Greeks with their profligate spending, inability to collect taxes, and luxurious welfare state (retirement at fifty-five versus the recent raising of the retirement age to sixty-seven in Germany). Eventually, the pressure was unrelenting and in May 2010, she agreed to a EURO110 billion loan guarantee for Greece (the German share of which is EURO 22.4 billion), a EURO 750 billion guarantee for other potentially troubled EURO members, and a shift towards more "political" European Central Bank policy–despite the domestic unpopularity of all of these measures. Pundits considered the overall cost of these measures to be much higher than was necessary, had Merkel not equivocated for so many months.

The delayed, but long-expected budget cuts were also highly unpopular. A 3.3 percent deficit in 2009 was followed by 5.2 percent (and a debt level of 78.5 percent of GDP) in 2010. In early June 2010, the government announced plans to reduce spending by EURO 80 billion between 2011 and 2014 and increase revenues, mainly to reduce a structural deficit of 2.5 percent, efforts which are now constitutionally required.[64] On the revenue side, the FDP vetoed increases in consumption and income taxes, leading to a new "transaction tax" on banks and other measures. Redistributive programs will be reduced through ending a heating subsidy for the poor and government payments for welfare recipients into the pension system. The opposition mercilessly exploited this "social cold-heartedness" and the coalition took big hits in the polls.

Internationally and at home, extensive criticism of such Hayekian neoliberalism surfaced,[65] spurred by concerns that a double dip recession would result from the premature and ill-timed end of Keynesian stimulus spending, or perhaps even a deflationary spiral.[66] The return of the German export motor over late 2009 and 2010 renewed criticisms in other EU countries about the structural imbalances of the German economy (lack of consumer spending and excessive savings) and the unfairness to the other countries that are the markets for German goods and services (despite the fact that exports outside of the Eurozone now account for 23 percent of GDP versus 17 percent within).[67] Merkel's reputation for firm and masterful economic management (so important for her reelection victory) was eroded and her celebrated decision making style, i.e., patient and deliberative, was now criticized as being evasive, lethargic, and ineffective: "the hesitant and sometimes obstructionist manner in which the country has acted during the crisis has won it few friends."[68] International tensions– especially with Sarkozy and Obama–also sullied Merkel's previously stellar reputation abroad.

Electorally, the Land election in North Rhine Westphalia in May 2010 was a major test of the national coalition's popularity not long after the bailout of Greece and decline in the EURO's value–one that it failed. Although hardly surprising, the CDU lost ten points compared to the last election and achieved 34.6 percent of the vote, versus 34.5 percent for the SPD. The FDP did quite poorly at 6.7 percent, while the Greens emerged as the real victor with 12.1 percent (and the Left Party at 5.6 percent). Eventually a Red-Green minority coalition was formed in July.[69] Many had been out for blood and the media was vigorously pushing the "Merkel-is-irrevocably-damaged" frame, so the CDU defeat was made out to be much more apocalyptic than it actually was. Despite the marked decline in support, the party still won the most votes. The CDU-led government from 2005-2009 was already anomalous in this state, long a Social Democratic bastion (*rote Hochburg*) and continuously governed by that party between 1966 and 2005. In addition, contemporary German voters have revealed a strong preference for divided government in which the governing coalition in the Bundestag does not also control the upper house (Bundesrat). Indeed, the Red-Green coalition lost control of that chamber already in 1999. Nevertheless, all of the current national political trends were evident in North Rhine Westphalia–the quick and unexpected comeback of the SPD after the September 2009 debacle, the surging Greens, the stabilizing Left Party, and the sinking Liberals. More importantly, the loss of a majority in the Bundesrat for the governing coalition will greatly complicate law-making (although Merkel governed quite effectively under similarly constraining circumstances from 2005-2009) and already there have been greater difficulties with, for example, needed reforms to the financially strapped health care system.

Finally, there was the resignation of Merkel's ally, President Köhler, and the necessarily quick election for a successor. Shocking and angering many, Köhler precipitously resigned on 31 May 2010 over controversial remarks he made about an export-dependent country like Germany potentially needing to use military means to ensure markets for its goods and services.[70] The subsequent election for his successor on 30 June became a kind of confidence vote for the chancellor. One of the problems for her was that the opposition chose as their candidate the charismatic Joachim Gauck–pastor, East German dissident (a founder of Neues Forum), head of the Stasi Archive from 1990-2000 (an office that even today is referred to as the Gauck Behörde)–versus Merkel's rather staid, safe choice of Wulff, whom she chose because of internal party pressure over her rumored first choice, the much more intriguing von der Leyen. Despite a large majority for the governing parties in the Federal Assembly (Bundesversammlung) convened only for presidential elections, Wulff eked out a victory in an embarrassing third round of voting. Merkel and the government survived, but damaged.[71] In fact, by early August 2010, the CDU/CSU may have sunk to 29 percent support, only one point ahead of the SPD.[72]

Rarely has a politician looked so forward to the *Sommerpause.* Given the vicissitudes of the new government's first year and her rising unpopularity, it is likely that Merkel is already looking back at the 2009 election campaign with longing and nostalgia. Yet, if there is one thing that observers should have learned by now, it is that Merkel is a remarkable politician who cannot be underestimated. Despite her political gifts, however, the governing environment remains extremely challenging in the face of persistent economic difficulties and international instability. Much is outside of her control—not the least of which is the behavior of her coalition partners and the opposition. Coupled with the structural changes that the authors of this volume have analyzed—the decline of the *Volksparteien,* a stabilizing five-party system, the attenuation of partisanship, on-going value change, as well as the myriad of other factors like the aging of the population and increasing multiculturalism—the future will probably be even more uncertain and unpredictable. It will be difficult for Merkel or any other potential leader to govern, let alone govern decisively in the Germany and Europe of the second decade of the twenty-first century. I do not want to try to predict how long Merkel will stay in power (even though my money is on her surviving to fight another election). But, I will venture to say that the lackluster 2009 campaign will very likely not happen again.

Notes

1. See http://www.dw-world.de/dw/article/0,,3965092,00.html; accessed on 12 August 2010.
2. "Germany's oddly vapid election," *The Economist,* 10 September 2009; "Germany's uninspiring election: Set Angela free," *The Economist,* 17 September 2009.
3. Roger Cohen, "The Miracle of Dullness," *New York Times,* 23 September 2009; See also the "Battle for the Bundestag" election blog from the American Institute for Contemporary German Studies; http://aicgsgermanelection2009.blogspot.com/.
4. See http://www.stern.de/wahl-2009/bundestagswahl/dienstwagen-affaere-schmidt-will-konsequenzen-ziehen-707500.html; accessed on 4 August 2010.
5. See http://aicgsgermanelection2009.blogspot.com/2009/08/campaign-posters-are-back.html; accessed on 24 July 2010.

6. See Eric Langenbacher, "Introduction," in *Launching the Grand Coalition: The 2005 Bundestag Election and the Future of German Politics* (New York, 2006).
7. http://www.europarl.europa.eu/parliament/archive/elections2009/en/turnout_en.html; accessed 12 August 2010.
8. See http://www.telegraph.co.uk/news/worldnews/europe/germany/4933901/German-politician-Dieter-Althaus-guilty-of-manslaughter-in-Austrian-ski-death.html; accessed 12 August 2010.
9. The two Land elections on the same day as the Bundestag election in Brandenburg and Schleswig-Holstein did not really influence the federal results.
10. Rajiv Chandrasekaran, "Sole Informant Guided Decision On Afghan Strike," *The Washington Post*, 6 September 2009.
11. http://www.worldpublicopinion.org/pipa/pdf/jun09/WPO_Germany_Jun09_quaire.pdf; accessed on 23 July 2010.
12. Sebastian Fischer, "Jung-Rücktritt: Merkel zieht die Reißleine," *Spiegel on-line*, 27 November 2009; accessed 23 July 2010.
13. The German electoral system gives two votes simultaneously–the first for a constituency seat and the second for a closed party list. The second vote is all-important for the final distribution of seats. If a party received more constituency seats than it would get in a proportional allocation process, however, it gets to keep those extra seats, the "overhanging mandates," and the parliament is expanded accordingly. As a result, the size of the Bundestag always exceeds the 598 minimum. After 2009, it had twenty-four overhanging mandates and hence 622 total seats.
14. An additional minister, Franz Josef Jung was also re-appointed but resigned just two months after the election. Also, Liberal Justice Minister Sabine Leutheusser-Schnarrenberger had previous ministerial experience in Kohl cabinets.
15. All results are from http://www.bundeswahlleiter.de/de/bundestagswahlen/ BTW_BUND_09/; accessed 4 August 2010. Arnold Schölzel, "SPD sieht kaum Fehler," *Junge Welt*, 29 September 2009.
16. Udo Zolleis, "Indeterminacy in the Political Center Ground: Perspectives for the Christian Democratic Party in 2009," *German Politics and Society* 27, no. 2 (2009): 28-44.
17. On party systems, see Arend Lijphart, *Patterns of Democracy: Government Forms and Performance in 36 Democracies* (New Haven, 1999). Conradt reports 4.60 effective parties based on votes.
18. See Peter Mair, *Party System Change: Approaches and Interpretations* (Oxford, 1997).
19. "Germany's Chancellor: Merkel is the message," *The Economist*, 25 June 2009.
20. "The neighbours fall out," *The Economist*, 10 July 2010.
21. See Eric Langenbacher, "Conclusion: The Germans Must Have Done Something Right," *German Politics and Society* 28, no. 2 (2010): 185-202.
22. "Country Report: Germany," *Economist Intelligence Unit*, July 2010, 8.
23. http://www.brookings.edu/articles/2009/03_g20_stimulus_prasad.aspx; accessed 4 August 2010.
24. See http://www.spiegel.de/wirtschaft/0,1518,638051,00.html; accessed 23 July 2010.
25. See http://www.spiegel.de/international/germany/0,1518,615613,00.html; accessed 23 July 2010.
26. http://www.realclearpolitics.com/articles/2008/12/an_empty_stocking_for_frau_mer.html; accessed 24 July 2010.
27. See Jeffrey J. Anderson and Eric Langenbacher, eds., *From the Bonn to the Berlin Republic: Germany at the Twentieth Anniversary of Unification* (New York, 2010).
28. See Joyce Marie Mushaben, *The Changing Faces of Citizenship: Social Integration and Political Mobilization among Ethnic Minorities in Germany* (New York, 2008).
29. See http://www.migration-info.de/mub_artikel.php?Id=060502; accessed on 11 August 2010.

30. http://www.das-parlament.de/2007/03/Thema/005.html; http://www.migazin.de/2009/09/29/20-bundestagsabgeordnete-mit-migrationshintergrund/; accessed 23 July 2010.

31. See http://www.spiegel.de/international/germany/0,1518,705237,00.html; accessed 24 July 2010.

32. See http://www.youtube.com/watch?v=0Vav32M36WQ; accessed on 5 August 2010.

33. See http://www.nytimes.com/2010/01/18/world/europe/18iht-womenside.html?_r=1&scp=1&sq=von%20der%20leyen&st=cse; accessed 4 August 2010.

34. See http://www.forbes.com/lists/2009/11/power-women-09_The-100-Most-Powerful-Women_Rank.html; accessed 23 July 2010.

35. Mention should also be made of Louise Schroeder, Oberbürgermeister of Berlin 1947-48; Ingrid Pankraz, Mayor of East Berlin in 1990; Helga Elstner (1978-1984), Krista Soger (1997-2001), Brigitte Schnieber Jostran (2004-2008) and Christa Goetsch (2008-) all Second Mayors of Hamburg; and Anne Marie Mevissen (1967-1975) and Karoline Linnert (2007-) the Mayor Senators of Bremen. There have also been many female ministers at the Land level.

36. http://www.weforum.org/pdf/gendergap/rankings2009.pdf; accessed 9 February 2010.

37. http://homepages.wmich.edu/~m0kintz/ASGPTables-web.pdf; accessed 22 July 2010.

38. See http://www.spiegel.de/international/germany/0,1518,635822,00.html; accessed 4 August 2010.

39. Sebastian Fischer and Philipp Wittrock, "Union ohne Alphatiere: Merkel sucht die Superstars," *Der Speigel*, 19 July 2010.

40. See http://www.sueddeutsche.de/politik/wirtschaftsminister-warum-guttenberg-beliebtester-politiker-ist-1.174476; accessed 24 July 2010.

41. See http://www.independent.co.uk/news/world/europe/tony-paterson-from-big-brother—to-foreign-minister-1794708.html; accessed 23 July 2010.

42. See http://www.welt.de/politik/bundestagswahl/article4874088/Das-Leid-der-Konservativen-mit-Kanzlerin-Merkel.html; accessed 3 August 2010.

43. The contributions assembled here were originally published as a special issue in *German Politics and Society* 29, no 3 (2010).

44. See http://www.timesonline.co.uk/tol/news/world/world_agenda/article7001488.ece; accessed 22 July 2010.

45. http://aicgsgermanelection2009.blogspot.com/search?updated-max=2009-09-28T14%3A33%3A00-04%3A00&max-results=7; accessed 20 July 2010.

46. See http://www.zeit.de/politik/deutschland/2009-10/gabriel-scheswig-spd-vorsitz; accessed 20 July 2010.

47. http://www.spd.de/de/politik/100_Tage/index.html; accessed on 3 August 2010.

48. See http://www.spiegel.de/flash/flash-21634.html; accessed 24 July 2010.

49. See Dan Hough and Michael Koß, "Populism Personified or Reinvigorated Reformers? The German Left Party in 2009 and Beyond," *German Politics and Society* 27, no. 2 (2009): 76-91.

50. http://www.die-linke.de/; accessed 3 August 2010.

51. See http://www.welt.de/politik/nrw-wahl/article7553405/Die-Gruenen-sind-die-Koenigsmacher-in-NRW.html; accessed 3 August 2010.

52. See http://www.welt.de/politik/deutschland/article8797846/Wahl-2011-Wowereit-warnt-Gruene-vor-Uebermut.html; accessed 3 August 2010.

53. Florian Gathmann , "Grünes Umfragehoch: Der Machiavelli-Quassel-Mix," *Der Spiegel*, 9 July 2010.

54. See http://www.spiegel.de/politik/deutschland/0,1518,707628,00.html; accessed 20 July 2010.

55. "Angela's clashes," *The Economist*, 19 June 2010.

56. See http://www.taz.de/1/politik/deutschland/artikel/1/tiraden-des-bizarren-onkel-guido/; http://www.spiegel.de/politik/deutschland/0,1518,679220,00.html; accessed on 20 July 2010.

57. There have been scandals surrounding his mistress and "second" family. See http://www.nytimes.com/2008/09/30/world/europe/30iht-germany.4.16593417.html; accessed 4 August 2010.
58. See http://www.nytimes.com/2008/09/28/world/europe/28iht-bavaria.4.16539767.html; accessed 3 August 2010.
59. http://www.csu.de/partei/unsere_politik/index.htm; accessed 3 August 2010.
60. http://www.bild.de/BILD/politik/2010/08/05/geheime-umfrage-bayern-horst-seehofers-csu/unter-40-prozent.html; http://www.spiegel.de/politik/deutschland/0,1518,710232,00. html; http://www.stern.de/politik/deutschland/seehofer-kritisiert-cdu-als-unkonservativ-keine-demokratisch-legitimierte-partei-rechts-der-union-1589566. html; accessed on 5 August 2010.
61. See http://www.spiegel.de/politik/deutschland/0,1518,657008,00.html; accessed on 11 August 2010.
62. Arguably as challenging for her career was the 2002 Bundestag election campaign, when intraparty rivals outmaneuvered her and were able to select Stoiber as the CDU/CSU chancellor candidate, who was defeated by Schröder.
63. Graham Bowley, "Debt Worry for Europe Fades a Bit," *The New York Times*, 19 July 2010. Nevertheless, the decline of the EURO may have helped the recovering German export sector.
64. "Germany's budget deficit: Slash and bounce," *The Economist*, 12 June 2010.
65. See http://blog.heritage.org/2010/06/25/keynes-vs-hayek-obama-vs-merkel/; accessed 3 August 2010.
66. See http://www.spiegel.de/international/business/0,1518,701894,00.html; accessed 3 August 2010.
67. "The euro-area economy: Lemon aid," *The Economist*, 10 July 2010.
68. "Country Report" (see note 23).
69. See http://www.nytimes.com/2010/05/10/world/europe/10germany.html; accessed 3 August 2010.
70. See http://www.dw-world.de/dw/article/0,,5636499,00.html; accessed 3 August 2010.
71. "Angela Merkel rebuked," *The Economist*, 3 July 2010.
72. See http://www.spiegel.de/politik/deutschland/0,1518,708795,00.html; accessed on 5 August 2010.

$\mathcal{L}$ose-Lose Proposition

Policy Change and Party Politics in the Grand Coalition

• • • • • • • • • • • • • •

Clay Clemens

Introduction

Grand coalitions between a parliament's two largest parties enjoy the
capacity to enact major change, whether such power sharing arrangements are common, as in Austria, or mere episodic experiments, as in
countries ranging from Iceland to Israel–and Germany. For where more
narrowly based governments run afoul of the Federal Republic's "institutional pluralism," an alliance of Christian Democratic Union/Christian
Social Union (CDU/CSU) and Social Democratic Party (SPD) can "avoid or
overcome structural gridlock" due to a huge Bundestag majority and
enough Bundesrat seats to pass any bill.[1] Less clear is whether two traditional co-equal rivals will *agree* on policy change. One view is that sharing
the risks and benefits of power leads both to see it as a possible win-win
proposition, thus fostering cooperation. A second perspective, by contrast,
suggests that the two partners instead see all policy outcomes in zero-sum
terms, and, thus, seek to block each other, polarizing partisan competition
and yielding stalemate.[2] A third position is that variables like programmatic convergence, interest alliances, domination of each party by its
more moderate elements, a weak opposition, and leadership skill determine whether there is agreement or gridlock.[3]

For some, the first federal grand coalition's "rather impressive" record
from 1966-1969 vindicates the optimistic view.[4] Despite reneging on a
promised electoral law change, it would prove modern Germany's "most
successful long-term reform alliance."[5] Indeed, some saw the duopoly as

so efficient that it endangered democracy by overpowering parliamentary opposition and indulging anti-democratic longings for consensus, "a substitute for the strong man."[6] To be sure, the 1960s grand coalition was "ready and willing to act" on domestic issues by "expanding the state," but "fundamental polarization" did prevent an historic breakthrough in foreign affairs (Ostpolitik).[7] Moreover, facing weak mainstream opposition, the Union and SPD eventually drew apart as each sought to keep some supporters from defecting to more radical anti-system rivals.[8] Still, their alliance "optimally served the short and long term aims of both parties"—indeed, each gained votes in the 1969 Bundestag election.[9]

The second grand coalition formed by Angela Merkel in 2005 has drawn more critical reviews. With 73 percent of the Bundestag seats (448 out of 614), the government could pass any bill and—given that the Union, SPD, or both ran enough Land governments—had scant fear of a Bundesrat veto (until Hesse's 2009 election shifted the balance). Moreover, as a result of both majorities, it even had little reason for concern about the powerful Constitutional Court.[10] Yet, within the first year, *Der Spiegel* found this "coalition of the powerless" to lack decisiveness or readiness to accept any kind of risk, asking "who is governing Germany?" By late 2008, the liberal weekly newspaper *Die Zeit* accepted that the alliance was "pretty much over."[11] Scholars like Wolfgang Rudzio classify "the quality of its output as mixed," a "hodgepodge" that left key policy questions unresolved, or "reached solutions hardly capable of functioning."[12] Reimut Zohlnhöfer notes that the Grand Coalition did not use its power to pass many structural reforms, settling instead for "patch up jobs," many "partially contradictory."[13] While Merkel would defend her government's preference for "small steps" over bold leaps, others saw it as staggering and stumbling.

Blame for this record has been placed on polarized partisan competition. Zohlnhöfer highlights highly divergent positions: "the Grand Coalition's partners themselves blocked ... significant reform measures."[14] Journalists accused the Union and SPD of "doing nothing that could help the other side more than its own," as "black and red ... remained alien worlds."[15] Electoral considerations are likewise cited, mainly a scramble for centrist, swing voters that diminished any zeal for bold ventures.[16] Also, both Union and SPD entered the Grand Coalition at a time and as a result of declining support, having between them captured barely 70 percent of the popular vote (compared with 90 percent in the 1960s and 1970s). In a more fragmented party system, they faced three Bundestag rivals, each angling to lure away disaffected supporters. Finally, unlike in the 1960s, this Grand Coalition's partners had not sought to govern with each other, and settled for doing so out of desperation. That made for "an uninterrupted campaign," as each positioned itself for the next election and, ideally, thereafter a new liaison: for the Union, an alliance with the center-right, free-market Liberals (the Free Democrats or FDP); and for the SPD a duo with the environmental Greens (with whom they had co-governed from 1998 until 2005) alone if possible, and, if not, conceivably a three-way center or even all-left coalition including the Left Party.[17]

Yet, had interparty friction alone been decisive in constraining policy change under Merkel's Grand Coalition, one partner would have more often stood united against the other, generating gridlock. That was rare, or often merely a proximate cause of its "hodgepodge." The ultimate source was generally *intraparty* paralysis, with neither camp's leaders able to advance ideas that enjoyed solid support in its own ranks. In short, the Grand Coalition's main problem lay less in its own dynamic than at one level lower.

Three Partners in Crisis: The Parties of Merkel's Coalition

Fully explaining the policy record of Merkel government thus requires seeing it not only as two co-equal rivals waging a "War of the Roses," but as more fragmented with differences inside the CDU/CSU and SPD often as deep as those between them. For this Grand Coalition coincided with—and would exacerbate—an identity crisis within each of its camps. The root cause lay in societal changes that weakened the size and loyalty of each party's traditional support, making it vital, if not easy, to woo more swing voters away from each other, while simultaneously fending off three smaller rivals. This resulted in conflicts over orientation that fueled—and were, in turn, fueled by—strategic dilemmas and leadership struggles.

The CDU

Merkel's CDU entered the Grand Coalition amid unprecedented uncertainty about its traditional identity. For decades this broad center-right party had thrived (even coming close to an absolute electoral majority at times) based on representing Christian social values, economic liberalism, and cultural conservatism, a programmatic balance preserved by giving each faction an implicit veto. Yet, the social wing—protector of solidarity-based welfare state policies—had lost influence as Germany's Catholic labor movement (anchored in the Christian Democratic Employees Association) waned in the 1980s and 1990s, and it could no longer count on patronage long provided by Helmut Kohl after his 1998 defeat and tarnished reputation in light of the donations scandal. Meanwhile, the CDU's pro-business market wing had drawn more adherents as a neoliberal discourse gained currency in Europe amid stagnation and joblessness blamed on welfare state spending.[18] Seeking to trump reforms pushed by the SPD-led government, Merkel (Chairwoman of the CDU since 2000) had prodded her party to pursue a "fundamentally new policy," altering its old "social-market" balance by making an even bolder neoliberal shift. Her 2003 Leipzig Program proposed slashing labor costs (through more individual provision of social security), loosening job protections, cutting benefits, and reducing taxes. What she labeled "the most comprehensive reform package in history" was, others agreed, "all about upheaval, not continuity"—and it galvanized the market wing.[19] CDU fiscal conservatives—well-represented in the Bundestag caucus and among its regional minister-presidents—joined in, stipulating that any cuts in payroll or income taxes be offset so as not to increase debt.[20] Others went along mainly in the hopes that it would one-up the SPD and keep the party at 40 percent voter support.

This neoliberal turn seemingly invigorated the CDU in 2004-2005, but doubts soon mounted. Given SPD charges and voter concerns that the platform would gut welfare state benefits, the social wing urged shelving key parts and fiscal conservatives grew warier that bold reform might mean larger deficits after all. Market wing leaders had to fight to keep Leipzig at the heart of the 2005 Union campaign manifesto. But, as the party's huge initial opinion poll lead waned over the summer and it won just 35 percent of the vote in September, recriminations flew. The social wing blamed the manifesto's "lack of compassion" for scaring centrist voters.[21] A defensive market wing retorted that CDU half-heartedness had driven pro-reform voters to the FDP. Bitter though the Union was at having to settle for a grand coalition, Leipzig's now isolated advocates were poorly positioned to insist that Merkel press it. She all but dropped most planks in her bid to lead the new government, reaching a deal with the SPD by instead giving fiscal consolidation—even tax hikes—top priority.

Intraparty debate would thus rage during the Grand Coalition. Social wing leaders insisted on returning to "balance" and solidarity, even to a critique of capitalism. While not going that far, fiscal conservatives also repudiated large parts of the Leipzig Program. Thus, the market wing, while still better represented among party activists, could only deplore this CDU shift "away from a market-oriented policy."[22] Grand Coalition politics added to the confusion. Outflanking its new governing partner, the CDU Dresden

Congress in late 2006 voted to reverse even a key part of SPD-implemented reforms already in law. A year later in Hanover, the party adopted a new Basic Program again granting "justice" and "solidarity" equal weight with "freedom" among key CDU principles. It also gave the party a greener image by stressing environmental themes. By contrast, Leipzig proposals would appear only in vague form, if at all. Market wing leaders kept pressing the CDU to avoid further "social democratizing" itself. Yet, any momentum for returning to a pro-business or neoliberal path was blunted by the 2008 global financial crisis–instead it fueled fresh agonizing over where the party stood regarding its basic views on state intervention in the economy.

The CDU identity crisis had a second dimension. In opposition before 2005, the party had begun to revise its traditionally conservative cultural profile on family and immigration issues above all. This process accelerated in the Grand Coalition. Younger, culturally liberal Christian Democrats aligned with Merkel pushed such "modernization," insisting that their party recognize societal realities–the rising share of working women, single parent households, unwed couples, and gay partnerships, as well as a need to better integrate residents and citizens with migration backgrounds. They argued that adaptation would impress centrist voters and blunt efforts to depict the CDU as reactionary. Cultural conservatives fiercely resisted such "pandering" to the *Zeitgeist* and argued that abandoning the "family silver" of traditional religious or national values would demoralize core supporters, driving many into the ranks of non-voters or to radical fringe groups. While this wing increasingly lacked prominent national spokespeople, it found sympathy among older and even among some younger Land-level politicians and activists.[23]

These twin CDU identity crises were interwoven with questions of strategy. Diluting the Leipzig Program made a Grand Coalition easier, but would it risk driving more Union voters to the Liberals? A return to the Leipzig path might reduce that risk but drive away "the weak in society without a guarantee of a compensating [coalition] majority with the FDP."[24] Would the CDU's dilution of cultural conservatism foster eventual cooperation with the Greens? These issues, in turn, fueled and were fueled by questions about Merkel's leadership. Even as she had accumulated power, out-maneuvered rivals, and lengthened her tenure, the party chairwoman–an Easterner without the usual party resume–remained something of an outsider. Pushing Leipzig had alienated her from the social wing and abandoning it after 2005 earned market wing distrust. Moreover, uneasiness with a woman leader, a secularized Protestant from the formerly Communist East, remained strong in Catholic, conservative, and/or southern precincts, fueling resistance to the modernization of party positions on sociocultural matters. What for her was the flexibility of a scientist, experimenting to seek what worked best–and in the case of her 2005 campaign what did not–struck critics as a willingness to sacrifice a clear CDU identity solely in order to help keep her grip on the Chancellory. As one observer noted, her quest for the center seemed to avoid defining content: "the concept gives orientation only in a spatial sense."[25] No CDU peers could mount a direct challenge once she took office, especially as public approval–above all of her role on the world stage–soared from 2007 on, yet neither could she always control them effectively. While past Merkel rivals like Hesse's Roland Koch or Lower-Saxony's Christian Wulff broadly backed her policies, they and most others felt free to push Union positions more firmly than she did, or merely to stress regional interests. For his part, Baden-Württemberg's Günther Oettinger pressed her more bluntly to uphold fiscal restraint. By contrast, Jürgen Rüttgers of populous, industrial North Rhine Westphalia, championed social wing concerns. Nor could Merkel rein in her purged rival, former Union caucus chief Friedrich Merz, an advocate of pure market economics and cultural conservatism.[26] Thus, while serving as chancellor of a Grand Coalition enhanced her power in the overall political system and popularity with voters, it could not ensure policy coherence within her own party.

The CSU

When Merkel's Grand Coalition took office, the CSU seemed fairly secure in its mutually reinforcing roles–as a national champion of conservative values and the "state party" of Bavaria, where it had won an undreamt of 60 percent of the Landtag vote only two years earlier under the leadership of Edmund Stoiber. Yet, there was lingering unease that in a larger, unified Germany with a more fragmented party system, dominating just one Land meant less national influence than previously. Indeed, the CSU had once accounted for 10 percent of all Bundestag seats, after 2005, it held just 7.5 percent. Moreover, in a Grand Coalition, it was not vital to the majority and had just two cabinet portfolios (Economics and Agriculture). Nor could the CSU be as sure of leverage within a Union led by the eastern, culturally liberal Merkel. Indeed, association with her and her CDU's programmatic shifts risked alienating conservative supporters at home. That base faced a deeper-seated threat as well. Over decades, the CSU had constructed and embodied Bavaria's unique identity while fostering its economic transformation, yet–thanks to shrewd social policies–without endangering societal cohesion and an idyllic natural landscape.[27] "Innovation, social justice and regional patriotism" had been its formula. Yet, modernization ultimately was diversifying lifestyles in Bavaria, just as everywhere else, with "[the Catholic] church, beer tents and *Lederhosen* less and less a part of everyday [life]." [28] Unable to draw on as sizable a cultural conservative base as before, the CSU increasingly had to count on impressing a more diverse electorate by conveying an image of unity and competence in managing the Land–though such voters might prove fickle if the state party stumbled.

And stumble it did. In 2005, Stoiber's deep budget cuts and major administrative reforms angered local communities. Moreover, after first agreeing to join Merkel's cabinet he then declined, frustrating would-be heirs to his Bavarian post and irking party functionaries. This flap triggered a messy putsch in 2006, which, in turn, stirred up long-suppressed regional rivalries within CSU ranks.[29] Stoiber's successors as minister-president (Günther Beckstein 2007-2008) and chair (Erwin Huber 2007-2008) proved blandly ineffectual. A non-partisan Bavarian voter group (the Freie Wähler, Free Voters) began to feed off of local discontent with the long-dominant state party. In 2007, the CSU's leaders frantically pressed Merkel for policy concessions to shore up its poll ratings, but in October 2008, the party fell to a grim four-decade low of just 43 percent in Bavaria's Landtag election. "Maverick" politician Horst Seehofer, former federal Minister of Health and later Agriculture, became CSU chair and minister-president, weathering a controversy over his "second family" and an illegitimate child. Seehofer would constantly seek to bolster his shaky grip with a flurry of headline-grabbing demands– from tax cuts to new subsidies–unapologetically declaring "populism is not a four letter word!" Yet to critics it seemed proof of growing panic.[30]

The SPD

The SPD's concurrent identity crisis was generated by its most recent struggle over balancing social justice with economic growth and financial stability so as to retain a loyal if shrinking trade union base, yet also attract middle class voters–and ideally once again earn the 40 percent of the popular vote it had won in better times. Unification, Communism's collapse, and globalization had driven more Germans to the margins, while also raising questions about the welfare state's viability. In response, the SPD had first shifted left, attacking modest Kohl-era reforms as unjust. At the same time, eager to regain power, the party also put up popular centrist Gerhard Schröder as chancellor, who led it to a strong 41 percent in the 1998 Bundestag election. Insisting that social democracy not be "ideologically narrowed," this SPD "modernizer" urged a more pro-business, "new middle" that would liberalize labor markets and curb entitlements. Initially his Red-Green coalition did little on that front, absorbed by fiscal consolidation, immigration reform, and overseas military missions. In early 2003, however, record unemployment, collapse of quasi-corporatist talks on job creation, and an "ordo-liberal crisis narrative" among experts who blamed high labor costs for economic stagnation all led him to push through Agenda 2010. [31] This package of reforms subjected social benefits, especially for the jobless, to deep cuts and strict means-testing. An uneasy left wing went along only so as not to endanger his government, but hated this "cold" neoliberalism. The SPD remained "a reform party against its own will."[32] Schröder and party chair Franz Müntefering held them in line by attacking U.S.-style "turbo-capitalism," including Merkel's "heartless" Leipzig Program, in the 2005 Bundestag campaign, managing to keep their party at 35 percent. Yet, modernizers also still defended fiscal balance and Agenda 2010 as vital to the SPD's governing credentials. Warning that a turn back to leftwing ideology could cost it power, Müntefering scoffed that "opposition is crap."[33]

When the electoral math of November 2005 allowed them to remain in power, albeit with the CDU/CSU, party leaders leapt at the chance. They garnered top cabinet posts—labor for Müntefering, finance for former North Rhine Westphalian Minister President Peer Steinbrück, and the Foreign Office for Frank-Walter Steinmeier, another veteran of Schröder's team (Chief of the Chancellory from 1999-2005). Their SPD, however, "entered the Grand Coalition internally confused."[34] Leaders promised the party faithful that they would have the clout to block Union plans for slashing Germany's welfare state and labor protections, as well as its planned tax cuts for the wealthy and privatization of state assets. Meanwhile, they also vowed to uphold the Agenda 2010 legacy and fiscal balance, even to anchor them in a new SPD program. Modernizers like the Seeheimer Circle and Networkers endorsed this approach.[35] But, pushback from the party left and a change of leaders led the next chair, Kurt Beck (2006-2008), to declare that reform "had gone far enough." The new Hamburg Program of 2007 instead endorsed the old ideal of "democratic socialism," spoke of pursuing a "preventive welfare state," and demanded new policies, such as a minimum wage. At the same time, continuing to govern from the center while voicing more leftwing themes merely made the party's "political orientation ... even more confused."[36] The global financial crisis of 2008-2009 allowed SPD leaders to rally against "casino capitalism" (Steinmeier), declare "the time of market radicals is past" (Müntefering) and push for some corresponding government measures, yet they still resisted demands from the party left, such as a stiff tax on capital. Throughout this period, the SPD as a self-proclaimed party of peace, also remained deeply split on how far to honor Schröder's other legacy of backing Bundeswehr overseas military missions (e.g., Afghanistan) and strict counter-terrorism measures. Modernizers still prevailed in nominating Steinmeier as chancellor candidate for the 2009 Bundestag election and in producing an election manifesto that promised small measures (e.g., a tax bonus for low income workers) but "avoided bold vision."[37] By now, the left seemed to be regrouping, readying to re-orient the SPD once it returned to opposition. Polarized between "an institutionalized left wing" and a modernizing right, the slumping party seemed to lack "an organized center" that tied them together.[38]

Complicating the SPD's dilemma over its programmatic orientation was a strategic quandary. After bitterly breaking with Schröder in 1999, ex-SPD chair Oskar Lafontaine (in this office 1995-1999) had become the voice of swelling protest against Agenda 2010 among leftists and trade unionists. This movement's alliance with the larger, more established ex-Communist Party of Democratic Socialism in eastern Germany had earned 8.7 percent of the 2005 vote. Throughout the Grand Coalition, fear that Lafontaine's growing (newly named) Left Party would continue siphoning off still more of its voters intensified pressure within the slumping SPD to shift back toward traditional welfare state and anti-militarist policies. Some even hinted at teaming up with this new rival. Modernizers, especially federal ministers, fiercely resisted both ideas as fatal folly, and tacitly preferred extending the Grand Coalition.[39]

SPD power struggles would, in turn, be fueled by this identity crisis and strategic dilemma. Both—along with complaints about Müntefering's autocratic style—led to a fall 2005 executive committee vote against a key appointment that led him to quit as chair. His later successor, Rhineland-Palatinate minister-president Kurt Beck (after Matthias Platzeck had the job for five months), though long a pragmatist, would press SPD ministers to shift leftward in hopes of stemming losses to Lafontaine. This fueled friction over party and government policy in the months leading up to Müntefering's 2007 resignation from the cabinet. But, Beck would stumble into controversy over possible Land-level coalitions with the Left Party. That paved the way for his rival Müntefering's return, yet in a brief, second stint as party chair from 2008-2009 (he would later be succeeded by Sigmar Gabriel), he still faced the core dilemma: how to uphold his SPD's credentials as a centrist governing party without further demoralizing its faithful and driving more of them to an upstart challenger.

The Grand Coalition's Policy Process and Record

Thus, the disorientation of all three members of the Grand Coalition was such that each one's leaders could not easily judge what policies the party would support fully in government. Merkel and Müntefering did not even push to include some of their own sides' disputed campaign proposals when negotiating the November 2005 coalition contract, a two hundred page set of policy aims. Others appeared in vague form and were later dropped for lack of consensus in one party, let alone across the aisle, or for fear of exacerbating internal strains.[40] The large coalition committee, supplemented by a steering board of just four top leaders (and periodic retreats at country estates outside Berlin), did hash out bipartisan proposals. Such deals were facilitated by Merkel's pragmatic relationship with Müntefering early on and with Steinbrück throughout, bonds bolstered by mutual trust and a shared desire to see their government succeed. That camaraderie, however, made each leader suspect within parts of his or her own camp. Moreover, their deals could so inflame key factions that intraparty peace necessitated offering side payments or even changing course later, as the summary of government policy below indicates. Such a style of governance made for incoherent, contradictory policy and exacted a political toll on the parties.[41]

To be sure, coalition leaders sought to tie in key players. The two Bundestag caucuses had "an uncommonly large role" in policy formulation. Union chair Volker Kauder and his SPD counterpart Peter Struck—who also enjoyed a close working relationship—took part in all government talks, giving them early input on behalf of their memberships. Bills would move through their caucuses in parallel and deputies could modify them over ministerial objections. Inter- and intra-party meetings would further smooth passage.[42] Although party discipline was weakened by the fact that deputies knew voting against a bill would not endanger the government's majority, there was thus never "a threatening number of dissident" parliamentarians until the end of the Grand Coalition. Nevertheless, this dynamic did not dispel a "certain nervousness" among groups of deputies that ministerial-level deals would compromise their priorities.[43] Tying in the minister-presidents was also a chronic challenge, especially for Merkel whose Union controlled most Länder. Stressing their constitutional autonomy, they saw no obligation to "nod through Grand Coalition resolutions."[44] Each had his own take on the party's positions or his own region's interests, meaning—as a group—they could push in different directions at once, often long before bills reached the Bundesrat. Likewise, each party's annual congress or other gatherings gave factions critical of coalition policy a chance to vent against its own leadership.

Financial and Economic Policy

The cabinet's first order of business was fiscal consolidation. Merkel and SPD Finance Minister Steinbrück broadly agreed on "sustainable budget policy," although the former's party preferred spending restraint and the latter's revenue enhancements (so as to avoid deep social cuts). Early on, they agreed to end a large subsidy for homeowners and a tax break for commuters. Merkel's Union also accepted the SPD's proposed wealth tax, while Social Democrats swallowed her pledge of higher VAT rates (increased to 19 percent as of 1 January 2007)—on paper an even trade. Merkel and Steinbrück, with backing from CDU minister-presidents, continued to stress fiscal consolidation, warning that some cherished outlays would have to be cut or capped. As an economic boom began boosting revenues, a balanced budget was in sight by 2011. Moreover, the government also enacted a major change early on, hammering out a deal to enhance Germany's international competitiveness by lowering its business tax rates: the SPD resisted easing the burden on companies too much for fear of losing more revenue, while the Union market wing wanted even deeper reductions, yet both compromised on a 2008 deal that "did not represent an ideal solution for either side."[45]

To be sure, sustaining fiscal consolidation required appeasing opposition in both parties. The CDU market wing had never been enthusiastic about Merkel's VAT hike, which media headlines (and FDP speeches) called the largest tax increase in postwar history. For its part, the SPD left saw coalition policy as tilted toward higher earners and Steinbrück's emphasis on fiscal consolidation as overdone. By 2006, both the SPD and CSU were pressing for economic stimulus. As growth took off in 2007 the social wing in Merkel's CDU began urging tax relief for middle-income Germans and families, the SPD favored reducing employee payroll contributions instead, and the CSU talked of both. Yet, fiscally minded CDU caucus officials and minister-presidents insisted on "a clear commitment to budgetary consolidation as the top priority."[46] After sending unclear signals, Merkel split the difference, talking of tax relief, but only in the long term.

Specific levies also tested coalitional, but especially Union unity. With a tight Bavarian Land election looming, an uneasy new CSU leadership reversed course on the commuter tax break in 2008, insisting that its elimination had unduly hurt Bavarians given their longer driving distances.

Merkel's resistance to reinstating this benefit fueled deep intra-Union acrimony, though the Constitutional Court eventually forced her to do so. A similar feud broke out after judges ruled that the inheritance tax would have to be eliminated unless revised. SPD leaders insisted that a new law was a matter of social justice, and provided that it did not unduly burden family businesses, the CDU market wing was ready to deal, as were Union Länder who relied on the revenue. But, after a compromise was reached, CSU leaders began demanding a row of exclusions from any new law and urged that each Land be able to set its own rates. This intra-Union spat held up the bill in late 2008, and an angry SPD warned Merkel against being blackmailed by her CSU ally. Ultimately, the coalition deal passed, with Bavaria abstaining in the Bundesrat.

Unsurprisingly the 2008-2009 global financial crisis massively raised pressure on Merkel/Steinbrück's fiscal restraint. Both initially assigned "sole responsibility" for the crisis to an "Anglo-Saxon drive for double-digit profits and massive bonuses."[47] They urged tighter regulation of transactions, but resisted spending to prop up financial firms or as stimulus. A hasty bank loan guarantee was still only optional. Merkel defended "swimming against the tide" of cheap money and massive bailouts for reckless firms, insisting that debt was the problem, not the answer.[48] Yet, pressure mounted on "Frau Nein" and her finance minister from abroad and from within their divided parties. The SPD left derided them for seeking too little state control over banks and executive pay. Many in the party began edging away from Steinbrück's fiscal caution, eager to outdo the Left Party in defending jobs. The CDU's social wing and even its market wing also began to call for some stimulus, while the CSU stepped up calls for tax cuts. When coalition leaders responded with a small spending package in November, it consisted mainly of infrastructure projects already in the pipeline. A plan to spur auto sales with a tax break for new car buyers ran into a "chorus of many voices," including SPD environmental objections and CDU fiscal concerns, resulting in a "typical compromise" that allowed all sides to "save face."[49]

That winter, jobless forecasts of five million forced Merkel and Steinbrück to approve a second, unprecedented 50 billion EURO stimulus, with something for everyone: an SPD-backed tax deduction for trading in old cars for fuel-efficient models, Rüttgers' proposed credit fund for hard-hit firms (derided by the CDU market wing as "state capitalism"), and CSU tax cuts (in place of SPD proposals for consumer vouchers). Even experts who welcomed a stimulus derided this "hodgepodge" that reflected "the art of politics" and omitted "hardly a single proposal" under discussion in the coalition.[50] As one commentator put it, "the claim that Grand Coalitions are best for solving big problems has been revealed as a myth." Its main aim was "to press through as many details as possible from each position paper."[51] In another reversal, Steinbrück arranged for a government stake in shaky Commerzbank, and an even more "extraordinary measure"–a bill expropriating investors and partially nationalizing troubled Hypo Real Estate. As *Der Spiegel* observed on 13 January 2009, "nothing is impossible in this crisis now."[52]

Yet, these moves touched off a furor in the Union that would hamper further action. As one commentator put it, "The more convictions are given away in the storm of crisis the more those in the CDU seek orientation."[53] The market wing deplored growing state intervention as a violation of "pure" CDU policies," and lamented that it left the call for tax cuts to CSU or FDP leaders. Fiscal conservatives called for an end to big bailouts and deficits, yet resisted further tax cuts. Merkel pledged to avert further expansion of the state's role or subsidies. Despite having balked when there was a surplus, now–with a massive deficit–she promised to push for tax cuts after the election. Moreover, despite her own stern denunciations of big bankers and reckless firms, she could not muster a consensus on how far to go in restricting them. Many in her Union sympathized with the strict SPD proposals, but the market wing balked, diluting at least part of that spring's bills on tax havens and executive salaries. It was not just Müntefering who argued that "no one knows anymore where the center of ideas of the CDU lies."[54]

Inter- but also intra-Union differences also plagued a decision on auto firm Opel, hard hit by the crisis of its U.S. parent General Motors. The SPD urged state investment so as to save jobs–the CDU social wing and minister-presidents with plants in their Länder (Koch and Rüttgers) agreed. But, the market wing and fiscal conservatives resisted, rallying behind the new CSU economics minister Karl-Theodore zu Guttenberg, who declared "an orderly insolvency" less risky for taxpayers. Merkel pledged not to let Opel go under and hinted at federal loan guarantees, but also voiced doubt that its collapse would threaten the economy and counted on private investors. In late spring 2009, she agreed to offer the auto firm a "bridge credit" before its sale to a Canadian-Russian consortium, pledging that it was a "special situation" and she could see "no second, similar" case for government aid."[55] Guttenberg led the resistance, but was overruled by Koch and Rüttgers. Talk of bailing out a major retail conglomerate that included the popular department store chain Karstadt/Quelle revived the same intra-Union conflict. When Guttenberg and others resisted a bailout, Merkel joined those chiding any such free-market dogmatism. Regardless how the current global crisis began, she declared, it shows that "it is good there are states [in the world]."[56]

All of the coalition's inter- and intra-party differences were epitomized in the earlier negotiations to partially privatize German Rail. The SPD left resisted any plan, citing the grim precedent of British Rail's breakup. Social Democratic leaders and key trade union allies conceded that the railways needed outside investment, but sought to limit private sector control for fear of layoffs, fare hikes, and service cuts, concerns also shared by he CDU social wing. Yet, in early 2008, the SPD accepted a deal drafted by its transportation minister Wolfgang Tiefensee and Merkel's Union, which envisioned selling a quarter of the rail service to private investors, with tracks and stations remaining in government hands. SPD leftists deplored this cave-in as a first step toward full privatization, and demanded more layoff protection, while Land governments led by the CDU also protested prospects of loss of local train service. Ultimately, the scheme had to put on hold given the 2008-2009 turmoil on global markets.

Social, Labor, and Family Policy

Throughout the Grand Coalition, SPD leaders defended Agenda 2010's welfare state cutbacks, while the CDU market wing had not given up on Leipzig's call for more individual provision of social security. With "most voters' preferences to the left of the *Volksparteien*," however, such retrenchment was risky for the coalition government.[57] The SPD left was ready to roll back the past half-decade of neoliberal reform, as was the CDU social wing. The result was a true cacophony on issues from entitlements to labor market policy.

The coalition contract had proposed delaying eligibility for wage-indexed pension benefits until age sixty-seven so as to conserve retirement funds. In 2006, Müntefering enacted this plan on a phased basis, eager to show SPD commitment to a sustainable social state. Modernizers and most of the Union backed him, his party's left and the CDU social wing only after much protest. But then, amidst the 2009 recession, new SPD Labor Minister Olaf Scholz proposed a government guarantee that falling wages not drag down benefit levels. With elections looming, few resisted this popular pledge, even though it broke with the basis of German pension policy—and undercut the earlier reform by rewarding seniors at the expense of younger employees. When Steinbrück noted this contradiction, much of his own party, the CDU social wing, and CSU leaders accused him of alarming seniors; only the CDU market wing defended him. Due to this intraparty disorientation and election politics, "the government only succeeded in confusing both groups, old and young."[58]

Differences within both partners sowed even more confusion over the coalition's public health care reform. At Leipzig, the CDU had endorsed replacing income-scaled employee-employer payroll contributions with a flat-rate premium, so as to lower wage costs and foster competition among statutory insurance funds. But many in the social wing and CSU had long seen this idea as socially unjust. By contrast, the SPD called for expanding the public system by hiking taxes on the wealthy, and on the surpluses of well-heeled private insurers. In 2006, the chancellor and Health Minister Ulla Schmidt agreed on a complex plan as a shaky step in both directions: a government-run pool into which payroll contributions and (eventually) tax revenue would flow, and out of which insurers would be compensated at a standard rate for each policy issued (though if their costs rose, they could impose a limited surcharge). CDU market wing supporters charged that this scheme flipped Leipzig on its head by centralizing control and initially raising payroll contributions. Social Democrats complained that it delayed the tax subsidy and let private insurers off scot-free. Late night Chancellory bargaining forced a compromise, but then Stoiber and southern CDU minister-presidents "brutally shredded" Merkel's plan further by charging that it would cost their Länder too much.[59] Even after an early 2007 deal satisfied the CSU chief, other CDU minister-presidents and market wing leaders bailed out, citing the lack of a real cap on costs, while many Social Democrats opposed the plan as socially unjust. Ultimately it passed, but with several CDU-led Länder voting no in the Bundesrat along with forty-three Bundestag deputies split between Union and SPD—and right through 2009, the CSU talked of abandoning Merkel's "state controlled medicine."

By contrast reform of statutory long-term care insurance failed due mainly to partisan differences. Initiated under Kohl, this entitlement had expanded to cover not just home nursing but nursing homes, and its costs—covered by equal employer-employee payroll contributions—were soaring (indeed, the Grand Coalition added to them by including care for dementia). The CDU had called for a shift to self-funded individual accounts over its social wing's resistance. The SPD insisted on taxing private long-term care insurance funds to subsidize the public system. Unable to compromise, the coalition ended up again raising payroll contributions, a solution no faction had advocated.

Both parties were even more divided over labor market reform, resulting in "a patchwork full of errors in craftsmanship."[60] Early on the government reduced the employee-employer payroll contribution for unemployment compensation in hopes of spurring job creation. But, the effect was offset by other increases (in pensions, for example) and by a revision of Agenda 2010. The Hartz IV law had limited jobless compensation (ALG I) to one year, after which there was only a flat rate, strictly means-tested benefit (ALG II) lower than welfare. The SPD left and CDU social wing long had seen this step as a social outrage. Others in the Union argued that it had cut neither unemployment nor costs. Given CDU/CSU calls for a "general revision," coalition leaders pledged to re-examine the unpopular Hartz IV laws. Yet, SPD ministers—led by Müntefering—resisted undoing such a key legacy of the Schröder era. Merkel did not push him, but her maverick party rival Rüttgers then endorsed extending ALG I levels for older employees who had paid into the system longer. Over resistance from the market wing, that idea won approval at a CDU congress in 2006. Uneasy about being "out-flanked," the SPD left stepped up pressure on Müntefering, but—despite waning support from modernizers—he still balked. This issue in particular fueled the SPD's 2007 leadership fight, as Beck demanded re-extending ALG I and easing ALG II means-testing. After several weeks, Müntefering at last gave in and several months later the coalition did lengthen jobless compensation for older workers. Though at CDU insistence this change was ostensibly to be "cost-neutral," intraparty pressures had pushed Merkel's cabinet to undercut the effect of its own earlier move to lower labor costs.

Cross-cutting alliances undercut another labor market proposal. Merkel's Union favored easing employment protection laws that it argued stopped firms from creating new jobs for fear of being unable to trim payrolls in tough times. A reluctant SPD had agreed to discuss change, but only for newly hired workers and only if companies offered them other protections. The CDU's social wing agreed with such conditions, but its market wing—having initially pressed Merkel to seek total abolition of layoff protection—saw the resulting tradeoff as worse than the status quo. Thus, a divided Union could not press any version of change on the SPD.

Another debate ran more down party lines, but also cut across them. With their SPD eager to do something for workers, and fend off the Left Party, its ministers led the charge for a comprehensive federal minimum wage. The Union in general resisted a blanket requirement as sure to further undermine private sector job creation. While still upholding the freedom of employers and unions to negotiate contracts, however, the CDU social wing favored a compromise. Uneasy about being charged with indifference to stagnant and even "immorally low" pay, Merkel did as well. In mid 2007, the Grand Coalition agreed that an existing law on minimum labor conditions (including wage floors) in some transnational service industries facing cheaper foreign competition could be expanded modestly to include, first, the postal sector. Sensing they could push further, especially as public support rose, the SPD labeled this deal as just "step one." It proposed including more branches, and increased demands for an eventual blanket minimum wage. Despite market wing talk of opposing even the postal services deal, the Union caucus went along in late 2007. Backed by the social wing, Merkel agreed to negotiate half a dozen more sectoral minimum wage agreements the following year.

One of the government's main successes came in family policy. The Red-Green coalition had proposed but not implemented moving beyond aid for at-home mothers and toward public day care. With Merkel's backing, Family Minister Ursula von der Leyen–a telegenic mother of seven–actually would push this change through by generating a broad consensus within the CDU. Its social and market wings were won over by the idea of bringing more women into the labor force, while conservative resistance was diluted by the "brilliant strategy" of treating such policies as an answer to Germany's low birth rate.[61] Von der Leyen's first measure was a 2006 tax break to help employed couples afford nannies. Then she pushed a bill ensuring that parents who took time off from work to raise children still received up to two-thirds of their salaries (to a specified income limit) for ten months–and a year if both the mother and father did so. The SPD left grumbled that these steps favored the wealthy and Union conservatives found that they discriminated against traditional single breadwinner families, but–after minor concessions–coalition support solidified.[62] Next, von der Leyen pushed to triple public day care facilities and make access to them a basic right, both initially the SPD's ideas. Yet, while the Social Democrats favored funding them by slashing Union-backed per-child tax breaks and subsidies, the family minister sought an alternative based on federal and Land revenue. Working this out took until late 2007 and the eventual deal also required an "offset." Conservatives led by the CSU demanded a commensurate payment to traditional families raising children at home. Fearing diversion of such funds, von der Leyen and others in her CDU instead held out for a coupon for public child care. This intra-Union dispute and SPD resistance held up the day care bill nearly a year before there emerged what one journalist called "a typical compromise of the Grand Coalition–full of question marks" and based on "interesting fronts" within the government.[63] Nevertheless, the net result of all these steps was a rare success–a revolution even–in family policy.

Other Policy Areas

The Grand Coalition's other main achievement also had a long history. For years governments under both parties had complained that Germany's complex system of federalism hampered efforts to enact policy change, though talks underway since 2003 to rationalize policy making had stalled. The Grand Coalition pledged to complete this reform process (as some said in part to prove a capacity for more than "small steps"), but avoided one divisive issue altogether by not discussing geographical consolidation of the Länder, and then broke the massive task into two phases. The first focused on disentangling federal and Land legislative jurisdiction, cutting the share of laws needing Bundesrat consent so that a government's partisan foes in that body could not blockade bills passed by a Bundestag majority. Over some SPD resistance, the federal government, in turn, passed more power over education and environmental affairs to the Länder. This "most comprehensive reform of the Basic Law since its inception" passed both chambers easily in mid 2006[64] and early assessments indicated that the reform met its main goal.[65] For two years, work advanced on the second phase, reordering the financial powers of different levels of government–among the coalition's "last great tasks" and "proof of its reason for being."[66] Yet, even this agenda had been pared down by leaving out the complex intra-Länder revenue sharing scheme (Bundesfinanzausgleich). The result was a constitutional change barring Land governments from amassing deficits–though those worst off could draw on a joint reserve fund–and subjecting the federation to a new, more flexible if still significant debt brake. While elements in both parties disliked some results of each stage of this reform project, it touched on comparatively few core issues of party identity.

Given partisan differences over energy and environmental policy, the Grand Coalition's 2005 contract pledged not to reverse bills passed by its Red-Green predecessor. Eager to show her party's more modern, greener image, Merkel–earning broad acclaim–took the lead in pressing European Union partners and the U.S. to accept new global climate talks in 2007. CDU-led Länder and almost all factions of her Union, however, warned that Germany could cut carbon emissions and meet energy demands only by reversing the previous government's phase-out of nuclear power plants. Warning that such a step would violate the original coalition agreement, SPD leaders pledged to support Merkel against "hardliners" in her own camp who were threatening to "make the Chancellor seem weak."[67] Despite voicing her general support for atomic power, Merkel affirmed the coalition accord. At its 2007 retreat in Meseberg, the coalition agreed on a plan to cut greenhouse gasses by 2020 by 40 percent from 1990 levels. It stressed new limits on power generation, home construction, and aircraft or ship emissions. But squabbling continued over cost estimates for increasing use of renewable energy sources. After more bickering, the coalition agreed to tax vehicles based on their carbon dioxide emissions but, at Union insistence, excluded older cars. Finally, a Grand Coalition pledge to streamline and codify Land-level environmental regulations in federal law failed in early 2009, with the SPD pushing it, the CSU resisting, and a divided CDU unable to find a solution. On this, as on most environmental issues, the coalition stalled in large part because Merkel's party could not reconcile its new, greener image and its more traditional pro-business stance.

On domestic security, Interior Minister Wolfgang Schäuble pushed for tough counterterrorism measures. Merkel and Union colleagues backed him, even while disavowing some of his more dire warnings and stricter proposals. SPD Justice Minister Brigitte Zypries worked to modify Schäuble's agenda, though colleagues pressed her to resist more firmly.[68] In 2006, the coalition set up a joint federal-Land anti-terror database, and by 2008, it had agreed on a bill allowing federal police to use informants, conduct surveillance, monitor electronic communications, and search computers. Facing an SPD-led Bundesrat veto, the measure was softened to require that authorities secure a warrant. Schäuble also pressed the coalition for an amendment to the Basic Law permitting the Bundeswehr to protect targets within Germany from attack by air or sea, but an SPD revolt scuttled the plan. Both parties did back a measure that made visiting terrorist training camps abroad illegal.

Unlike the Red-Green coalition, Merkel's sought no major reform of immigration laws, but instead focused on better integration of minorities. Her coalition launched the German-Islamic Conference and an annual Chancellory summit, bringing representatives of the Muslim community together with officials. It produced an action plan of proposed policy changes to foster integration. Yet, the effect of these efforts was partly undercut by a revision of the Red-Green immigration law to fix perceived loopholes. It assured some non-citizens a right to remain, but set age limits and language tests for spouses from abroad so as to bar wives from arranged marriages. The new law also penalized aspiring citizens who did not attend integration courses that—after intra-Union debate over Land-level naturalization tests—required familiarity with Germany's constitutional order (conservatives also sought to require questions about culture and beliefs). Younger migrants now would also have to be able to support themselves financially. Qualms on the left of both coalition parties did not block the bill's passage in 2007. On another front, the CDU market wing and SPD leaders agreed to meet a shortage of technical specialists in areas like information technology by allowing targeted immigration, akin to a point system used elsewhere, whereas Union conservatives and some in the SPD insisted on training German-born personnel. The coalition ultimately agreed on a modest quota for eastern European engineers and a small reduction in the minimum salary that firms could pay skilled immigrant employees.

On one other rights issue, Merkel agreed in 2006 that an EU equal opportunity law be broadened in line with an SPD-Green draft, which would bar discrimination based not only on race, gender, and ethnicity, but also sexual preference, age, disability, and religion, as well as offering unions or worker's councils legal recourse. Her CDU's social wing was supportive, but Union minister-presidents and the CDU market wing blasted this step as a burden on employers that also violated a coalition deal to enact EU measures verbatim rather than expand on them.

Unlike its 1960s forerunner, this grand coalition did not fall apart over foreign policy, mainly because neither party sought fundamental change. Indeed, its contract explicitly pledged continuity. Union and SPD leaders extended Schröder's troop deployment in Afghanistan, albeit without expanding it. They faced criticism from within their parties for failing to give this mission a clear rationale—and growing pressure in each for a clear exit strategy. There was consensus as well on diplomatic pressure on Iran over its nuclear program and on Merkel's high-profile role in shaping the EU's Lisbon Treaty. Partisan differences over Turkey's membership played little role in part because events in that country continued to stall its prospects. On relations with Russia and China, the Chancellory and SPD-led Foreign Office did squabble over turf, especially given Merkel's abandonment of Schröder's purely business-oriented approach to both countries' regimes. That left Steinmeier in an uneasy position of chiding her emphasis on human rights and her meeting with Tibet's Dalai Lama—although both of these moves by the Chancellor had some sympathy within his own party.

Conclusion: The Cost of Incoherence

The second Grand Coalition would leave a mixed legacy. It did pass major reforms regarding federalism and family policy, though both built heavily on previous work and still required eliminating controversial items or buying off critics with side payments. Such expedients were even more evident on other measures–raising the pension age, but issuing a benefit guarantee, or reducing some non-wage labor costs only to raise others. In many areas the government produced often-inconsistent packages meant to satisfy constituencies within one or both parties, most notably during the 2008-2009 economic crisis. Elsewhere it settled for continuity. But only relatively rarely did the Grand Coalition reach stalemate entirely along purely partisan lines: caution or confusion within each party was as much a constraint upon major policy change as clashes between them.

This legacy would shape the 2009 Bundestag campaign. As one commentator noted, voters had trouble discerning "conceptual distinctions" between the governing parties, while "positions within each … appear farther apart than [do] the Union and SPD."[69] As chancellor candidates, Merkel and Steinmeier were "perhaps accidental, but honest expression of a years-long process of assimilation" at the top.[70] Thanks to the consensus at this level having "expanded enormously," theirs would be a boring contest.[71] Yet, at lower levels there was only further disorientation, as "the more social democratic the policies of the Grand Coalition … the more harshly [the Union had to] delineate itself from the SPD." Likewise, Social Democrats were reduced to attacking Merkel's party for a "market radicalism" that she and most of her CDU had already abandoned.[72] Still, any such rhetorical radicalism on both sides was too little too late. With the Grand Coalition hardly associated with the kind of major change they advocated, both the CDU market wing and SPD left had trouble holding onto large numbers of their supporters, and (unlike in 1969) both governing partners suffered voter defections.

In September 2009, many in both the Union and SPD were relieved to see their Grand Coalition end, yet given the root cause of its problems, neither could take much solace. Even in a seemingly more congenial alliance with the FDP, the Union's struggle over orientation would go on, while the SPD would find regenerating in opposition easier said than done given the depth of its own identity crisis and established partisan competitors such as the Greens and the Left Party. While the Grand Coalition had compounded the challenges facing both parties, these problems would by no means end when it did.

Notes

1. Ludger Helms, "The Grand Coalition: Precedents and Prospects," *German Politics and Society* 24, no. 1 (2006): 47.
2. Herbert Kitschelt, "Partisan Competition and Welfare State Retrenchment: When Do Politicians Choose Unpopular Policies?" in *The New Politics of the Welfare State*, ed., Paul Pierson (Oxford, 2001), 285-88.
3. Angelika von Wahl, "From Family Policy to Reconciliation Policy: How the Grand Coalition Reforms the German Welfare State," *German Politics and Society* 26, no. 3 (2008): 30.
4. "No other [postwar] government ... passed so many major bills" in just three years. Helms (see note 1), 58.
5. Robert Leicht cited in Lothar Probst, "Grosse Koalitionen als Sanierungsmodell? Erfahrungen aus Bremen," *Zeitschrift für Parlamentsfragen* 37, no. 3 (2006): 630.
6. Probst (see note 5), 629; Klaus Hildebrand, "Die erste Grosse Koalition 1966 bis 1969: Gefährdung oder Bewährung der parlamentarischen Demokratie in der Bundesrepublik, *Zeitschrift für Parlamentsfragen* 37, no. 3 (2006): 616.
7. Hildebrand (see note 6).
8. Karlheinz Niclauss, "Kiesinger und Merkel in der Grossen Koalition," *Aus Politik und Zeitgeschichte* 16 (2008): 8-9.
9. Heribert Knorr cited in Probst (see note 5), 630.
10. The bicameral reconciliation committee was convened only eight times, mainly to address minor issues and with a compromise resulting. Moreover, it took one-third of the Bundestag or a Land government–neither of which the Grand Coalition's opposition had–to seek an abstract judicial review ruling from the Constitutional Court. Reimut Zohlnhöfer, "Grosse Koalition: Durchregiert oder im institutionellen Dickicht verheddert," *Aus Politik und Zeitgeschichte* 38 (2009): 9-14.
11. *Der Spiegel*, 30 October 2006; *Zeit Online*, 13 November 2008.
12. Wolfgang Rudzio, "Informelles Regieren: Koalitionsmanagement der Regierung Merkel," *Aus Politik und Zeitgeschichte* 16 (2008): 17.
13. Zohlnhöfer (see note 10), 10.
14. Ibid., 13.
15. Eckart Lohse and Markus Wehner, *Rosenkrieg: Die grosse Koalition, 2005-2009* (Berlin, 2009), 261.
16. Zohlnhöfer (see note 10), 13.
17. Lohse and Wehner (see note 15), 263.
18. Franz Walter, "Zurück zum alten Bürgertum: CDU/CSU und FDP," *Aus Politik und Zeitgeschichte* 40 (2004): 34, 37; Viola Neu, *Die Mitglieder der CDU: Eine Umfrage der Konrad Adenauer Stiftung*, 2007, http://www.kas.de; accessed 24 May 2010.
19. *Financial Times Deutschland*, 2 December 2003.
20. Examples included CDU Bundestag Business Manager Norbert Röttgen, Deputy Caucus Chair Michael Meister, and Finance Spokesperson Steffen Kampeter, along with Hesse's Roland Koch, Baden-Württemberg's Günther Oettinger, and Saxony-Anhalt's Wolfang Böhmer.
21. Gerald Weiss cited in *Welt Online*, 6 October 2005.
22. Heiner Geissler, Karl-Josef Laumann and Kurt Lauk, cited in *Welt Online*, 23 April and 27 April 2006.
23. *Die Welt*, 27 April 2007; Stefan Mappus, Markus Söder, Philipp Missfelder, and Hendrik Wüst, "Moderner bürgerlicher Konservatismus: Warum die Union wieder mehr an ihre Wurzeln denken muss," http://www/stefan-mappus.de; ccessed 24 May 2010.
24. Uwe Thaysen, "Regierungsbildung 2005: Merkel, Merkel I, Merkel II," *Zeitschrift für Parlamentsfragen* 37, no. 3 (2006): 609.
25. Stefan Braun, "Verunsicherte CDU," *Süddeutsche Zeitung*, 29 January 2009.

26. Clay Clemens, "Modernization or Disorientation? Policy Change in Merkel's CDU," *German Politics* 18, no. 2 (2009): 121-39.
27. Eva Hepburn, "The Neglected Nation: The CSU and the Territorial Cleavage in Bavarian Party Politics," *German Politics* 17, no. 2 (2008): 184-202.
28. Christoph Seils, "Christsoziales Wetterleuchtern," *Zeit Online*, 2 April 2008.
29. Heinrich Oberreuter, "Stoibers Sturz: Eine Beispiel für die Selbstgefährdung politischer Macht," *Zeitschrift für Parlamentsfragen* 39, no. 1 (2008): 112-19.
30. Angela Köckritz, "Seine erste Wahl," *Die Zeit*, 4 June 2009.
31. Kenneth Dyson, "Economic Policy Management: Catastrophic Equilibrium, Tipping Points and Crisis Interventions," in *Governance in Contemporary Germany: The Semisovereign State Revisited*, eds., Simon Green and William Paterson (Cambridge, 2005), 126, 135-37.
32. "Einmal Agenda und Zurück," *Zeit Online*, 25 October 2007.
33. Detlev Lücke, "'Opposition ist Mist: Lasst das die anderen machen—wir wollen regieren,'" *Das Parlament* 14, 29 March 2004.
34. Herbert Kremp, "Die SPD entkernt sich selbst," *Welt Online*, 5 July 2009.
35. Franz Walter, *Die SPD: Biographie einer Partei* (Reinbeck, 2009), 266.
36. Christoph Egle, "No Escape from the Long-term Crisis? The Social Democrats' Failure to Devise a Promising Political Strategy," *German Politics and Society* 27, no. 2 (2009): 19.
37. Susanne Höll, "Solide und nicht besonders links," *Süddeutsche Zeitung*, 4 April 2009.
38. Walter (see note 37), 270.
39. Lohse and Wehner (see note 15), 258.
40. "Gemeinsam für Deutschland: Mit Mut und Menschlichkeit. Koalitionsvertrag von CDU, CSU und SPD," http://www.cducsu.de; accessed 24 May 2010.
41. Margaret Heckel, *So regiert die Kanzlerin: Eine Reportage* (Munich, 2009), 77-80.
42. Otto Bernhardt and Anne Deter, "Zum Erfolg verurteilt: Die Willensbildung in der grossen Koalition seit 2005 am Beispiel der Finanzpolitik," *Zeitschrift für Parlamentsfragen* 40, no 1 (2009): 215.
43. Rudzio (see note 12), 15.
44. *Welt Online*, 9 June 2006.
45. Bernhardt and Deter (see note 42), 211, 214.
46. Michael Meister cited in *Focus-online*, 13 May 2008.
47. "Germany blames U.S. for global crisis," Marketplace, 25 September 2008, http://www.marketplace.publicradio.org; accessed 24 May 2010.
48. CDU, Speech by Angela Merkel, 22nd Party Congress of the CDU of Germany, Stuttgart, 2 December 2008, http://www.stuttgart08.cdu.de; accessed 24 May 2010.
49. Lohse and Wehner (see note 15), 247, and Heckel (see note 43), 145-50.
50. Christoph Schmidt, "Ein Sammelsurium, das hilft," *Süddeutsche Zeitung*, 7 February 2009.
51. *Hamburger Abendblatt*, 14 January 2009.
52. *Der Spiegel*, 13 January 2009.
53. Braun (see note 25).
54. Cited in www.bild.de; accessed 12 April 2009.
55. *Die Welt*, 3 June 2009.
56. Die Bundesregierung, Speech by Chancellor Angela Merkel, "Erfolg mit Verantwortung—Made in Germany—die Soziale Marktwirtschaft," 2 June 2009, Bulletin no. 66-1, 2 June 2009, http://www.bundesregierung.de; accessed 24 May 2010.
57. Armin Schafer, "Die Reform des Sozialstaats und das deutsche Parteiensystem," *Zeitschrift für Parlamentsfragen* 38, no. 3 (2007): 660, 666.
58. Kommentar, "Garantie mit Pferdefuss," *Zeit Online*, 7 May 2009.
59. Bernd Ulrich, "Putschisten aus Prinzip," *Zeit Online*, 12 July 2006.
60. Gabriela Holtzner, "Erst Reförmchen, dann der Kampf gegen die Krise," *Tagesschau*, 18 August 2009.
61. von Wahl (see note 3), 36-38.

62. Müntefering noted that this change was "confusing for some men in the Union," resulting in an "ideological debate." *Spiegel online*, 22 April 2006.
63. *Spiegel-online*, 15 May 2007.
64. Arthur Gunlicks, "German Federalism Reform Part One," *German Law Journal*, 1 January 2007, 115.
65. Special Issue, "German Federalism in Transition," *German Politics* 17, no. 4 (2008).
66. Katharina Schuler, "Was wichtig ist bleibt liegen, *Zeit Online*, 23 June 2008.
67. *Der Spiegel*, 9 January 2006.
68. Many were already outraged at military surveillance of protesters during the 2007 G-8 summit.
69. Brigitte Fehrle, "Lob dem Lagerwahlkamp," *Berliner Zeitung*, 25 May 2009.
70. Heribert Prantl, "Lob der Langweile," *Süddeutsche Zeitung*, 26 August 2009.
71. Matthias Geis, "Seid umschlungen, Gegner!" *Zeit Online*, 20 August 2009.
72. Matthias Geis, "Aggressive Nähe," *Zeit Online*, 23 April 2009.

$\mathcal{T}$HE SHRINKING ELEPHANTS

The 2009 Election and the Changing Party System

• • • • • • • • • • • • • • •

David P. Conradt

> "The good old times of stability and continuity in our party system when the only question was which of the 'Small Ones' would be chosen by one of the 'Big Ones' are definitely gone."[1]

On one level, there was nothing surprising about the results of the 2009 election, the seventeenth in the Federal Republic of Germany's history. Contrary to the widespread speculations about "Germany's Gathering Crisis,"[2] a renewal of the Grand Coalition or even an unprecedented three-party coalition, a familiar pair of parties emerged with enough votes and seats to govern for the next four years. The Christian Democrats (CDU/CSU) and their long-time "junior" partner, the Free Democrats (FDP), were supported by 48.4 percent of the voters, which, thanks to the vagaries of the electoral system, yielded a comfortable majority of forty-two seats (53.4 percent). An old partnership was thus renewed–the CDU/CSU and FDP had governed from 1949 to 1966 and again from 1982 until 1998. Why then, has this rather mundane or traditional result been termed the "real sensation" of the 2009 election?[3] Did Germany dodge the bullet of another grand coalition or a three-party government? Or has this "normal outcome" merely slowed down a long-term trend toward realignment and a new party system.

This chapter attempts to explore these questions. I begin with a delineation of the "elephants'" features. What exactly is a *Volkspartei* (people's party) today? I then examine the dealignment process–the long-term and irreversible erosion of party attachments.[4] Next, I attempt to explain this development both with reference to the demand side–the voters and their motivations–as well as the supply side of the political equation–the role of parties, their leaders, strategies, and policies. Finally, the consequences of these changes for the future of the party system and the Federal Republic's political process are discussed.

The term *Volkspartei* came into vogue during the late 1950s when the Christian Democrats and Social Democrats (SPD) emerged as the two largest parties and, with the exception of the two grand coalitions (1966-1969; 2005-2009), alternated as the dominant party in the two-party coalitions that have been the norm for the Federal Republic. Peter Lösche has provided us with a useful definition, followed, in his case, by the pronouncement quoted at the outset of this chapter. He identifies four characteristics: 1) a broad social base that need not mirror society, but must be supported by multiple classes, secular groups, and religions; 2) a generalized, media-based appeal focused on voter maximization—a *Volkspartei* must have the support of at least 35 percent of the electorate, a minimal membership base of 1 percent of the registered electorate (about 600,000) with about 10 percent of this membership active as functionaries; 3) a focus on governing and assuming major responsibility for the policies and personnel of government, including an openness and ability to negotiate the necessary coalitions and compromises to form a government; 4) a supportive milieu—a dense network of social, economic, and cultural organizations that reinforces the parties' core electorate of about 20-25 percent.[5] Only with such a secure milieu-based foundation can a *Volkspartei* make successful forays into the new center of modern societies. Based on this conception and criteria, Lösche essentially declares the SPD finished as a *Volkspartei* with the CDU/CSU not far behind it, teetering on the edge of extinction.

An even direr prognosis for the CDU was given by Wolfgang Stock. Writing before the actual 27 September 2009 Bundestag election, he observed that:

> the CDU appears to be headed for what happened to its European sister parties some twenty years ago; they fragmented into smaller, more focused parties. In Germany, the general election of 2009 will prove the end of the concept of the *Volkspartei*, a party able to integrate all strands of society ... Indeed the future of the CDU is bleak: If Merkel wins the election she will buy some time but is unlikely to stop the trend of losing her best and brightest party members and voters.[6]

He predicts the Union will fragment into a "Christian values" party, a small-town, rural party with its base in the south and southwest, and a Conservative party similar to that found in Sweden.

Dealignment

The major assumption behind these analyses of the major parties is partisan dealignment. Indeed, there is wide-spread consensus within the scholarly community on the indicators of partisan de-alignment.[7] There is, however, much less agreement on the structure and politics of a realigned party system.

Declining Turnout

Most analysts of party dealignment/realignment consider a declining voter turnout as a major indicator of impending change in the party system. This certainly applies to the Federal Republic. In fact, the decline of the CDU and SPD correlates strongly with declining voter turnout ($r = .87$). At their zenith in the mid1970s, their combined share of over 90 percent of the vote was accompanied by a similarly exceptionally high turnout. In 2009, an all-time low was reached as only 70.8 percent of the electorate participated. Of course, the 2009 campaign did little to encourage participation because neither the candidates, nor the parties had any polarizing effect on the voters. The highly touted television "duel" between Angela Merkel and Frank-Walter Steinmeier quickly was dubbed a "duet" by the press—with the moderators of the debate provided more drama than the participants. It was, indeed, "the shortest and softest" campaign in the Federal Republic's history.[8]

When asked about the campaign in post-election surveys, over 80 percent of voters stated that it was of little or no help to them in reaching a decision.[9] Both the Land elections held prior to the national vote (in Thuringia, Saarland, and Saxony on 30 August 2009) and the opinion polls indicated a known outcome. Merkel would remain chancellor—even U.S. President Barack Obama assured her at a July 2009 White House meeting that she should not worry about the election. With the outcome "known" there was little incentive especially for the marginal voter to cast a ballot.

The combined vote of the elephants in 2009 reached its lowest level in the history of the Federal Republic. The Social Democrats, Germany's oldest party and the prototype of the European mass membership party, dropped to their lowest level since 1893. Even among the "other" parties, the Pirates (advocating civil and privacy rights on-line), who did not even exist until 2006, received the support of about one in every ten new, first-time voters.[10]

Figure 1: Major Party Vote, 1949-2009

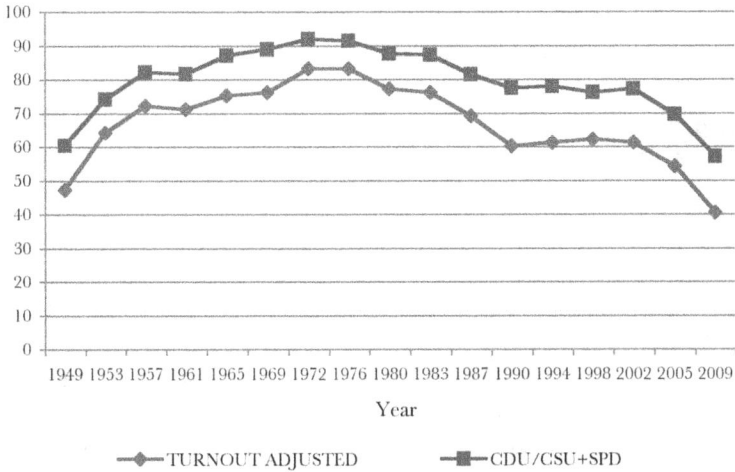

Figure 1 presents this combined vote from 1949-2009 both in absolute terms and adjusted for turnout, which shows an even more drastic decline for the major parties. In 1976, for example, 83 percent of the registered electorate voted for either the CDU/CSU or the SPD with their second ballot—the remainder supported the FDP, smaller parties, or did not vote. In the September 2009 Bundestag election, only 40 percent of the eligible electorate supported the elephants as the majority of voters either stayed home, or supported the opposition parties. The big parties find it increasingly difficult to mobilize the ordinary citizen or marginal voter. In the eastern regions, the combined CDU/CSU-SPD share of the total electorate has dropped from 55.7 to only 47.7 percent in 2009. When crossing the Elbe one no longer changes countries, but certainly party systems.

Party Identification

The steady decline in identification with political parties continued in 2009. Since 1972, the proportion of German voters with a "very strong" or "strong" attachment to a political party has dropped from 55 percent to only 30 percent at the 2009 election.[11] Party identification also relates to the time of the electoral decision: the weaker the voter's identification with a party, the later he or she will have decided.[12] Almost half of all voters with a weak or very weak party identification in 2009 decided late, as compared to 32 percent with a moderate identification and only 17 percent with a strong or very strong party identification. Among strong identifiers in 2009, the decision of

83 percent had been set for a long time or "for months," for those with a moderate identification 68 percent had it set, but for those with a weak or very weak identification only 53 percent had made up their minds.[13]

Weaker Party Organizations

Steady declines in membership have accompanied the elephants' electoral decline. As Figure 2 shows, the SPD's membership peaked in 1976 at slightly over one million. In that year's national election the party received 42.6 percent of the vote, but by 2009, both the SPD's membership and its electorate had dropped by about 50 percent. The peak year for the Union was 1984 when the combined CDU/CSU membership reached the 900,000 mark. At the national election the preceding year, the Union, led by Helmut Kohl, received 48.8 percent, the second best result in its history. Perhaps even more disturbing for the parties is the age composition of the remaining members: over half of the membership of the CDU/CSU and SPD are now over sixty years of age and only about 5 percent are under thirty.[14] Fewer members mean a weaker ground game, a reduced ability to engage voters in face-to-face discussions, and reduced party visibility between elections. Interestingly, this also correlates with increased volatility. With fewer members and activists, it becomes increasingly difficult for the parties to mobilize their own supporters, much less reach out to potential new voters. This is a pattern also found in other established democracies.[15]

Figure 2: SPD and CDU/CSU Membership 1946-2009

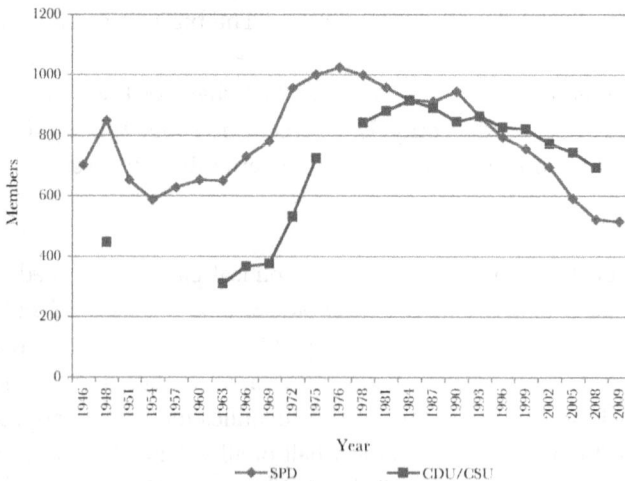

Source: Oskar Niedermayer, "Parteimitglieder in Deutschland: Version 2008," Bonn: Bundeszentrale für politische Bildung, 2008 and Frankfurter Allgemeine Zeitung, November 12, 2009, p. 4.

Ticket Splitting

This indicator of dealignment requires, of course, an electoral system and/ or institutional structure that enable voters to divide or split their support. While this is impossible in unitary, majoritarian systems such as Great Britain, it is relatively easy in countries with a federal structure with a separation of powers structure, as in the United States. In Germany, the two ballot system provides an easier means to split, or in this case divide the two ballots. Nonetheless, it was only after the 1976-1980 electoral cycle that splitting became widespread. Prior to that time, there had been periodic episodes of splitting, but usually at state elections. The increase in splitting correlates strongly with the decline of the two *Volksparteien*. This reached a new record in 2009 as about 26.4 percent of the electorate supported different parties with their two ballots.

Late-Deciders

As noted above, another component of the dealignment syndrome is an increase in voters deciding late in the campaign, i.e., in the "final weeks," "final days," or on election day. As the data presented in Figure 3 show, there have been major increases in both of these indicators, especially since unification. Turning to "late deciders," the jump since 2002 has been extraordinary and has prompted considerable research interest. Not surprisingly, ticket splitting and deciding late are closely related—indeed, the

Figure 3: Ticket Splitters and Late Deciders, 1953-2009

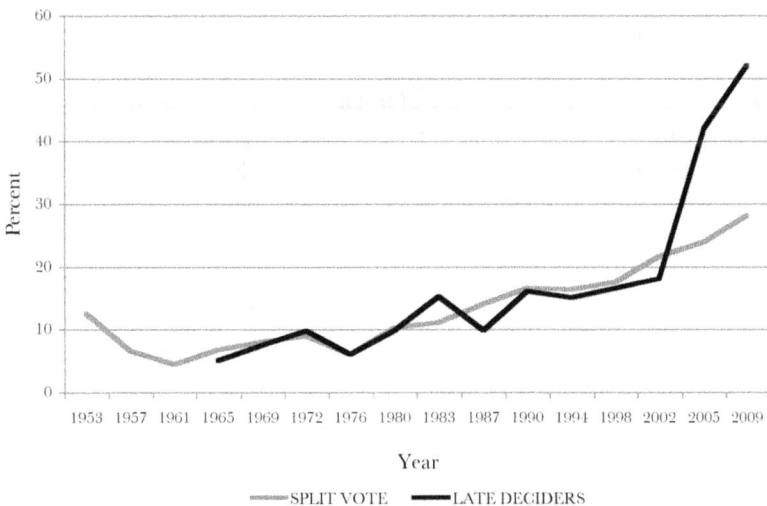

Source: Federal Statistical Office; Schmitt-Beck (see note 12); 2009 Mannheim post-Election study.

correlation between the two is very strong (r = .90) and significant. It appears that voters who split their ballots also decided late.[16] Preliminary examination of survey data from the 2002, 2005, and 2009 elections indicate, that this is a correct inference.

Volatility

Consistent with the other indicators of dealignment, electoral volatility in 2009 reached its highest level since the Federal Republic's first national electoral cycle in 1949-1953. In addition as Table 1 shows, for the first time since unification, volatility was higher in the western states. Indeed, volatility in the East has actually been quite stable–at a high level–since the first postunification election. There is no longer a volatility gap between the two regions of the once-divided nation: voters are moving because they perceive new political choices and opportunities. Christian Democrats concerned about the party's lack of a clear commitment to economic liberalism and less attached to the Catholic Church have an alternative– the Free Democrats. Disappointed SPD supporters have two viable alternatives–the Greens and since 2005, the Left Party.

Table 1: Voter Volatility, West-East 1990-2009 (in percent)

Year	West	East
1994	11.2	31.8
1998	12.8	23.2
2002	13	18.6
2005	14.2	24.6
2009	27.5	24.9

Source: Pederson Volatility Index

By moving into the center, the SPD left much of its traditional clientele with a sense of abandonment. As Table 2 shows, this was filled in 2005 and 2009 by the Left Party. In the western states, the SPD received the support of 50 percent of unemployed and 52 percent of manual workers in 1998. The then-PDS was not a factor. While the Social Democrats lost about 5 percent of its support among these groups in 2002, the PDS remained very weak in this region. Three years later, the newly formed Left Party had a foothold among the western unemployed (14 percent) and blue collar workers (6 percent).

If the SPD's goal was to regain or even retain its western blue-collar core, the decision to enter into the Grand Coalition was a huge mistake. In 2009, only 22 percent of unemployed workers in the West supported the party. The Left Party is now the stronger party among unemployed workers. Among blue collar workers, the results were similar. With only 27 percent of the blue collar vote, the SPD has lost about half of this electorate since 1998. The Left Party now enjoys double-digit support among western blue collar voters. In the East, the SPD's level of support was stable at around 40 percent in both the 1998 and 2002 elections. The other alternative for these voters was to stay home, which millions did in 2005 and 2009.

Table 2: Support for SPD and Left Party among Unemployed and Blue Collar Workers 1998-2009 (West-East)

	1998	2002	2005	2009
Unemployed SPD West	50	45	38	22
Unemployed Left Party West	2	3	14	25
Worker SPD West	52	45	40	27
Worker Left Party West	1	1	6	12
Unemployed SPD East	37	37	26	14
Unemployed Left Party East	25	21	42	44
Worker SPD East	39	41	29	17
Worker Left Party East	18	15	29	32

Source: Forschungsgruppe Wahlen

Explanations

A variety of explanations have been offered for this dealignment trend. I focus first on the supply side—the changes in the electorate and its socio-economic and cultural environment—and then on the parties own behavior—their strategies, leadership and policies—both within government and opposition.

Erosion of the Core Milieu

This argument and its close cousin, the "milieu" thesis, focus on the decline of the parties' core electorates. The numbers are well known and extensively analyzed elsewhere.[17] In 2009, these trends continued. Back in 1953, six of every ten Catholics reported attending services every Sunday or almost every Sunday, whereas by 2009, only two out of ten Catholics regularly did so. Within this group, support for the CDU/CSU has also declined from 84 percent in 1953 to 67 percent in 2009.[18] Thus, the combined (size x vote) contribution of strong Catholics to the CDU electorate has dropped from over 50 percent in the 1950s to only 14 percent in the 2009 vote. While the decline in party loyalty among strong Catholics is less than the decline in the size of this group, both contribute to the erosion of its Catholic core. The SPD's core—unionized manual workers—also continued to decline in 2009. Among unionized workers in the West, the Social Democrats dropped from 54 percent to only 37 percent; its largest drop among any occupational group.[19] In 1953, almost three-fourths (73 percent) of all unionized manual workers voted for the party.[20] Since 2005, the Social Democrats unlike the Christian Democrats, however, have also had a formidable competitor for their core, the Left Party.

Decline of Milieu

Both *Volksparteien* emerged in the postwar period out of much older, distinct working-class and Catholic subcultures supported by an organizational network of trade unions, lay organizations, youth, women's, cultural, and recreational associations. There was even once a Social Democratic burial society, The Red Flame, which encouraged cremation. Like the CDU and SPD, the Bavarian CSU also has had a distinct milieu, which has been in decline. Indeed because of its dominance of this state, the CSU became the victim of its own success. In modernizing Bavaria, transforming it from a small-town, rural region into a high-tech powerhouse, it created the conditions for its decline. Higher levels of education, especially in rural areas, the successful integration of eastern and northern Germans, and the steady urbanization of the state gave Bavarians not only a higher standard of living, but also the resources, increasing choices, and options that have had political consequences.[21] Thus, the prime cause for the demise of the *Volksparteien* is the erosion of these working-class, Catholic, and Bavarian subcultures.

This milieu explanation is largely identified with Peter Lösche and his Göttingen colleague, Franz Walter. They argue that this erosion is irreversible because the milieus cannot be replaced with new ones of comparable size and relevance. Of course, the Greens and the Left also have milieus, but they are limited in size and scope—and are not built overnight. Lösche predicts that the parties will soon change at a much faster rate then over the past six decades. New smaller parties organized by parliamentary *Fraktionen*, social movements, and narrowly based clientele groups will challenge and replace the elephants.[22]

The Parties: Strategies, Policies, and Leaders

On the supply side, voter discontent with the Grand Coalition is one explanation for the decline in *Volkspartei* support and turnout at the 2009 election. In contrast to 1966-1969 Grand Coalition when the SPD made substantial gains in the 1969 election, neither party profited from the

2005-2009 version. As Figure 4 shows, both parties ended their alignment in 2009 with support levels below their 2005 totals. The SPD, of course, lost more than the CDU/CSU—the correlation of its support level with time is a robust -.92. Internal party conflicts over proposed revisions to Agenda 2010, relations with the Left Party in Hesse, and leadership disputes took their toll. By mid 2008, only about 25 percent intended to vote for the party—a level from which it could not recover. The Grand Coalition was also difficult for the CDU's electoral fortunes. Its support level never exceeded 42 percent and beginning in early 2008, it began a steady decline. Like the SPD, the CDU in the Grand Coalition supported policies that alienated its base, although not to the same extent as for the Social Democrats. The family leave program was seen by many traditionalists as an abandonment of the Union's support for traditional gender roles, i.e., stay-at-home moms. In response to Chancellor Merkel's criticism of the Pope over rehabilitating a Holocaust-denying bishop in early 2009, several thousand additional members left the party.

Figure 4: Support for CDU/CSU-SPD During the Grand Coalition 2005-2009

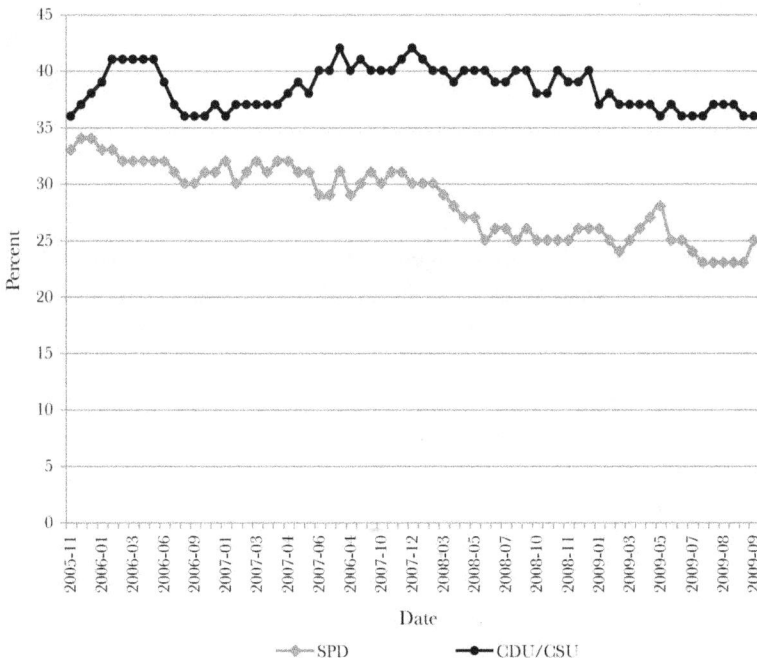

Source: Forschungsgruppe Wahlen

Grand Coalitions in State Elections

In addition to the periodic polls cited above, the decline of the Grand Coalition parties was accompanied throughout the four-year tenure of the government by the results of state elections–Germany's functional equivalent to mid-term elections. Between 2005 and 2008, the last great regional bastions of the major parties–North Rhine Westphalia for the SPD and Bavaria for the CDU/CSU–also fell victim to deconsolidation. In September 2008, the CSU suffered its worst defeat in a Land election in its history. Long the anchor of the national party, the Bavarians since 2002 have lost 34 percent of their voters.

A similar pattern was evident at the other state elections held between 2006 and 2009. The CDU saw its support drop at fourteen of these elections. It made a miniscule gain of 0.4 percent in Hesse (January 2009) and Brandenburg (September 2009). Included in these losses were the Bavarian disaster (a decline of over 17 percent), about 12 percent in Thuringia (August 2009) and Hesse (January 2008) and almost 9 percent in Schleswig-Holstein (September 2009). The SPD did not fare much better. Their decline in state elections began earlier following the 2002 election, a trend that continued during the Grand Coalition. It suffered double digit losses in Mecklenburg-Vorpommern (September 2006), Hesse (January 2009), the Saarland (August 2009) and Schleswig-Holstein (September 2009). It did manage very modest gains at six of these elections and had one lone triumph, albeit short-lived, when it nearly toppled the CDU/FDP government in Hesse in January 2008 (7.6 percent gain).[23]

Party Policies: The Bitter Fruits of Neoliberalism

In explaining the decline of the SPD in 2005 and 2009, no single factor has received more attention than Agenda 2010, the series of economic and social welfare reforms initiated by the Red-Green government in 2003 and passed in 2004 with the support in the Bundesrat of the CDU/CSU.[24] Ignoring his own party's history and the opinions of many of its activists, Chancellor Gerhard Schröder announced that "social welfare programs will be cut. Individual responsibility will be encouraged by government, which will also ask more of the individual in terms of financing social programs."[25] In short, government would do less and the individual would have to do more to sustain welfare benefits, pensions, and health care programs. The most controversial of the Agenda 2010 reforms was the so-called Hartz IV provisions that combined the second tier of unemployment benefits with the welfare program. This meant that after exhausting the insurance level of unemployment payments, further benefits would require a means test.

All of this was too much for many SPD supporters and, above all, the trade unions. Agenda 2010 was seen as an egregious violation of the core principles of social democracy: social justice and a commitment to the disadvantaged in society. Thousands of members and millions of voters left the party. The party chairmanship became a merry-go-round as four different chairmen led the party over the four-year Grand Coalition. In 2006, one of the architects of the Grand Coalition, Franz Müntefering, resigned over disputes with the party's Left. His replacement, Matthias Platzeck, quit after a few months, allegedly for health reasons. His successor, Kurt Beck, lasted until September 2008 when he resigned after a mini-putsch by party pragmatists who doubted his ability to lead the SPD during the 2009 campaign. Frank-Walter Steinmeier, the foreign minister under Merkel, became the party's standard bearer in the 2009 election. According to post-election surveys, the "electorally decisive" issues for those leaving the SPD in 2009 were social justice (42 percent), economic policy (31 percent) and labor market policies (28 percent)–all three could be considered as code words for Agenda 2010.[26]

The CDU and even the CSU also recognized the economic realities and tried unsuccessfully to introduce their own neoliberal reforms during the last two Helmut Kohl governments. The Union and Merkel at the fabled 2003 Leipzig *Parteitag* put forth a program that in its key components differed little from Agenda 2010. In short, both elephants were listening to and accepted the prevailing neoliberal messages coming from the economic and political research institutes in Berlin, Munich, and Cologne.

In the 2005 campaign, the Union essentially ran on the Leipzig Program and added a new economic and financial adviser, Professor Paul Kirchhof, to the campaign team. The Social Democrats, ignoring their own Agenda 2010, campaigned against the alleged cold, neoliberal policies as enunciated by Merkel and Kirchhof. Tax increases, cuts in pensions, health care, unemployment support and job security would all be part of a Merkel-led center-right coalition. Only the Social Democrats stood between this Merkel-Kirchhof experiment and the German people. This trope, played to near perfection in the final weeks of the campaign by Schröder almost salvaged his Red-Green government and profoundly shocked Merkel and the CDU. This was the ghost that haunted her during the Grand Coalition and above all the 2009 campaign and she was determined to avoid any hint of an ideological direction in her campaign or that of the CDU. Thus, both parties tried to avoid their own records and programs and the result was a short and content-free campaign.

Once returned to power, albeit in a grand coalition, the SPD proceeded to support or even initiate many of the programs they rhetorically opposed during the campaign, but supported or even initiated through Agenda

2010. The VAT was increased not by the 2 percent as advocated by Merkel during the campaign, but rather by 3 percent. It was the SPD labor and social programs minister who initiated the increase in the full retirement age from sixty-five to sixty-seven.

Indeed, this has been the pattern of SPD campaigns and governance at least since 1994. In his analysis of voter policy positions, state and federal election manifestos, and coalition agreements from 1994 to 2006, Marc Debus finds that the SPD's core clientele (blue collar and unionized workers) "prefers a left-wing profile for the party. When participating in government, however, Social Democrats implement a more liberal economic policy than originally promised before elections." This, he demonstrates, leads "to a further alienation of the core voter clientele from the SPD."[27]

The Irony of Agenda 2010: The CDU/CSU Profits, the SPD Bleeds

But, Agenda 2010 actually began to produce the intended results. After heavy political and fiscal start-up costs, many of the measures passed by the Schröder government started to work under the Grand Coalition. From late 2005 until the final quarter of 2008, over 1.5 million new jobs were created, many of them taken by older workers responding to the reduced unemployment benefits of Agenda 2010. The economy grew by 3.2 percent in 2006 and 2.5 percent in 2007 in spite of a steep increase in the VAT. Even in 2008, a modest growth rate of 1.3 percent was recorded, albeit most of it in the first nine months of the year. This solid economic performance also meant increased tax revenue and a sharp reduction in national debt. The finance minister in fact predicted a balanced budget by 2011, if not earlier. By 2008, the federal deficit had dropped from EURO 47.4 billion to EURO 14.1 billion. Alas, the world-wide economic crisis dramatically changed this outlook, and the 2009 deficit returned to the EURO 40 billion mark with much higher deficits forecast for 2010.

Table 3: The Grand Coalition Economic Record

	2005	2006	2007	2008	2009
Real GDP Growth	0.8	3.2	2.5	1.3	-5.0
Employment (millions)	38.9	39.1	39.8	40.3	40.2
Unemployment (millions)	4.9	4.5	3.8	3.3	3.4
Unemployment (percent)	10.8	9.8	8.3	7.8	8.2
Inflation (consumer prices)	1.5	1.6	2.3	2.6	0.4
Federal Deficit (billion EURO)	47.4	34.5	18.9	14.1	40.3
Public Deficit* (percent GDP)	3.3	1.6	+0.2	0.0	3.2
Trade Balance (percent GDP)	5.2	6.5	7.9	6.7	4.4

*Federal, State, Local and Social Programs
Source: Statistisches Bundesamt, "Bruttoinlandsprodukt 2009 für Deutschland," (Begleitmaterial), Wiesbaden, 13 January 2009; Deutsches Institut für Wirtschaft, Wochenbericht, Nos. 1-2, 7 January 2010, 11.

Frank-Walter Steinmeier, the SPD's chancellor candidate and one of the major architects of Agenda 2010, ruefully remarked on the evening of the party's greatest loss since 1893 that the voters apparently gave the chancellor's party the credit for the economic upturn during the Grand Coalition and punished his Social Democrats who introduced the program six years earlier. Indeed, early analysis of survey data shows that independent voters, about 37 percent of the total, were more likely to give credit to the perceived economic recovery to the CDU/CSU and not the Social Democrats. In their analysis of the vote, under the heading "Life is not Fair," Robert Rohrschneider and Rüdiger Schmitt-Beck calculated that positive evaluations of the Grand Coalition's economic record among independent voters added about 9 percent to the Union's aggregate vote in the West and about 5 percent in the eastern states. The corresponding figures for the SPD were about 3 percent in both regions.[28] While there is a generally strong relationship between attitudes towards the economy and judgments about the role of the government in producing the perceived favorable developments, i.e., people who think the economy is good will be more likely to give the government some credit, this relationship in 2009 was much stronger among CDU/CSU voters than among SPD supporters. In other words, even the SPD's own voters were less likely to give their party's members of the Grand Coalition credit for the economic upturn than were CDU supporters.[29]

Generally the economy or the international economic crisis, which began in the fourth quarter of 2008, was not a major issue in 2009.[30] There were several reasons for this. First, the Grand Coalition alignment meant that neither party had any incentive to politicize the financial, credit, and economic distress. Sharing governmental responsibility also meant that it was difficult to stake out an advantageous campaign position. Second, the measures that were taken by the Grand Coalition after September, 2008–a multi-billion euro bank bailout, deposit guarantees, two stimulus packages, "cash for clunkers" (*Abwrackprämie*), together with well-established safety nets such as the *Kurzarbeit* program–has enabled Germany thus far to weather the storm in better condition than most of its neighbors and trading partners. Participation in the *Kurzarbeit* program increased from only 39,000 workers in September 2008 to 1.5 million by May 2009. *Kurzarbeit* enabled firms to reduce the hours of its employees with the Federal Labor Institute covering about two-thirds of the workers' income loss. Employers are also compensated for their contributions to their short-time workers pension, health insurance, and other social funds. Workers on short-time are not considered unemployed.

At the time of the September 2009 election, over 1 million employees were still benefiting from the program. Thus, Germany's unemployment level in the fourth quarter of 2009 was 7.9 percent, as compared to 10 percent in the United States, 9.5 percent in France, and 8.8 percent in Britain. Barring an economic upturn, this program could well run out of funds in 2010 and the impacted employees would join the ranks of the unemployed.[31] Third, as shown above in Table 3, the Grand Coalition's economic record throughout most of the legislative period, i.e., until the fourth quarter of 2008, was quite strong. The economy grew in 2006 and 2007 by a combined total of 5.5 percent. The 2007 growth performance occurred in spite of a record increase in the VAT. Unemployment dropped from 10.8 percent in 2005 to 7.8 percent in 2008. Hartz IV provided a strong incentive for older workers to re-enter the labor market and by 2007, the job growth among older, long-term unemployed workers was above the national average. Indeed, until November, 2008 Germany had experienced thirty-eight consecutive months of job growth. This solid economic performance greatly reduced the federal deficit until the fateful fourth quarter of 2008. Overall, under Agenda 2010, the economy and labor markets became leaner and more efficient. In comparison to other large market economies, Germany is less of a problem child. Even with record projected deficits in 2010, total debt as a percentage of GDP is estimated at about 5 percent as compared to 13 percent in the United States.

If the economy in 2009 was the "dog that did not bark,"[32] it was because it had been well-muzzled by its two owners. Only one, however, would reap some benefit from this record. In the view of most observers, while SPD ministers such as Steinbrück and Steinmeier deserved at least as much credit as Merkel's team, the voters did not agree.

The Empty Nets and Globalization

This argument, developed by Christopher Allen, Peter Mair, and others, focuses not on the erosion of the parties' demographic core or milieu, but rather their over-reaction to this erosion. The SPD, as it abandoned its traditional role as the guardian of social justice and went fishing for voters in the "new center," came up with "empty nets."[33] In other words, if the SPD had continued to emphasize its support for the German model, it would have attracted enough votes from the center in addition to maintaining its hegemonic position among workers. Allen contends that "the issues that created social democracy over a century ago—persistent unemployment, the struggle for publicly provided welfare benefits, and social fragmentation—have all developed new 21st century incarnations." In Germany, the combination of globalization, European integration, and the dislocations of unification severely challenged the assumptions of the social market economy. In both Germany and Sweden, according to this analysis, "when Social Democratic parties assume that they can retain their core constituency by undercutting their core values and using broader, less focused appeals to unattached voters, it appears that they do so at their peril ..."[34] Moreover, "there is space to the left of social democracy occupied by more natural potential allies then exist to social democracy's right. Can they cast their nets where their potential supporters are?" By moving into the new center and identifying with the winners in the new globalized economy the SPD, like their counterparts in Sweden and other PR states, were paradoxically leaving a "lucrative space" of globalization losers for smaller left parties to occupy.

Likewise the CDU/CSU in abandoning its core is now vulnerable on its right flank. Intra-party critics charged that during the 2009 campaign the CDU appeared no longer interested in its version of "values voters," including Catholics, but also church-going Protestants and what is left of the refugee block. Party elites ignored the misgivings of the base about gay marriage, out-reach to Muslims, and the family policies of the CDU modernizers, i.e., state support for working mothers and alleged neglect of stay-at-home moms. As mentioned above, Chancellor Merkel's remarks critical of the (German and Bavarian) Pope reportedly cost the Union thousands of once loyal members. Following the 2009 election, the debate intensified when four state-level leaders published a *Thesenpapier* in a leading newspaper sharply critical of the campaign and Merkel's leadership. They emphasized that the chancellor's focus on the center of the electorate was causing it to lose its profile, i.e. identity.[35] Another group of concerned CDU activists formed a "Working Group of Engaged Catholics" within the party to emphasize the perceived lack of the "high C" in Merkel's CDU. This would be the equivalent, as one commentator put it, "of a working group for environmentalists" being formed within the Green party.[36]

A similar thesis is provided by Hans Peter Kriesi et al.'s analysis of cleavage structure and party support in several West European societies.[37] Globalization, they argue, has produced a new cleavage—integration versus demarcation—in established democracies, which has redefined the classic (Lipset-Rokkan) two dimensional, economic and cultural, cleavage structure. The SPD with Agenda 2010 attempted to deal with the same problems—sluggish growth, high unemployment, soaring public debt, and a funding crisis in the welfare state that the Kohl governments had faced.

In addressing these specific policy problems, it was also redefining its ideological profile as were its counterparts in other established European democracies. In their six nation study, Kriesi et al. found a mismatch between the positions of political parties, especially those on the Left, and the demands of the losers of globalization, unskilled manual workers, the unemployed, and the less well-educated.[38] The result: "In all cases, with the partial exception of the UK, party systems have been destabilized and are becoming more fragmented and polarized."[39]

Conclusions

Clearly, a major dealignment has now taken place in the Germany party system. If, when, and in what form realignment will follow is not clear. But, the *Volksparteien* will not return in their traditional form. Their social, economic, and cultural bases have eroded and will not be replaced by any new cleavages of comparable importance or quantity. The global, post-industrial knowledge economy is too individualized and fragmented to be mobilized by mass parties with broad, general appeals. Many analysts of German voting behavior contend that in the future no party can hope to secure more than 35 percent of the vote.[40] Certainly, the institutional structure, above all the proportional electoral law and federalism, do not hinder, but rather invite new interests to enter the electoral arena. In 2009, a single issue party, the Pirates, received only 2 percent of the vote, but over 10 percent among young, first-time voters. At the Greens first foray into national elections in 1980, they received 1.5 percent of the party vote.[41]

As always some hedging must be added to the *Trauerrede* for the elephants. While both the Free Democrats and Greens are firmly based in their respective, but modest milieu, how stable is the Left Party? Its record-setting performances in 2005 and 2009 were clearly related to the SPD's policy and strategy problems as well as the presence of two of Germany's most gifted campaigners, Oskar Lafontaine and Gregor Gysi.[42] In opposition, the SPD can distance itself from the neoliberal sins of the Schröder-Müntefering era while at the same time attempting to cooperate or if possible co-opt Left Party voters. As one observer put it, "[2009] will be the last election at which the SPD limits its coalition options."[43] It is also increasingly unlikely that either Lafontaine or Gysi will play major roles in the 2013 campaign. One is also reminded that the failure of the PDS in 2002 to clear the 5 percent electoral threshold largely was attributed to Gysi's (temporary) absence from the party's leadership.[44]

Matthias Jung has also pointed out there are two sides to volatility. It can produce both sharp declines and advances–high volatility can also mean a relatively quick comeback.[45] The SPD in 2009 with a poor strategy, a suboptimal campaign, and a poor coalitional constellation encountered a perfect storm, which will probably not be repeated in the immediate future. Just a partial mobilization of its considerable (2.1 million) stay-at-home electorate would bring it to within striking distance of the Union.

In the aftermath of the 2005 and 2009 elections, some observers expressed concern about the continued decline of the major parties. The former SPD Mayor of Bremen alluded to the Weimar Republic and its ineffective party system. *The Economist* opined that "if the *Volksparteien* are in trouble, Germans fear democracy may be too."[46] Charles Lees argues that the party state concept is "at the heart of the Federal Republic's political settlement."[47] Moreover, he considers the decline of the major parties' integrative role "alarming" with possibly adverse effects on the system's legitimacy.[48]

There is no evidence thus far that the changes analyzed in this chapter represent any challenge to the Federal Republic's stability or legitimacy. Given its electoral system and federal structure, the *Parteienstaat*, based on the strong constitutional position of the parties, will survive a more complicated, albeit fluid party system. While Lösche and others have emphatically pronounced the end of the *Volksparteien*, they also are quick to add that is no cause for alarm or concern about the viability of the Federal Republic. Indeed, most democracies do not have party systems dominated by large, catch-all parties. As Table 4 shows, the Federal Republic's current number of effective parties is still well below those of such well-established democracies as the Netherlands, Denmark, Sweden, Finland, and Switzerland. In fact, most democracies with proportional representation do not have large *Volksparteien*. The half-century period of dominance by the CDU/CSU and SPD could be viewed as a unique development, an outlier so to say, conditioned by uniquely favorable historical conditions including the postwar culture of consensus and conflict avoidance. In future research on the party system, unification and globalization may well be seen as the "critical junctures" which led to a more fluid multi-party system.[49]

Table 4: Effective Number of Parties in West European Democracies (based on vote)

Country	Year	Number
Finland	2007	5.88
The Netherlands	2006	5.80
Switzerland	2007	5.61
Ireland	2009	5.48
Denmark	2007	5.41
Sweden	2006	4.66
Germany*	2009	4.60
Norway	2009	4.55
France	2007	4.32
Luxembourg	2009	4.25
Italy	2008	3.82
Great Britain	2005	3.59

* CDU/CSU are considered a single party.

Source: Author's calculation from Michael Gallagher, Electoral Systems Website, available at www.tcd.ie/Political_Science/staff/michael_gallagher.htm. The measurement of effective number of parties at the electoral level is based on the Laaskso-Taagepera formula. See Markku Laasko and Rein Taagepera, "'Effective' Number of Parties: A Measure with Application to West Europe," *Comparative Political Studies* 12, no. 1 (1979): 3-27.

Notes

1. Peter Lösche, "Ende der Volksparteien." *Aus Politik und Zeitgeschichte* 51 (2009): 6.
2. Alister Miskimmon, William E. Paterson, and James Sloam, *Germany's Gathering Crisis: The 2005 Federal Election and the Grand Coalition* (London, 2009).
3. Matthias Jung, Yvonne Schroth, and Andrea Wolf, "Regierungswechsel ohne Wechselstimmung," Aus *Politik und Zeitgeschichte* 51 (2009): 12.
4. On dealignment see Russell J. Dalton and Martin P. Wattenberg, eds., *Parties without Partisans* (New York, 2000). For the German case, see Rüdiger Schmitt-Beck, "Kampagnenwandel und Wählerwandel. 'Fenster der Gelegenheit' für einflussreichere Wahlkämpfe," in *Machtdarstellung und Darstellungsmacht*, eds., Ulrich Sarcinelli, Jens Teschner (Baden-Baden, 2003), 199-218, here 205.
5. This definition is quite comparable with Otto Kirchheimer's famous "catch-all" party concept and its emphasis on vote maximization and a general, leadership-based appeal rather than programmatic rigor and goal-oriented policy specificity. For new research on the catch-all party see Michelle Hale Williams, ed., "Catch-All in the Twenty First Century?" Special Issue, *Party Politics* 19, no. 8 (2009): 539-664.
6. Wolfgang Stock, "The CDU: Still a Party for the Future?" *Transatlantic Perspectives*, (Washington, 2009), 24-27.
7. Russell J. Dalton, *Citizen Politics*, 5th ed. (Washington, 2008), 180-190.
8. Matthias Jung, "Das sozialdemokratische Lagerdilemma, *Berliner Republik*, 6 (2009).
9. University of Mannheim, Post-Election Survey, 2009, variable pos 034.

10. Infratest Dimap surveys and Federal Statistical Office.
11. David P. Conradt, "The Tipping Point: The 2005 Election and the De-Consolidation of the German Party System?" *German Politics and Society* 24, no. 1 (2006): 18. Data for 2009 are from Forschungsgruppe Wahlen, Survey No. 1828, 2 October 2009.
12. Rüdiger Schmitt-Beck, "Better Late Than Never: Campaign Deciders at the 2005 German Parliamentary Election," Paper presented at the Fifth ECPR General Conference, Potsdam, 10-12 September 2009.
13. Mannheim (see note 9).
14. Lösche (see note 1), 8; Data from Oskar Niedermayer, "Parteimitglieder in Deutschland: Version 2008," (Bonn, 2008).
15. Dalton and Wattenberg (see note 4).
16. Note that the definitive test of this statement would, of course, require individual level data and is beyond the scope of this chapter.
17. Conradt (see note 11).
18. Forschungsgruppe Wahlen, "Bundestagswahl. Eine Analyse der Wahl vom 27. September, 2009", Bericht No. 138, Mannheim: Forschungsgruppe Wahlen, 129. The 1953-2009 figures are only from western Germany.
19. Forschungsgruppe Wahlen (see note 18), 118.
20. Institut für Demoskopie Survey No. 066, September 1953.
21. Franz Walter, *Herbst der Volksparteien?* (Bielefeld, 2009), 51.
22. Lösche (see note 1), 11.
23. At the state level, lower turnout and increased party system fragmentation are usually characteristic of post-grand coalition elections. Melanie Haas, "Auswirkungen der Großen Koalition auf das Parteiensystem," *Aus Politik und Zeitgeschichte* 35-36 (2007): 21-23.
24. For an excellent analysis of the role of both major parties in passing Agenda 2010 see Thomas Saalfeld, "Conflict and Consensus in Germany's Bi-Cameral System: A Case Study of the Passage of the Agenda 2010," *Debatte* 14, no. 3 (2006): 247-269.
25. Cited in Matthias Geyer, Dirk Kurbjuweit, and Cordt Schnibben, *Operation Rot-Grün: Geschichte eines politischen Abenteurs* (Munich, 2005), 260-261.
26. Infratest dimap Post Election Surveys; available at http://stat.tagesschau.de/wahlen/umfrage.
27. Marc Debus, "Unfulfilled Promises? German Social Democrats and their Policy Positions at the Federal and State Level between 1994 and 1998," *Journal of Elections, Public Opinion and Parties* 18, no. 2 (2008): 201-224.
28. Robert Rohrschneider and Rüdiger Schmitt-Beck, "Understanding the 2009 Election Outcome," unpublished presentation, Rice University Conference on Germany, Houston, October 2009.
29. Mannheim (see note 9).
30. This is the consensus of most post-election survey analysts. See Forschungsgruppe Wahlen (see note 18). A careful analysis of the 2009 pre- and post-election surveys by Anderson and Hecht came to a similar conclusion. They found "no effects of sociotropic retrospective voting in the 2009 German election...voters did not punish the government for the country's past economic performance, nor did they reward any of the opposition parties with support because they viewed the country's economy as having gotten worse." Christopher J. Anderson and Jason D. Hecht, "Voting When the Economy Goes Bad, Everyone is in Charge, and No One's to Blame: The Case of the 2009 Election," Paper presented at the 2009 German Federal Election Conference, University of Kansas, 26 April 2010, 21.
31. *Der Spiegel,* 21 December 2009, 68-72.
32. Rohrschneider and Schmitt-Beck (see note 28).
33. Christopher Allen, "'Empty Nets.' Social Democracy and the 'Catch-All Party Thesis' in Germany and Sweden," *Party Politics* 15, no. 5 (2009): 635-653. For a similar argument applied to all the parties that emerged out of the Rokkan-Lipset "frozen parties and

cleavages thesis" see Peter Mair, "Ruling the Void? The Hollowing of Western Democracy," *New Left Review* 42 (2006), 25-51.

34. Allen (see note 33), 644.
35. Gerd Langguth, "Gefahr von der Basis," *Spiegel online*, 11 January 2010.
36. *Der Spiegel*, 11 January 2010, 23. According to the group's leader its primary goal is to ensure that the party is "firmly anchored in fundamental Christian values."
37. Hans Peter Kriesi, et al., "Globalization and the Transformation of the National Political Space: Six European Countries Compared," *European Journal of Political Research* 45 (2006): 921-956.
38. Ibid., 327.
39. Ibid., 344. In the British case, the authors stressed the institutional barriers to new party formation, i.e., the electoral system and absence of subnational opportunities. But as recent elections in Britain have shown, a single-member district system may delay major party erosion, but it cannot prevent it. On further changes in European party systems see Oskar Niedermayer, "Von der Zweiparteiendominanz zum Pluralismus: Die Entwicklung des deutschen Parteiensystems im westeuropäischen Vergleich," *Politische Vierteljahresschrift* 51, no. 1 (2010): 1-13.
40. *Spiegel online*, 13 January 2010.
41. In addition to being young, the Pirate voters were male, with a natural science or engineering educational background and little, if any, prior political activity. The party's major issue was free and uncensored access to the Internet. Many were mobilized by the Grand Coalition's efforts to police the Internet. See Felix Neumann, "Die digitale Opposition," *Berliner Republik* 6 (2009); available at www.b-republik.de.
42. For an analysis of the Left Party's 2005 vote and its relationship to the SPD, see Oliver Nachtwey and Tim Spier, "Political Opportunity Structures and the Success of the German Left Party," *Debatte* 15, no.2 (2007): 123-154. They conclude: "... the Left Party's gains truly are meat from the social democratic table," 154.
43. Bernd Ulrich, "Der Boden zittert," *Die Zeit*, 3 September 2009; available at www.zeit.de/2009/37/01-Wahlen.
44. On the PDS in the 2002 election, see Gerald R. Kleinfeld, "The PDS Implodes" in *A Precarious Victory. Schroeder and the German Elections of 2002*, eds., David P. Conradt, Gerald R. Kleinfeld, and Christian Søe (New York, 2005), 135-152.
45. Matthias Jung, "Das sozialdemokratische Lagerdilemma," *Berliner Republik* 6 (2009).
46. Jörg Siegmund, "The Decline of the *Volksparteien, German-American Issues* 11 (Washington, 2009), 7.
47. Charles Lees "The Paradoxical Impact of Party System Change in Germany," Paper presented at the American Political Science Association Annual Meeting, Toronto, 3-6 September 2009, 2.
48. Ibid., 23.
49. In his path dependent analysis of the origins of the West German party system, Marcus Kreuzer stresses the importance of early conditions such as the licensing of the political parties and the five percent clause of the Basic Law as critical for the institutionalization of the postwar Bonn system. Marcus Kreuzer, "How Party Systems Form: Path Dependency and the Institutionalization of the Post-War German Party System," *British Journal of Political Science* 39, no.2 (2009): 669-697.

Chapter 3

$\mathscr{B}$UNDESTAG ELECTION 2009
Solidifying the Five Party System

● ● ● ● ● ● ● ● ● ● ● ● ● ●

Steven Weldon
and
Andrea Nüsser

Even before the final polls closed and initial results were reported, it was evident there was something different about the 2009 German Bundestag election. Whereas recent election campaigns had been highly partisan and full of excitement and uncertainty, this one failed to capture the public's imagination. *Der Spiegel* lamented that the campaign was "the dullest in living memory," while the *Economist* called it "soporific."[1] This apathy was reflected in the record low voter turnout of 70.8 percent, a near seven point drop from the previous low set in 2005.[2] Indeed, there seemed to be little at stake in this election as the customary battle between the Christian Democrats (CDU/CSU) and Social Democrats (SPD) over which one would lead the new government never materialized. The Christian Democrats held a double digit lead in opinion polls before and throughout the campaign,[3] and it was clear Angela Merkel would continue as chancellor–the only question was whether the CDU would partner with the center-right Free Democrats (FDP) or continue in a grand coalition with the SPD.

The lack of competition between the top two parties, however, was not the only contributing factor to the lackluster campaign. The German party system had undergone a dramatic change in the four years since the previous election and especially since the 2002 election. It had stabilized into a five-party system and no longer was there uncertainty about each of the three minor parties surpassing the five percent threshold and securing representation in the Bundestag.[4] Throughout the 1990s and first half of the 2000s, this was not the case.

While the campaign may have failed to spark much interest, the results of the election were significant and likely represent a fundamental shift in the nature of German politics. The three minor parties all made notable gains at the expense of the two traditional *Volksparteien,* and the SPD saw its worst performance in its history, capturing just 23 percent of the vote. Despite holding on to the chancellorship, the CDU/CSU also sank to a sixty year low with less than 34 percent. In contrast, the three minor parties each posted historical bests and each received more than 10 percent of the vote.

These developments raise important questions about the future of German politics. Will the two major parties continue to lose votes to the three smaller parties? Following an over three decade trend of voter dealignment, does the 2009 election represent the beginnings of a realignment? Or, are we likely to see a more fluid five-party system with many independent or swing voters up for grabs in each election cycle?[5] Finally, is there a single German party system or are there effectively two separate systems in the former East and West?

In this chapter, we explore these questions with a focus on the general electorate and the core supporters for each party. We draw primarily on the 2009 German Longitudinal Election Study (GLES), which the principal investigators graciously made publicly available within three months of the election. We begin with an overview of the fundamental changes in the party system over recent decades and the establishment of the current five-party system. We then examine general patterns of support for the parties for the 2009 election and provide a more detailed analysis of each party's core and swing voters. In the final section, we explore the dramatic drop in SPD support between the 2005 and 2009 elections, focusing on the motivations of those supporters who remained loyal to the SPD and those that defected to the other parties.

Development of the Five-Party System

The rise of the three minor parties and solidification of the five-party system in the 2009 election was momentous, but it has its roots in the well documented dealignment processes that began in the latter half of the twentieth century.[6] Modernization and the rise of the welfare state in postwar Germany led to a gradual weakening of traditional partisan attachments and a decline in salience of religious and class cleavages.[7] This was a double-edged sword for the two major parties. On the one hand, each party's traditional supporters were becoming less dependable at election time. On the other, so were those of their main competitor. Indeed, the party system as a whole was becoming more fluid and this opened the door for the two traditional *Volksparteien* to adopt more centrist policies that would attract new voters at the expense of each other.[8]

While the rise of the catch-all party model initially had little impact on the make-up of the party system,[9] in time it further fueled the dealignment trends and contributed to the weakening grip that the CDU/CSU and SPD jointly held on German political life. Electoral volatility rose as voters not only were increasingly likely to switch parties from one election to the next but they were also more likely to split their ballot in the same election. Turnout steadily dropped, as did party membership numbers, and the public became ever more disenchanted with political parties and their leaders.

These developments, as well as the increased salience of postmaterialist issues, set the stage for the Greens' emergence in Germany. The Greens first gained Bundestag representation following the 1983 election, breaking the over two decade monopoly of the CDU/CSU, SPD and FDP. In 1998, the Greens achieved another historic first when they entered government as the junior coalition partner to the SPD. This gave Germany its first democratically elected, fully leftist government and formally ended the two-and-a-half-party system that had characterized German federal politics for most of the postwar period.

Table 1: Results of Bundestag Elections (1949-2009)

Year	CDU/CSU	SPD	FDP	Greens	Left Party
1949	31.0	29.2	11.9		
1953	45.2	28.8	9.5		
1957	50.2	31.8	7.7		
1961	45.3	36.2	12.8		
1965	47.6	39.3	9.5		
1969	46.1	42.7	5.8		
1971	44.9	45.8	8.4		
1976	48.6	42.6	7.9		
1980	44.5	42.9	10.6	1.5	
1983	48.8	38.2	7.0	5.6	
1987	44.3	37.0	9.1	8.3	
1990	43.8	33.5	11.0	5.1	2.4
1994	41.4	36.4	6.9	7.3	4.4
1998	35.1	40.9	6.2	6.7	5.1
2002	38.5	38.5	7.4	8.6	4.0
2005	35.2	34.2	9.8	8.1	8.7
2009	33.8	23.0	14.6	10.7	11.9

Source: http://www.bundeswahlleiter.de

In spite of the Greens' success, their situation remained quite precarious throughout their early history. As Table 1 shows, their vote share regularly hovered just over the 5 percent threshold with an average of 7 percent for the seven federal elections from 1983 to 2005. In 1990, they failed to get over the threshold in the West, their traditional region of strength—despite their impressive performance in 1987 when they captured 8.3 percent of the vote in the last election before unification. In this sense, the 1990 results effectively underscored the tenuous position of the German Greens in federal politics, even if this election was historically unique in other respects.

The beginnings of the Party of Democratic Socialism (PDS/Left Party) were even less auspicious. The successor to the former SED ruling party of East Germany, the PDS competed in the first election after unification in 1990. While it failed to register support in the West or get over 5 percent nationwide, it performed strongly in the East, securing seventeen Bundestag seats and attaining full Fraktion caucus status. The PDS failed to get over the threshold again in 1994, but because it won four directly elected constituency seats from the first ballot (*Erststimme*), it was eligible for full proportional representation. The 1998 election marked the high point for the PDS when it finally slipped just over the national threshold.

It appeared at the time that the PDS was well on its way to playing a more prominent role in German politics. Its support had grown steadily in the years since unification and the party seemed to be feeding off Easterners' growing disaffection with the established parties and the pace of economic progress.[10] It also had entered state government and gained legitimacy as a junior partner to the SPD in Saxony-Anhalt, Mecklenburg West Pomerania, and Berlin.[11] Yet, its strength also proved to be its weakness—the PDS was never able to gain a foothold outside the former East and in the 2002 elections it had its worst showing. Not only did it fall below the 5 percent hurdle, but it also failed to win three direct constituency seats and hence was not eligible for any additional seats from the second or proportional vote.

The far left in Germany was reeling at that time, however, there would be a silver lining in the disastrous 2002 result, setting in motion the process that would lead to the solidification of a strong five-party system.[12] Based at least partly on its poor results from 2002, the PDS formed an electoral alliance for the 2005 elections with Electoral Alternative for Labor and Social Justice (WASG). Led by Oskar Lafontaine, a former SPD party leader and its chancellor candidate in 1990, WASG broke away from the SPD due to dissatisfaction with the centrist policies of Chancellor Gerhard Schröder's Red-Green government. Competing across all of Germany, this newly formed leftist alliance captured nearly 9 percent of the federal vote in 2005, a marked improvement on what the PDS was able to do on its own.

Until now, we have focused our attention on the decline of the two *Volksparteien* and the tenuous rise of the two newest minor parties. Nevertheless, as one can also see in Table 1, although the FDP was able to secure nearly 15 percent of the vote in 2009, it too was on less firm ground over much of the previous three decades. As recently as 1998, the party hit its nadir with just 6.1 percent support.

The weak position of the three minor parties, however, is not just reflected in their relatively low vote share since unification. Indeed, it is important to note that much of their expressed support, especially for the FDP and Greens, actually came from weak supporters or even party identifiers of the CDU and SPD respectively. These voters were presumably casting strategic second ballot votes to ensure that their junior partners got over the 5 percent hurdle.[13] Consider this. The results above and throughout most of this chapter refer to the *Zweitstimmen*. Yet, if we looked instead at the *Erststimmen* for the direct constituency elections, we would find that the FDP averaged a mere 4.9 percent of the vote for the five federal elections from 1990 to 2005, while the Greens averaged 5.6 percent.[14] In the 1994, 1998, and 2005 elections, the FDP would have failed to get over the electoral threshold if that hurdle applied to this vote or in a simple proportional representation system.

While it is surely true that many supporters of the two minor parties also cast strategic first votes for their respective major partners, it is more telling for our purposes to compare these results with those from the 2009 election where the FDP received 9.4 percent of the *Erststimmen* and the Greens received 9.2 percent. Including the performance of the Left Party, which received 11.1 percent, it seems clear that the German party system has undergone a fundamental change since the electoral alliance and subsequent merger of the PDS and WASG into the Left Party. To further underscore this point, in the last election before the establishment of the leftist alliance in 2002, the CDU/CSU and SPD combined to receive 83 percent of the *Erststimmen* and 77 percent of the *Zweitstimmen*, whereas in 2009 they managed just 67 percent and 57 percent respectively.[15]

The final aspect of the new five-party system that we examine is the extent to which the parties' support varies between East and West. As discussed above, following unification, the PDS fared quite well in the East, regularly securing upwards of 25 percent of the federal vote. Yet, in the West it was unable to establish a foothold at the federal or state level. In contrast, the SPD, and especially the Greens, ran disproportionately strong in the West. This has prompted some to suggest that Germany effectively has two separate party systems despite over two decades since the fall of the Berlin Wall.[16]

Table 2: Official Results of the 2009 Bundestag Election by Land (in percent)

	CDU/CSU	SPD	FDP	Greens	Left Party
Schleswig Holstein	32.2	26.8	16.3	12.7	7.9
Hamburg	27.8	27.4	13.2	15.6	11.2
Lower Saxony	33.2	29.3	13.3	10.7	8.6
Bremen	23.9	30.2	10.6	15.4	14.3
North Rhine Westphalia	33.1	28.5	14.9	10.1	8.4
Hesse	32.2	25.6	16.6	12.0	8.5
Rhineland-Palatinate	35.0	23.8	16.6	9.7	9.4
Bavaria	42.5	16.8	14.7	10.8	6.5
Baden-Württemberg	34.4	19.3	18.8	13.9	7.2
Saarland	30.7	24.7	11.9	6.8	21.2
Berlin	22.8	20.2	11.5	17.4	20.2
Mecklenburg West Pomerania	33.1	16.6	9.8	5.5	29.0
Brandenburg	23.6	25.1	9.3	6.1	28.5
Saxony-Anhalt	30.1	16.9	10.3	5.1	32.4
Saxony	35.6	14.6	13.3	6.7	24.5
Thuringia	31.2	17.6	9.8	6.0	28.8

Source: http://www.bundeswahlleiter.de

Table 2 examines this notion with results from the 2009 election broken down by the Land level. In one sense, there is some evidence for such a divide. The Left Party continues to fare much better in the former East with the other four parties performing better in the West. Yet, what we find more striking is that all five political parties were able to get over the 5 percent threshold in each of the sixteen Länder, and, moreover, they were able to do so rather comfortably. In other words, any one of the sixteen Länder serves as a microcosm for Germany as a whole, insofar as each would reproduce on its own the five-party system that we see at the national level. We take this as convincing evidence of a strong five-party system that is likely here to stay at the federal level, as well as the state and municipal arenas. We now examine in greater depth the nature of this new five-party system with a focus on the voters for each party.

The Nature of the Five-Party Systems—Patterns of Support for Each Party

The erosion of core voters (*Stammwähler*) since the early 1990s and the increasing number of swing voters (*Wechselwähler*) present a growing challenge to the political parties and election prognosticators alike. Voters are making their decisions later in the campaign–and there is a significant number who do so in the last days before or even the day of the election.

For example, in the most recent election, more than 40 percent of voters report making their decision within the last week of the campaign.[17] This is a large number of potential swing voters and it means that they play a critical role in determining the parties' fates and the overall election outcome. It also provides preliminary evidence against the idea that we may be seeing a realignment of the German electorate–at least in the sense of a large share of the electorate having strong ties to the different parties.

In this section, we explore the challenge that the parties face in maintaining their support and achieving electoral success, looking more closely at their respective core and swing voters from the recent election. We also examine how the voters for each party in 2009 recall voting in the 2005 election, as well as levels of party identification. Core voters are those who routinely vote for the same party, often out of tradition and convention, rather than because of its current performance. In contrast, swing voters have no fixed party preference and are more likely to switch their vote from election to election. They represent the fluid element of each party's support base and the party system in general. Swing voters then are the main targets of an election campaign as they make their voting decision during that period of time.

The data for this part of the analysis come from the 2009 GLES, which includes both a pre- and post-wave survey of the same respondents. Following the logic above, we distinguish a party's core and swing voters based on the time point that respondents report having made their voting decision. Voters who made their voting decision well in advance of the election are coded as core voters, while those who made their choice at some point during the campaign are coded as swing voters.

Table 3 shows the voters for each party broken into core and swing voters in terms of the percentage points that each group contributed to each party's overall vote share. Among everyone who voted in the 2009 election, 43 percent are coded as core voters and 57 percent as swing voters.[18] Despite the large number of swing voters, it appears that even the minor parties have a solid enough base of core voters to ensure getting over the 5 percent threshold and securing representation in the Bundestag. As noted above in regards to the discussion on the first ballot votes, this appears to be a relatively new development and lends support to our argument that the German party system has developed into a stable, but fluid five-party system.

A closer look at each party's share of core versus swing voters reveals interesting differences between the five parties. Despite their declining vote share and their historical lows in the 2005 and 2009 elections, the

Table 3: Core and Swing Voters of Each of the Five Parties (in percent)

	Core Voters	Swing Voters	All Voters
CDU/CSU	17.0	14.4	31.4
SPD	11.2	12.1	23.3
FDP	5.6	10.8	16.4
Greens	4.5	9.4	13.9
Left Party	4.5	5.9	10.4
	42.8	52.6	95.4

Source: 2009 German Longitudinal Election Study (GLES)

Christian Democrats have the most solid support base of all parties. Not only does the CDU/CSU have the highest share of core voters (17 percent of all voters), it is also the only party for which the share of core supporters is larger than the share of non-core supporters (14.4 percent). Moreover, this pertains despite quite a few CDU party identifiers deciding during the 2009 campaign to cast their vote for the FDP (see Table 5). If we assume that this group simply was voting strategically and in more dire circumstances would return to the CDU, then this party's core voters increase to approximately 20.5 percent of the electorate.

To explore the extent of core support further, Table 4 shows how the voters of each party in 2009 recall voting in the 2005 election. The values represent the percentage of voters for each party from the 2005 election that cast votes for the respective parties in the 2009 election. Even though core voters make up just over half of the voters, 63.5 percent of CDU/CSU voters in 2005 stayed loyal to the party in 2009. Moreover, most of those who defected did so to the FDP with nearly a quarter from 2005 opting for the traditional junior coalition partner. To put this in further perspective, an astounding 53.9 percent of FDP voters in the 2009 election actually voted for the CDU in 2005. This suggests that many CDU/CSU supporters cast a strategic vote for the FDP with the hope of ensuring their favored Black-Yellow governing coalition.

Table 4: Comparison between Voting in 2005 and 2009 (in percent)

Vote in 2005	Vote in 2009					
	CDU/CSU	SPD	FDP	Greens	Left Party	Other
CDU/CSU	63.5	5.2	22.4	2.1	2.3	4.4
SPD	8.8	58.7	4.2	13.2	9.2	5.8
FDP	16.7	3.3	63.7	3.3	4.1	9.0
Greens	4.6	12.2	2.1	65.4	11.3	4.2
Left Party	1.2	5.6	1.9	4.3	79.6	7.4
Other	18.7	7.9	10.4	9.8	10.4	42.7

Source: 2009 German Longitudinal Election Study (GLES)

The SPD's support base is significantly smaller and weaker than that of the Christian Democrats. Apart from its size, the distribution of its core and swing voters is fairly even with 11.2 percent core and 12.2 percent swing voters. In other words, core voters constitute just 48 percent of the SPD's support, while 52 percent made their decision at some point during the campaign. The most notable development though, and one to which we already have alluded, is the remarkable drop in SPD's vote share from the 2005 to the 2009 election—a full 11.2 percentage points.

Where did these former SPD voters go? Table 4 shows that a majority did, in fact, stay with the SPD (58.7 percent)–perhaps surprisingly, this was only a five point lower retention rate than that of the CDU/CSU. While CDU/CSU defectors went overwhelmingly to the FDP, however, SPD defectors spread themselves more evenly across the other parties. Interestingly, in spite of a variety of factors that would seem to have worked against the SPD, including Merkel's popularity, the comparatively strong position of the CDU/CSU, and the turmoil within the SPD leadership over the previous four years,[19] the SPD lost a relatively small share of its voters to its grand coalition partner (8.8 percent). Coupled with the fact that 5.2 percent of CDU/CSU voters in 2005 defected to the SPD in 2009, it is difficult to conclude that the CDU/CSU benefited much from the Social Democrats' woes–at least not directly in terms of attracting disillusioned voters.

Instead, most 2005 SPD voters who defected in the 2009 election chose to support the Greens or the Left Party. This may seem surprising since it was evident before the election that the Greens and the Left Party would remain in opposition–the Social Democrats' statement prior to the election, ruling out the possibility of a Red-Red-Green coalition, only further reinforced their likely opposition status. This suggests former SPD supporters did not so much cast a strategic vote for the Greens and the Left Party as they did a sanctioning vote to express their dissatisfaction with the policy direction of the two major parties forming the grand coalition.[20] This interpretation is further supported by the fact that many voters who still identify with the SPD nonetheless voted for the Greens and the Left Party in the 2009 election (see Table 5).

With 14.6 percent of the vote, the FDP secured its historically best result in 2009, nearly five points better than in the 2005 election. While the FDP's result was the best of the three small parties, the support bases of the Greens and the Left Party actually appear to be stronger than that of the FDP. As Table 3 shows, only 5.6 percent of all voters can be considered FDP core voters, or 34 percent of its total vote share. As noted above and in Table 5, the 66 percent support from swing voters was predominately

Table 5: Party Identification by Vote Choice 2009 (in percent)

Party Identification

	CDU/CSU	SPD	FDP	Greens	Left Party	No/other party
CDU/CSU	65.8	5.4	2.7	1.4	0.3	24.5
SPD	5.0	66.3	0.7	5.0	0.6	22.3
FDP	34.2	3.0	28.0	1.1	0.7	33.0
Greens	4.3	18.6	0.6	48.0	1.6	26.9
Left Party	4.2	16.3	0.6	4.8	43.1	31.0

Source: 2009 German Longitudinal Election Study (GLES)

from CDU/CSU identifiers, many of whom had voted for the CDU/CSU in 2005. This provides further evidence that the FDP's support base is significantly weaker than the 2009 election results suggest.

The Greens fell to the fifth-largest party behind the FDP and the Left Party, but they too scored a historical best. Like the FDP, the Greens had a relatively small share of core voters (4.5 percent) and attracted significant support from former voters of its historical coalition partner. Indeed, 13.2 percent of SPD voters from the 2005 election defected to the Greens, which amounts to over 30 percent of the Greens total vote share. This suggests that they too may have some difficulty in duplicating their success in future elections. At the same time, however, in comparison to the other two minor parties, it appears the Greens have a much stronger and stable support base. As Table 5 indicates, Green voters tend to have much higher rates of party identification than those for the FDP.

Despite its exceptional result, the Left Party is in a difficult position. Located left of the SPD, the only possible coalition partners for the party are the SPD and the Greens. Yet, before the election, the SPD indicated it would not form a coalition with the Left Party on the federal level. Also, although it fared better than the Greens, the Left Party has the smallest support base of all parties, combining 4.5 percent core voters and 5.9 percent swing voters (see Table 3). Unlike the FDP's and the Greens' vote share, the Left Party's vote share is fairly evenly split between core (43.5 percent) and swing voters (56.5 percent). Despite its small size, the fairly balanced vote share and comparably large share of core voters suggest that its support base is small, but relatively solid. Nevertheless, at some point before the election, 20 percent of Left Party voters considered voting for the SPD. Similar to the Greens, this party might have benefited from frustrated SPD supporters who cast sanctioning votes.

The Fragmentation of the SPD

The results so far suggest that the fragmentation of the German electorate poses much more of a hurdle to the SPD and the ideological left than to the CDU/CSU, FDP and center-right. In this final section, we examine this in greater detail with a closer look at the voting behavior of the voters who recall voting for the SPD in the 2005 election. As is evident in Table 4, 58.7 percent stayed loyal to the SPD in 2009, 8.8 percent switched to the CDU/CSU, 4.2 percent to the FDP, 13.2 percent to the Greens, and 9.2 percent to the Left Party. Understanding the motivations and attitudes of these voters is critical to understanding the SPD's long-term fate and any possibility of a genuinely leftist governing coalition in the near future.[21] We focus on three factors known to influence voting decisions, particularly for voters who make their decision during the campaign: issue positions, images of the political parties, and candidate or leadership images.[22]

Table 6: Left-Right Ideology and Issue Competence: Former SPD Voters by Current Party Choice

	Mean Left-Right Ideology (Self-Reported)	Percentage who believe their party is the most competent to solve key issues	
		1st Issue	2nd Issue
CDU/CSU	5.42	50.0	44.7
SPD	4.72	55.6	58.6
FDP	5.81	45.0	17.5
Greens	4.23	16.5	34.4
Left Party	3.50	21.6	30.0

Source: 2009 German Longitudinal Election Study (GLES)

Note: left-right ideology is measured on an eleven point scale running from 1 to 11 with 6 as the midpoint. For issue competence, respondents were first asked to identify in an open-ended question the most important and second most important problems facing the country. They were then asked to identify which party would be most competent in solving those problems. The values reported are the percentage of respondents who identified their own party as most competent to solve the problems, regardless of the specific problem identified.

We begin with issue positions as outlined in Table 6, which first shows former SPD voters' mean left-right ideological positions based on the party they supported in the 2009 election. The findings indicate that voters were quite rational in their voting decisions for this election, even if they tend to be more moderate than the traditional voters of the respective political parties. The most conservative SPD defectors chose the FDP, which appears to be consistent with the electorate as a whole for this election. CDU/CSU defectors are to the right of the SPD loyalists, and then come the Green voters, and finally those that defected to the Left Party–clearly the most ideologically leftist. In short, it appears that most voted for the party that was closest to them on the left-right spectrum. Nevertheless, it is important to note that regardless of the party supported in 2009, all groups of former SPD voters are located on the left side of left-right divide, including those of the CDU/CSU and FDP. This suggests that the latter two parties may have some difficulty in retaining these cross-over voters.

The final two columns in Table 6 get at the role of issue positions in voting behavior in a different and more direct way. Here respondents were asked in an open-ended format to identify up to two key problems that they think Germany is facing. They were then asked to identify the party that could best solve those problems. We do not examine the specific problems raised, because our chief interest is simply whether there is a correspondence between perceived issue competence and vote choice. Thus, the reported values are the percentage of former SPD voters for each party for whom there is such a correspondence. Overall, the results are mixed. Voters of the two major parties are more likely to see those parties as the most competent in handling the key problems, while minor party voters are less likely to have such confidence in their preferred parties. Nonetheless, taken into consideration with the findings on left-right ideological placement, there is good evidence that many voters who left the SPD between 2005 and 2009 did so because they believed that another party better represented their interests.

Table 7: Mean Ratings of Parties: Former SPD Voters by Current Party Choice

	CDU	CSU	SPD	FDP	Greens	Left Party
CDU/CSU	2.31	0.72	0.76	0.45	0.20	-2.93
SPD	0.21	-1.11	2.76	-1.06	1.81	-1.70
FDP	1.43	-0.06	0.66	2.52	0.62	-2.70
Greens	-0.02	-1.46	1.78	-1.16	2.78	-1.38
Left Party	-0.98	-1.48	0.59	-1.25	0.97	1.64

Source: 2009 German Longitudinal Election Study (GLES)

Note: values are the mean ratings of the parties in 2009 by the voters of the respective parties. The universe is restricted to respondents who recall voting for the SPD in the 2005 election. Ratings are on an eleven point scale running from -5 to +5 with 0 feeling neutral.

Turning now to party and candidate images, Table 7 shows former SPD voters' mean ratings for each of the six political parties broken down by the party they supported in the 2009 election, while Table 8 shows the ratings for the party leaders. It is important to note that these attitudes were assessed in the pre-election wave of the survey, and hence, before many of the respondents had decided which party to support on election day. Not surprisingly, voters tended to rate their respective new parties and their leaders the highest.

The more interesting results are the assessments of the other parties and leaders as well as comparisons between the party and its leader. For example, those who defected to the CDU/CSU did rate the CDU highly, but they rated Merkel even higher. They failed to give equally high marks to the FDP or its leader, and in fact rated Frank-Walter Steinmeier notably higher than Guido Westerwelle. They were relatively ambivalent toward the Greens, but harbored extremely negative feelings toward the Left Party and its co-leader Oskar Lafontaine. Taken together, these results suggest that the CDU/CSU defectors were driven primarily by a positive orientation toward the CDU party leader and an intense aversion toward the Left Party, and especially any possibility of a Red-Red-Green coalition.

Table 8: Mean Ratings of Party Leaders: Former SPD Voters by Current Party Choice

	Merkel	Guttenberg	Steinmeier	Westerwelle	Künast	Lafontaine
CDU/CSU	3.29	2.01	1.41	0.04	-0.43	-2.19
SPD	1.79	1.29	2.65	-1.26	1.27	-1.39
FDP	2.64	2.65	0.78	2.27	0.15	-2.57
Greens	1.63	1.22	1.45	-1.61	1.60	-1.74
Left Party	0.57	0.94	0.37	-0.97	0.72	1.49

Source: 2009 German Longitudinal Election Study (GLES)

Note: values are the mean ratings of the party leaders in 2009 by the voters of the respective parties. The universe is restricted to respondents who recall voting for the SPD in the 2005 election. Ratings are on an eleven point scale running from -5 to +5 with 0 feeling neutral.

Voters who stayed loyal to the SPD in 2009 also present an interesting picture. These voters were not particular fond of the CDU or CSU as political parties, clearly favoring their historical junior partner, the Greens. The ratings, however, were reversed for the respective leaders, with Merkel garnering more positive feelings than Renate Künast. This suggests that many SPD loyalists, while preferring a Red-Green coalition, would have been quite content with a continuation of the Grand Coalition, so long as Merkel remained chancellor.

Turning to the Green defectors, we see that their ratings were quite similar to those of the SPD loyalists. Yet, notably, along with the FDP defectors, they were the only voters who failed to rank their own party leader the highest, actually giving the highest marks again to Merkel by a small margin. Finally, the Left Party clearly sticks out from the others. Despite favoring the SPD and Greens over the CDU/CSU and FDP, the defectors to the Left Party did not express very positive feelings to any of the other parties or their leaders. Moreover, these feelings were mutual.

In sum, the steep drop in SPD vote share between 2005 and 2009 appears to be the function of a variety of short-term factors that depended on the specific party. Those who crossed-over the left-right spectrum to vote for either the CDU/CSU or FDP stand out for their very positive assessment of Merkel and aversion toward the Left Party and Lafontaine. True, they are also more conservative than other former SPD voters, but CDU/CSU defectors still tend to be closer ideologically to the SPD. In contrast, ideological motivations appear to be the primary factor for defectors to the Greens and the Left Party. They remain somewhat positively oriented toward the SPD (Green defectors more so than those of the Left Party), but seem to have a better ideological fit with the more extreme parties.

The Future of the German Five-Party System

The 2009 German election likely will be remembered as the solidification of a relatively stable, but fluid five-party system. That fluidity, however, is not random. As Frank Decker and others suggest, it appears to be structured along the left-right ideological spectrum with the parties divided into two major camps and vote-switching much more likely within the respective camps rather than between them.[23] Indeed, most of the voters who defected from the CDU/CSU switched their support to the FDP, while SPD defectors favored the Greens and the Left Party. More to the point, based on findings from the GLES, only 8.5 percent of all voters reported voting for a party on the opposite side of the left-right ideological spectrum compared to their 2005 vote. Perhaps surprisingly, the cross-over between the two sides was split fairly evenly with only a slight advantage to the CDU/CSU and FDP (4.5 versus 4.0 percent).[24]

Nevertheless, there appears to be a clear difference between the two camps in terms of the risk that fragmentation poses for the respective mass parties and their prospects for forming a government in the future. The rightist camp looks relatively stable with the CDU/CSU maintaining a strong position and the vote-switching between the two parties more cooperative than adversarial. This is not the case for the leftist camp and the SPD. Not only has the SPD ruled out a coalition involving the Left Party for now, but the support bases of both the Greens and the Left Party appear more solid than that of the FDP.

The nature of the current party system can be traced to the 2005 electoral alliance of the PDS with the WASG, or perhaps more correctly, the efforts of the Schröder-led Red-Green coalition to implement the series of neoliberal economic and social welfare reforms known as Agenda 2010. Agenda 2010 was unpopular with the left wing of the SPD, which broke away to form the WASG, as well as the supporters of the two more leftist parties. At the same time, the SPD appears not to have been rewarded by more moderate voters for implementing these policies, despite the strong evidence that they worked as intended to reinvigorate the German economy.

This has put the SPD in a rather difficult situation. In the absence of cooperation with the Left Party, the SPD has virtually no hope of regaining the chancellorship in the near future and will be relegated to the opposition, or at best, a junior partner with the CDU/CSU in a grand coalition. While the Left Party currently is extremely unpopular within the SPD, it seems unlikely SPD party leaders or its supporters will accept this marginal role in German federal politics much beyond the most recent election. Already the media has begun to speculate that Lafontaine's stepping down from the leadership of the Left Party in January 2010 will help to warm relations between the two parties and pave the way for future pre-election alliances. With or without Lafontaine this is clearly necessary for the SPD—fighting the Left Party and trying to prevent its success appears to be a losing battle.

Notes

1. *Spiegel online*, 27 September 2009; available at http://www.spiegel.de/international/germany/, accessed on 15 January 2010; *The Economist* (website), 28 September 2009; available at http://www.economist.com; accessed on 15 January 2010.
2. The 70.8 percent represented a near 7 percent drop from the previous low set in the 2005 elections. See www.bundeswahlleiter.de; accessed on 15 January 2010.
3. Forschungsgruppe Wahlen; available at http://www.forschungsgruppe.de/; accessed on 15 January 2010.
4. The FDP, Greens, and the Left Party all polled above 10 percent throughout the campaign. See Forschungsgruppe Wahlen (see note 3).
5. See Oskar Niedermayer, "Die Entwicklung des deutschen Parteiensystems bis nach der Bundestagswahl 2002," in *Die Parteien nach der Bundestagswahl 2002*, ed., Oskar Niedermayer (Opladen, 2003), 9-41; Oskar Niedermayer, "Das fluide Fünfparteiensystem nach der Bundestagswahl 2005," in *Die Parteien nach der Bundestagswahl 2005*, ed., Oskar Niedermayer (Wiesbaden, 2008), 9-36.
6. On dealignment see Russell J. Dalton and Martin P. Wattenberg, eds., *Parties without Partisans* (New York, 2000).

7. Klaus von Beyme, *Parteien im Wandel: Von den Volksparteien zu den professionalisierten Wählerparteien* (Wiesbaden, 2000).
8. Ibid.
9. Otto Kirchheimer's influential article, for example, traces the shift to a catch-all strategy to the early 1960s. It would be nearly another quarter century before a new party would enter parliament with the Greens in 1983. See Otto Kirchheimer, "Der Wandel des westeuropäischen Parteiensystems," *Politische Vierteljahresschrift* 6 (1965): 20–41.
10. Russell Dalton and Steven Weldon, "Germans Divided?: Political Culture in a United Germany," *German Politics* 19, no, 1 (2010): 9-23; Robert Rohrschneider, *Learning Democracy: Democratic and Economic Values in Unified Germany* (New York, 1999); Henry Krisch, "From SED to PDS: The struggle to revive a left party," in *The New Germany Votes: Unification and the Creation of a New German Party System*, ed., Russell Dalton (Oxford, 1993), 163-84; Peter Doerschler and Lee Ann Banaszak, "Voter support for the German PDS over time: Dissatisfaction, ideology, losers and east identity," *Electoral Studies* 26 (2007): 359-370.
11. The PDS and SPD first cooperated in 1994 in Saxony-Anhalt. Rather than forming an official coalition, the SPD minority government was tolerated by the PDS—deemed the "Magdeburger Model." Official coalitions followed in Mecklenburg West Pomerania (1998-2006), Berlin (since 2002), and Brandenburg (since November 2009).
12. Niedermayer 2003, 2008 (see note 5).
13. Franz Urban Pappi and Paul W. and Thurner, "Electoral behaviour in a two-vote system: Incentives for ticket splitting in German Bundestag elections," *European Journal of Political Research*, 41 (2002): 207-32; Thomas Gschwend, "Ticket-splitting and strategic voting under mixed electoral rules: Evidence from Germany," *European Journal of Political Research* 49 (2007): 1-23; Susumu Shikano, Michael Herrmann, and Paul W. Thurner, "Strategic Voting under Proportional Representation: Threshold Insurance in German Elections," *West European Politics* 32, no. 3 (2009): 634-656.
14. Bundeswahlleiter (see note 2).
15. Ibid.
16. Russell Dalton and Wilhelm Bürklin, "Two German Electorates?: The Social Bases of the Vote in 1990 and 1994," *German Politics and Society* 34 (1995): 79-99; Russell Dalton and Willy Jou, "Is There a Single German Party System?," *German Politics and Society* 28, no. 2 (2010): 34-52; Robert Rohrschneider and Dieter Fuchs, "A New Electorate? Economic Trends and Electoral Choice in the 1994 Federal Election in Germany," *German Politics and Society* 13 (1995): 100-122.
17. German Longitudinal Election Study (GLES), Deutsche Gesellschaft für Wahlforschung, Mannheim.
18. If we define strategic voters as those who identify with one party but cast a vote for the established coalition partner, then this provides a more even split between core and non-core voters. Based on this criterion, 7 percent of coded non-core voters are in fact strategic voters.
19. Leading up to the election, the majority of Germans clearly preferred Merkel as chancellor to Steinmeier. In August 2009, the distance between both candidates reached a record high since 1977 (Merkel 65 percent, Steinmeier 23 percent). Similarly, during the entire election campaign the CDU/CSU had a clear lead ahead of SPD. See Forschungsgruppe Wahlen, Politbarometer August II 2009.
20. Before the election, 58 percent were satisfied with the CDU's performance in the Grand Coalition, while 46 percent of voters were content with the SPD's performance. GLES (see note 17).
21. The large sample size of the GLES (n=6008) allows us to examine this relatively small but key group with greater precision and confidence than is possible for a typical national survey. The sample size for all voters who recall voting for the Social Democrats in 2005 was n=1026, including n=602 who remained loyal to the SPD, n=90 who defected to the CDU or CSU, n=43 to the FDP, n=135 to the Greens, and n=94 to the Left Party.

22. See Angus Campbell, Philipp E. Converse, Warren E. Mille, and Donald E. Stokes, *The American Voter* (New York, 1960), 24-32; Mario Paul, "Warum überraschte das Votum der Wähler? Eine Antwort mit Hilfe eines integrativen Modells zur Erklärung des Wahlverhaltens," in *Bilanz der Bundestagswahl 2005: Voraussetzungen, Ergebnisse, Folgen*, eds., Eckhard Jesse and Roland Sturm (Wiesbaden, 2006), 189-210.

23. Frank Decker, "Koalitionsaussagen und Koalitionsbildung," *Aus Politik und Zeitgeschichte* 51 (2009): 20-26; Eckhard Jesse, "Parteiensystem im Wandel? Das deutsche Parteiensystem vor und nach der Bundestagswahl 2005," in Jesse and Sturm, (see note 22).

24. In reality, the split may have favored the CDU/CSU and FDP slightly more. This is because the GLES post-election survey slightly underestimates support for the CDU/CSU, while overestimating support for the Greens. Nonetheless, the general point still holds—there was limited vote-switching across the left-right spectrum and it did not appear to significantly benefit one side over the other.

$\mathscr{T}$HE SPD AND THE DEBACLE
OF THE 2009 GERMAN FEDERAL ELECTION
An Opportunity for Renewal

• • • • • • • • • • • • • • • •

William E. Paterson
and
James Sloam

Introduction

The 2009 federal election was a disaster for the German Social Democratic Party (SPD). Germany's oldest party slumped to its worst result in the history of the Federal Republic, polling only 23 percent of the vote (down from 34 percent in 2005).[1] Furthermore, the historically low turnout (70.8 percent) disguised the true calamity of the SPD's performance: the party lost over six million voters–almost 40 percent of the sixteen million Germans who had voted for the party only four years earlier–who either stayed at home or switched party.[2] Given the traditional stability of German party politics, this marked an extraordinary turn of events. Trust in the SPD's competence, identification with its values, and belief in its credibility all nosedived. While SPD-inspired reforms to the welfare state (particularly to unemployment benefits and provisions for retirement) blurred the boundaries with the center-Right, strategic uncertainty (illustrated by the SPD's damaging flirtation with the Left Party (LP) after the 2008 Hesse state election)[3] undermined the party's credibility. The resulting political catastrophe inspired a raft of political commentary from *Der Spiegel* to the British *Financial Times* that speculated about the "end of social democracy."[4]

Table 1: Results of the 2009 German Federal Election

	Percent Votes Cast in 2009 (change from2005)	Actual votes cast in 2009 in Millions (percent change from 2005)	Distribution of Seats in Bundestag (change from 2005)
CDU/CSU	33.8 (-1.4)	14.66 (-12 percent)	226 (-22)
SPD	23 (-11.2)	9.99 (-38 percent)	222 (-29)
FDP	14.6 (+4.7)	6.32 (+36 percent)	93 (+32)
LP	11.9 (+3.2)	5.16 (+30 percent)	76 (+22)
Greens	10.7 (+2.6)	4.64 (+21 percent)	68 (+17)

Source: Statistisches Bundesamt Deutschland, www.bundesstatistik.de

Although we do not wish to understate the devastating nature of the SPD's defeat, we argue that one must take into account broader developments in German and European politics. The first section of the chapter addresses the rise and fall of the SPD in the 1990s and 2000s–from the "loosely coupled anarchy" of the early to mid 1990s,[5] to the emergence of the "Neue Mitte" (new center) after the party came to power in 1998, to the Grand Coalition with the CDU/CSU between 2005 and 2009. We examine the defeat of the SPD within the context of broader developments–the long-term decline of the German catch-all parties (the SPD and the Christian Democratic Parties–CDU/CSU) and the rise of the three smaller parties (the Free Democratic Party–FDP, LP, and the Greens), and the more recent retreat of social democracy across much of Western Europe. In that context, we draw parallels with the problems faced by the Christian Democrat parties as well as the survival (and demise in 2010) of the New Labour project in the UK. We argue that the SPD's catastrophic defeat paradoxically presents a good opportunity for renewal and profiling against a Black-Yellow (CDU/CSU-FDP) government that must deal with a resource crunch in public finances.[6]

The Rise and Fall of the SPD

Claims predicting the demise of social democracy in Germany and elsewhere in Europe are not new,[7] but have often been overstated.[8] These predictions were based on the premise that changes in society–in particular, the shrinkage of the blue-collar workforce,[9] the individualization of values and lifestyles,[10] and voter dealignment[11]–would fatally damage social democratic parties by:

1. Undermining organizational models reliant upon bottom-up power structures, (supported by a large membership base and crystallized in the party conference);

2. Weakening solidarity and ideological coherence in a more diverse society;
3. Increasing strategic uncertainty with the emergence of the new postmaterialist left as a political force (reflected in the rise of the Green Party).

These arguments were used to explain the internal divisions in the SPD that led to the fall of the Helmut Schmidt chancellorship in 1982. Indeed, the German SPD from the early 1980s to the mid 1990s was riven by internal tensions, suffering from organizational, ideological and strategic pluralism,[12] and was forced to adapt.

A destructive consequence of organizational pluralism was that it allowed ambitious Länder princes to agitate against each other and official SPD policy from their regional power bases. In the 1990s, Oskar Lafontaine, Rudolf Scharping and Gerhard Schröder–minister presidents in the Saarland, Rhineland-Palatinate, and Lower Saxony, respectively–would regularly launch attacks on their rivals and party policy in a battle for power within the SPD. One example is the dramatic coup d'état staged by Lafontaine at the 1995 Mannheim party conference to depose Scharping as party chairman. A further illustration is Schröder's attacks on SPD policy on European integration (e.g., calling for a postponement of European Economic and Monetary Union as late as 1997). Party discipline was temporarily restored in the mid to late 1990s through the dual leadership of Lafontaine (party chairman) and Schröder (chancellor candidate).

Ideological pluralism in the SPD in the 1980s and 1990s was characterized by three competing streams of social democratic ideology.[13] The first stream–the old left–emphasized the traditional social democratic values of "solidarity" and "social justice" and was closely affiliated with the trade union movement. This stream is often portrayed as representing the core values of the party. The second, new left stream stressed postmaterialist and individualist issues such as environmentalism and human rights and reached its height in the SPD in the 1980s when many of its ideas were incorporated into the Berlin Basic Program.[14] A third, centrist stream, indicative of the views of the party establishment, favored moderate positions (including economic orthodoxy) in support of the existing social market economy–reminiscent of the policies pursued by the SPD under the Schmidt chancellorship (1974-1982). With the increase in material concerns after unification and the change in perception of the Greens as a potential partner rather than a rival, the postmaterialist stream became somewhat absorbed into the traditional left-right axis. On the road to power in the late 1990s, a compromise was reached: "Lafontaine embodied the soul of the party, its social conscience ... against that Schröder portrayed himself as a driving modernizer, who talks about the harsh truths."[15] Despite the political success of this approach, i.e., the federal election victory in 1998, the SPD never really overcame its ideological divisions. Thus, the emphasis on a centrist reform agenda under Schröder's second Red-Green Government (2002-2005) caused a huge split within the party.

Ideological pluralism was mirrored by strategic uncertainty—in particular the party oscillated between appeals to the center ground (CDU/CSU voters) and the postmaterialist left (Green voters). Herbert Kitschelt explains that the SPD "oscillated over the entire range of alternatives," after it lost power in 1982, enabled by "a leadership constrained in its strategic autonomy," which found it "difficult to find a new strategic equilibrium with a consistent approach."[16] One important example of the SPD's strategic uncertainty was the party's response to German unification: while Lafontaine focused on the problems that unity would bring, Willy Brandt strongly endorsed a swift process to achieve unity. In programmatic terms, strategic uncertainty was reflected in the SPD's Berlin Program—a postmaterialist policy platform launched just at a time when Germany was faced by the huge material concerns posed by unification.[17] Nevertheless, as the Greens entered government at regional level and the "Realo" (pragmatist) wing began to take control (gradually displacing the radical "Fundis,") they were increasingly viewed as allies. The SPD could now concentrate on its battle with Chancellor Helmut Kohl and the Christian Democrats.

The Rise of the Neue Mitte and the Fall of the SPD

A solution to the problems of the 1980s and 1990s was found in the dual leadership of Lafontaine (appealing to the left and core voters) and Schröder (appealing to the center and floating voters), which together mobilized enough support for the SPD to come to power in 1998. The so-called leadership "troika" was completed by the dull but reliable Scharping (as head of the parliamentary party).[18] Once Lafontaine had resigned as finance minister and party chairman in 1999, the way was open for the SPD—in coalition with a pragmatic Green Party under Joschka Fischer—to move to the center in government in the strategic and ideological direction of the Neue Mitte. The Neue Mitte explicitly wanted "to have recourse to the values of pragmatism and *anti-dirigisme* ... to create an effective synthesis of liberal principles and the basic values of the SPD incorporating the idea of a welfare state that is 'well-made' rather than 'well intended.'"[19]

After the early departure of Lafontaine, it initially appeared that the Neue Mitte course, supported by Chancellor Schröder, would prevail. Schröder took over the chairmanship of the party and attempted to reposition the SPD in favor of a more pro-market and less *dirigiste* policy platform. Furthermore, he sought to align the SPD with Tony Blair's New Labour project in the UK, and the two leaders published a joint paper (the Blair-Schröder Paper), which stated—among other things—that "public expenditure as a proportion of national income has more or less reached the limits of acceptability."[20] Although the paper did not mark a shift in policy for New Labour, it provoked a storm of controversy in the SPD. Schröder thought that he could mobilize an electoral majority to achieve change within the party, but had underestimated the power of the traditionalists. The SPD's left-labor (old left) wing was able to veto the proposed reform agenda at that time.[21]

Although the term Neue Mitte was jettisoned for the sake of party unity, its reform program was to return with a vengeance after the 2002 federal election. The poor state of the German economy—rising unemployment (above the politically sensitive five million mark), sluggish growth, and increasing national debt[22]—pressed the case for change, and manifested itself in the Red-Green government's Agenda 2010 reform program.[23] The reform agenda was also a response to the failure to achieve change through traditional routes (e.g., the neo-corporatist Alliance for Jobs) under the 1998-2002 administration. Agenda 2010 represented a serious effort to rein in public finances (e.g., freezing pension rates) and introduce welfare-to-work employment policies (i.e., the so-called Hartz IV laws, which reformed the unemployment benefit system).[24] In the face of the resource crunch in German public finances and given the constraints (real and perceived) of European integration and economic globalization, Schröder warned in 2003 that the old left must "modernize or die."[25]

Under the Schröder Chancellorship, the strategic purpose of the SPD was transformed from a catch-all party to more of a rally party in support of the chancellor (sometimes referred to in the German media as a *Kanzlerwahlverein*).[26] Schröder was able, with the assistance of Franz Müntefering (as general secretary and later party chairman), to establish de facto hierarchical power structures that circumnavigated factions within the party by appealing over their heads to the electorate or drawing on the expertise of "independent" commissions (in particular, the 2002-2003 Hartz Commission on Modern Services in the Labor Market and the

2002-2003 Rürup Commission on Healthcare and Social Security). Agenda 2010, the centerpiece of the second Schröder government, nevertheless proved to be a step too far for the party, and resulted in the implosion of SPD membership, a breakdown in party discipline, and a collapse in support for the party in the polls (enabling the eventual emergence of the Left Party).[27] In May 2005, the SPD suffered a dramatic defeat in regional elections in North Rhine Westphalia (Germany's most populous state governed by the SPD for the previous thirty-nine years), precipitating the collapse of the Red-Green government as Schröder made a last desperate bid for support for his policies from the electorate.

Under Schröder's charismatic leadership, the SPD was able to achieve a competitive result and enter government in 2005 (though without Schröder himself),[28] despite the fact that the party had lost four million votes (approximately 20 percent of SPD voters) and nearly a quarter of its members in only seven years.[29] Yet, within the Grand Coalition, the SPD lacked both Schröder's ability to lead the party from the center and the luxury of being able to fall back on its core support. Successive party chairmen–Müntefering (twice), Matthias Platzeck, Kurt Beck, Frank-Walter Steinmeier (as acting chair)–failed because they were not capable of differentiating the SPD from the Grand Coalition dominated by Angela Merkel. Merkel profited from the widely-acknowledged *Kanzlerbonus*–she was able to take credit for initial improvements in the German economy under the Grand Coalition without being identified with specific unpopular measures.[30] For the SPD, Steinmeier was dwarfed in his role as foreign minister by Merkel's success in that area,[31] and Finance Minister Peer Steinbrück was dominated by the goal of budgetary consolidation.

The technocratic leadership of Müntefering and Steinmeier was effectively fenced in by a chancellor who was happy to steal the center ground from the junior coalition partner, and an opposition Left Party that successfully mopped up SPD voters that were disaffected by the party's role in the Grand Coalition. While centrist welfare and labor market policies–such as the raising of the retirement age to sixty-seven pushed through by Müntefering as Minister for Labor and Social Affairs–gained no new voters in the center, more traditional left-wing policies, such as the introduction of a basic minimum wage in a few sectors of the labor market, gained no new voters on the left. Agenda 2010 and participation as the junior partner in the Grand Coalition had essentially robbed the SPD of its identity as the party of social justice. The leaders who had helped pioneer these reforms in government–primarily Steinmeier, Müntefering, and Steinbrück–lacked the credibility to mobilize the party's support base.

Even before the federal election in autumn 2009, the SPD's dire predicament was illustrated vividly by poor regional elections that year in Hesse (down 13 percentage points from the previous election), Saarland (down 6), and Saxony and Thuringia (up 0.6 and 4 respectively, but only from disastrous performances previously).[32] The nationwide European election in June 2009 was particularly telling. In the run-up to the European elections, the SPD had sought to present itself as the protector of jobs and the social market economy in the face of the global financial crisis–the party supported bailouts for the car manufacturer Opel and retail group Karstadt (amongst others). This strategy failed: "The SPD could not win back its traditional clientele, and had a structural disadvantage in relation to the Union, given the integration of the WASG (the Agenda 2010 protest party) and the PDS in the Left Party."[33] The SPD's share of the vote fell to only 20.8 percent

Putting the Defeat into Context

Although the decline of the SPD has been dramatic since 1998, losing approximately half of its voters and a third of its members,[34] the defeat in 2009 must be put into context. First, the SPD was in power for eleven years. One of the reasons why governments tend to have a shelf-life is that parties inevitably lose some of their distinctiveness within the constraints of government, which, in turn, weakens their representative capacity.[35] This was especially true for the SPD within the Grand Coalition. In this sense, opposition can be seen as an opportunity for renewal.

Second, the decline of the SPD must be related to the steady decline in the fortunes of both Germany's catch-all parties.[36] In federal elections, the CDU/CSU and SPD combined won on average over 90 percent of the vote in the 1970s, 85 percent in the 1980s, 77 percent in the 1990s, and only 68 percent in the past decade (see Figure 1).[37] This is a reflection of the fact that neither of Germany's two main parties is trusted to deal with the economic problems that emerged in the 1970s and accelerated after unification (e.g., mass unemployment and public debt). In fact, the CDU/CSU received almost two million fewer votes in 2009 than in 2005 (losing over 10 percent of its voters–see Figure 1) and almost six million votes fewer (nearly 30 percent of its voters) than in the historic unification election of 1990.[38] In this context, SPD strategist Matthias Machnig has referred to a "double modernization crisis:"

> The Union became more socially liberal in 2001 and economically social democratic in 2005 [through the Grand Coalition] with the consequence of

alienating economic liberals and catholic core voters. The SPD became more economically liberal… which led to the alienation of unionized workers.[39]

Figure 1: Catch-all Parties' Election Results in the Federal Republic of Germany

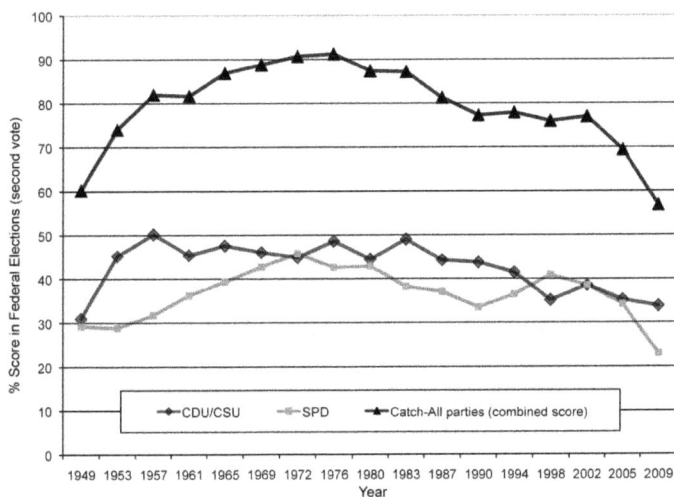

Thus, what we have seen is a gradual evolution away from the two-and-a-half party system that characterized the Bonn Republic towards a more complex five-party system, opening up the possibility even of three-party coalitions (as in the case of the CDU-FDP-Green "Jamaica" coalition established in the Saarland in October 2009). Are we seeing the "normalization" of the German party system towards a European model of bloc politics?[40] As yet, we cannot be sure. The dramatic fall in support for the catch-all parties and the dramatic increase in support for the three smaller parties in 2009 must (at least in part) be attributed to the short-term effects of the Grand Coalition (i.e., the ability of the smaller parties to profile themselves against the government), but, as Figure 1 shows, this trend is part of a long-term development. In this multiparty system, the SPD will have to adopt a more flexible attitude to potential coalition partners (including the LP) if it stands a chance of returning to power in the near future.

It is helpful to take a further step backwards, to look at the bigger picture for European social democracy to examine the substance behind some of the more alarming commentary on the future of the center-left. Social democracy is certainly in decline if one looks at the political map of Europe today compared to the highpoint of 2000 when center-left parties were in power in twelve of the (then) fifteen European Union states.[41] Social democratic parties in government indeed have had to face some existential challenges that have heaped pressure on public spending: from the increased costs of looking after a rapidly ageing population, to the constraints of the EU's Stability and Growth Pact and the Internal Market (with rules on deficit spending and the subsidization of industry), to the impact of the global financial crisis on the Eurozone. Yet, there is no clear evidence that the center-right has found it easier to cope with these challenges than the center-left. Furthermore, the comparison with the buoyant state of European social democracy at the turn of the century is unfair, ignoring, as it does, the cyclical nature of party politics. Between 1993 and 1997, social democrats were in opposition in the EU big three (France, Germany, and the UK) and after the British general election and the formation of the new Conservative-Liberal Democrat government in May 2010, we are back in the same situation.[42] The re-election of José Luis Zapatero and the Spanish Socialist Party in 2008 and the victory of the Greek Socialist Movement (PASOK) in 2009 showed that–given the right political circumstances–social democratic parties can continue to prosper. Today, we should therefore talk of the retreat rather than the defeat (and certainly not the end) of European social democracy.

The defeat of the SPD does, however, show the limits of revisionism for social democratic parties. Here, the story is not dissimilar to that of New Labour in the UK. For social democratic parties to move to the center and recast social democratic values in new policies, they require a strong charismatic leader, such as Blair or Schröder, capable of establishing a direct relationship with voters and individual party members. That leader then pursues a reformist path in government, but at the cost of alienating the party's core supporters. There is a natural shelf-life for this type of leader–eventually their political capital runs out (e.g., Blair over Iraq, Schröder over Agenda 2010) and their charisma wears thin. The new, less charismatic leaders who replace these reformers (Gordon Brown and Steinmeier) are then unable to bring back core supporters because they either: a) lack credibility/trust (to return to core values when they helped pioneer revisionist policies in the first place); and/or, b) lack the charisma to unite the party or the country. This is certainly true of the Steinmeier-Müntefering leadership that took the SPD into the 2009 federal election. Meanwhile, center-right parties have adopted centrist policy platforms (Merkel after the failure of her Leipzig Agenda in the 2005 federal election, David Cameron in his rebranding of the British Conservative Party), claiming in some way to be compassionate conservatives. The correction of the paths of the SPD and the British Labour Party in opposition–towards more traditional social democratic values–is, thus, highly likely.[43] We might call this the revisionist cycle.

European social democracy does, however, face some genuine challenges:

- to rejuvenate party organizations in the context of voter dealignment and collapsing membership;
- to provide a distinctive ideological narrative taking into account the huge pressures on public spending;
- to develop effective strategies to build electoral alliances within a diverse electorate.

An Opportunity for Renewal

The SPD must overcome a number of problems–organizational, ideological, and strategic. As we have argued previously,[44] one the reasons why many social democratic parties were only "failing successfully" in the late 1990s, was because they had had neglected underlying linkage issues with core supporters.[45] Center-left parties increasingly have seen the need to re-think the "social" dimension of social democracy. With its focus on the battle for the center ground of politics (from a political marketing perspective), modern revisionist social democracy has emphasized ideological pragmatism (in which ends are more important than means) and party discipline (involving hierarchical leadership structures), but rather neglected grass roots socialization and mobilization of party members and core supporters. The missing ingredient of the Neue Mitte (and the Third Way more generally) was therefore the communitarian aspect of progressive politics–building up democracy form the grassroots up through horizontal relationships between members (or voters) that stress rights and obligations. In the personalized, hierarchical leadership networks established by Schröder and Müntefering, there was little room for or attention paid to this approach. Nevertheless, even among senior SPD politicians, there was a sense of uneasiness about the development of an increasingly authoritarian leadership under Müntefering.[46] In organizational terms, the party needs to open up its structures and encourage outsiders to engage, as it tried to do (unsuccessfully) in the 1990s and again in 2001[47]–for example, returning to the idea of primary elections for parliamentary candidates and party leaders. Of course, the opening up of social democratic parties to new political, economic and social groups is not a new phenomenon. Brandt encouraged the

SPD to "dare more democracy" and integrate new political forces (particularly from the student movement) into the party in the 1960s and 1970s. The new SPD leadership says it will place greater emphasis on internal groups within the party–as part of the process of internal renewal, Sigmar Gabriel and Andrea Nahles embarked on a program of regional and local meetings with party activists after their election to the posts of party chair and general secretary in November 2009. Consolidation of support amongst party activists has been a necessary first step, from which the new party leadership hopes to engage more widely with SPD sympathizers "in all parts of society."[48] In this sense Machnig has written of the need to develop "networked centers of political activity, to hold together voter coalitions that are more socially and culturally heterogeneous."[49]

If the SPD wishes to remain a catch-all party in any meaningful sense, it must redefine its image to appeal to the centre of society.[50] In particular, the party must decide the extent to which it will amend the centrist policies put into place under Agenda 2010 and during the Grand Coalition. These policies include the Hartz IV laws on unemployment benefits, German participation in the NATO mission in Afghanistan, and the raising of the retirement age to sixty-seven.[51] One complication here was Steinmeier's reluctance to disavow Agenda 2010. Another major challenge for the SPD is to redefine its policies in response to the large cuts in public spending that will come over the next few years given the surge in deficit spending in the aftermath of the global financial crisis and the Eurozone crisis, and the fact that federal governments are now constitutionally obliged to deliver a balanced budget.[52] In this regard, the SPD has the opportunity to sharpen its focus on core areas of social investment, while having the strategic advantage of being in opposition when the axe falls on public spending.

Once the SPD has constructed a convincing narrative, it will have to sell this to the electorate. To achieve this successfully, it needs to find the right personnel to keep activists happy, mobilize core supporters and appeal to the center. The Gabriel-Nahles-Steinmeier axis seemingly is moving in this direction if the protagonists can actually work together.[53] A major obstacle for the SPD, however, is the lack of talent post Schröder (Gabriel is one of the few rhetorical talents in the party). [54] How the new narrative is deployed–at the next stage–will also depend on strategic choices.

The SPD nevertheless faces a trilemma of recapturing votes at the center (from the CDU/CSU), on the left (from the LP), while managing its relationship with the Greens. Within a multiparty system it would be unwise to choose too narrow strategic options (flexibility is required).[55] After all, its competitor parties have challenges of their own—the Christian Democrats in government must manage the gathering crisis in public expenditure (and take responsibility for large spending cuts), which is now even more difficult to manage given the budgetary impact of the Eurozone crisis. The FDP must cope with its supporters' disappointment that much of their liberal economic program will not be achieved given Chancellor Merkel's determination to occupy the political center. The Left Party must hold together after the departure of Lafontaine and in the context of ongoing tensions between East and West and left-wing social democrats and hardline socialists. The Green Party has the fewest challenges and is now a desired coalition partner for both catch-all parties. The SPD needs to build up support at state and local levels, in order to provide a springboard to power at federal level. Here, the Land election in North-Rhine Westphalia in May 2010 was crucial. Although the result was inconclusive (and not a great electoral success for the SPD), it damaged the governing parties in Berlin—removing their majority in the Bundesrat and intensifying preexisting erosion tendencies.

In the face of the humiliation in the 2009 federal election, what are the central goals for the SPD? At this stage, the party might concentrate on remotivating the two million SPD supporters who voted in 2005 but stayed at home in 2009. The rehabilitation should concentrate on reorganization and mobilization—developing and communicating a distinctive policy—rather than moving too much to the left or center, even though some move to the left is inevitable given the strong rejection of Agenda 2010 and imminent cuts in public spending. Opening effective channels for interaction, socialization, and mobilization through the new media is one way this might be pursued.[57] It is not, however, the end, or even the beginning of the end of social democracy. Although social democracy is at the low point of the cycle across much of Europe, recent setbacks for social democratic parties (primarily the German SPD) should be viewed as part of a general crisis of political parties and representative politics in advanced democracies.

What is now needed is a new generation of charismatic leaders, a convincing post financial crisis narrative, and more porous and responsive organizational structures that "dare more democracy." Achieving any one of these three desiderata would strengthen the position of the SPD, and its position will also be assisted by the forthcoming cuts in public spending of the CDU/CSU-FDP Government, the fractiousness of the coalition and the collateral damage of the Eurozone crisis. The crisis in the Eurozone was a windfall opportunity for the SPD who were able to unite all their constituencies in opposing the massively unpopular bailout of Greece. In the parliamentary debate to approve the bailout on 21 May 2010, the SPD withheld support for European legislation for the first time since the early 1950s.[56] A more likely (but less ambitious) solution might be found in coalition politics.[58] The departure of Lafontaine removes a huge barrier to coalition with the Left Party and the formation of a Red-Green coalition with the toleration of the LP in North Rhine Westphalia (in July 2010) points in this direction. Increasing distance from the German Democratic Republic and the changing nature of German views on foreign policy renders the LP less toxic as a junior coalition partner. In this scenario, either a new Grand Coalition or a SPD-Green-LP alliance could offer a route back to government at the federal level.

Notes

1. Statistisches Bundesamt Deutschland (SBD 2009a) *Bundesergebnis: Endgültiges Ergebnis der Bundestagswahl 2009*, available at http://www.bundeswahlleiter.de/de/bundestagswahlen/ BTW_BUND_09/ergebnisse/bundesergebnisse/index.html; accessed October 2009; Statistisches Bundesamt Deutschland (SBD 2009b) *Wahlberechtigte, Wähler, Zweitstimmen und Sitzverteilung bei den Bundestagswahlen seit 1949*, available at http://www.bundeswahlleiter. de/de/bundestagswahlen/downloads/bundestagswahlergebnisse/btw_ab49_ ergebnisse.pdf; accessed October 2009.
2. Ibid.
3. Prior to the 2008 Hesse state election, the Hesse SPD stated that it would not lead a coalition containing the LP. Yet, after the election Andrea Ypsilanti, the leader of the Hessen SPD sought to form a government with the Greens and the LP. Ypsilanti's planned coalition was embarrassingly vetoed by members of her own Hesse SPD who refused to enter into government with the LP, allowing Roland Koch (CDU) to continue as minister president—until his abrupt resignation in May 2010.
4. This phrase was originally used by Ralf Dahrendorf to interpret the poor electoral performance of social democratic parties in the 1980s. Ralf Dahrendorf, *Reflections on the Revolutions in Europe* (London, 1990).
5. Peter Lösche, "Lose verkoppelte Anarchie: zur aktuellen Situation von Volksparteien am Beispiel der SPD," *Aus Politik und Geschichte* 43 (1993).
6. Alister Miskimmon, William Paterson, and James Sloam, eds., *Germany's Gathering Crisis: The 2005 Federal Election and the Grand Coalition* (Basingstoke, 2008).
7. Adam Przeworski, *Capitalism and Social Democracy* (Cambridge, 1985); Dahrendorf (see note 4).
8. William Paterson and James Sloam, "European Social Democracy: Failing Successfully," in *When Parties Prosper*, eds., Kay Lawson and Peter Merkl (Boulder, 2007), 43-60.
9. Between 1950 and 1985, the proportion of blue-collar workers in the SPD membership fell from 50 percent to 40 percent and the proportion of white-collar, middle-class

members grew from 20 percent to 50 percent. Stephen Padgett and William Paterson, "The Rise and Fall of the West German Left," *New Left Review* 186 (1991): 46-77.

10. Anthony Giddens, *Modernity and Self Identity: Self and Society in the Late Modern Age* (London, 1991); Ronald Inglehart, *Modernization and Post-Modernization: Cultural, Economic and Political Change in 43 Societies* (Princeton, 1997).

11. Russell Dalton and Martin Wattenberg, eds., *Parties Without Partisans: Political Change in Advanced Industrial Democracies* (Oxford, 2000).

12. Lösche (see note 5); James Sloam, *The European Policy of the German Social Democrats: Interpreting a Changing World* (Basingstoke, 2004).

13. Sloam (see note 12), 111-112.

14. Padgett and Paterson (see note 9).

15. Frank Unger, Andreas Wehr, and Karen Schönwalder, K *New Democrats, New Labor, Neue Sozialdemokraten* (Bonn, 1998).

16. Herbert Kitschelt, *The Transformation of European Social Democracy* (Cambridge, 1994), 39.

17. Stephen Sylvia, "Loosely coupled anarchy: the fragmentation of the Left" in *Parties and Party Systems in the New Germany*, ed., Stephen Padgett (Aldershot, 1993), 171-89.

18. The troika model had also been important under the Schmidt Chancellorship when power was divided between Schmidt (chancellor), Herbert Wehner (parliamentary party leader) and Brandt (party chairman). "Despite internal conflicts and tensions, this trio–which can be taken as representative of the party as a whole–has functioned splendidly." *Die Zeit,* 22 December 1978.

19. Bodo Hombach, *The Politics of the New Centre,* Oxford, 2000), xxxv.

20. Tony Blair and Gerhard Schröder, *Europe: The Third Way/ Neue Mitte* in B Hombach *The Politics of the New Centre* (Oxford, 1999), 157-77.

21. Between autumn 1999 and autumn 2002 (up until the 2002 federal election), Schröder adopted a more rounded approach that sought to balance appeals to the centre (e.g., Finance Minister Hans Eichel's *Sparplan*) with appeals to Left, particularly the extension of workers' rights to smaller companies. In addition, the new post of general secretary was created for Franz Müntefering, who would use his knowledge of the party to maintain unity.

22. Germany breeched the 3 percent deficit criteria laid down in the EU Stability and Growth Pact every year between 2002 and 2005. See Wolfgang Streeck, "Endgame? The Fiscal Crisis of the German State," in Miskimmon et al. (see note 6), 38-63.

23. Andreas Busch, "Schröder's Agenda 2010: From 'Plan B' to Lasting Legacy?" in Miskimmon at al. (see note 6), 64-79.

24. Wolfgang Streeck and Christine Trampusch, "Economic Reform and the Political Economy of the German Welfare State," *German Politics* 14, no. 2 (2005): 174-195; Busch (see note 23).

25. Gerhard Schröder, "Modernise or Die," *The Guardian*, 8 July 2003, available at http://www.guardian.co.uk/politics/2003/jul/08/eu.policy; accessed March 2010.

26. The SPD's movement towards a French-style *rassemblement* was mirrored by Angela Merkel's more recent efforts to place herself above party politics with regard to the CDU/CSU. Both Schröder and Merkel were able to achieve change in this way due to the fact that their own personal popularity ratings tended to far outstrip support for their respective parties.

27. The Left Party was an electoral alliance formed of disgruntled SPD supporters and trade unionists and the Party of Democratic Socialism (PDS, the communist successor party in East Germany).

28. The CDU/CSU's naïve campaign strategy–Merkel advocated a pro-market agenda reflected in the nomination of economic liberal Paul Kirchhof as the party's tax expert for the campaign–allowed Schröder to appeal to SPD supporters by depicting the Christian Democrats as "socially cold." See James Sloam, "A Tale of Two Parties: The Failure of the Catch-All Parties in the 2005 German Elections', *Politics* 26, no. 2 (2006): 140-147

29. See SBD 2009b (see note 1); Sozialdemokratische Partei Deutschlands (SPD 2009) *Mitgliederbestand; Stichtag: 30.9.2009*, available at http://www.spd.de/de/pdf/mitglieder/ 090930_Mitgliederbestand.pdf; accessed October 2009.

30. In addition, the difficult ministerial portfolios in the Grand Coalition were taken by SPD ministers, who were forced to reign in public expenditure (Finance Minister Peer Steinbrück) and defend cuts in welfare expenditure (Minister for Labor and Social Affairs, Franz Müntefering).

31. See William Paterson, "The Foreign Policy of the Grand Coalition," *German Politics*, (forthcoming 2010).

32. In the previous regional election in Saxony, the SPD scored below 10 percent for the first time in any election since the creation of the Federal Republic in 1949. In the previous regional election in Thuringia, the SPD vote had fallen below 15 percent.

33. Oskar Niedermayer, "Die Wahl zum Europäischen Parlament vom 7. Juni 2009 in Deutschland: SPD-Debakel im Vorfeld der Bundestagswahl", *Zeitschrift für Parlamentsfragen* (4/2009): 711-731, 729.

34. BD 2009a and 2009b (see note 1); SPD (see note 29).

35. Some observers of political parties claim that–given the constraints and complexities of modern governance (domestic, European, and international)–they lose the capacity to represent. See Peter Mair, "The Challenge to Party Government," *West European Politics* 31, no. 1&2 (2008): 211-234.

36. James Sloam, "Catch-All Parties Catching Less: The 2005 Election and the Decline of the German Volkspartei," in Miskimmon, Paterson and Sloam (see note 6), 123-39.

37. SBD 2009b (see note 1).

38. SBD 2009b (see note 1). Furthermore, the CDU/CSU also has suffered from organizational, ideological, and strategic pluralism. Although this was mostly kept under control during the Kohl Chancellorship, Merkel has frequently been challenged by competing factions: the (economically) liberal wing formerly represented by Roland Koch (Minister President of Hessen); and, the social wing formerly represented by Jürgen Rüttgers (Minister President of North Rhine Westphalia) and Horst Seehofer (CSU Minister President of Bavaria). While Merkel has remained popular, this in-fighting has damaged the electoral performance of the Christian Democratic Parties.

39. Matthias Machnig, "Das Modell Volkspartei in der Krise," *Berliner Republik* 1 (2010), available at http://www.b-republik.de/aktuelle-ausgabe/das-modell volkspartei-in-der-krise; accessed February 2010.

40. Thomas Poguntke, "Perspectives: Implications for the German Party System," Paper presented to The New Government: Political Implications of the Elections in Germany conference, 21 October 2005, London. In these terms, there has been relatively little change in the share of the vote between the left (SPD-Green-PDS/LP) and right (CDU/CSU-FDP) blocs in recent elections. In the three elections between 1998 and 2005, the SPD-Green-PDS/LP vote captured between 51 percent and 53 percent of the vote. The share of the vote captured by the Left bloc fell below 50 percent in 2009, for the first time since 1994.

41. By the beginning of 2010, center-left parties were still in power in eight of the EU-15 member states (but had lost power in three of the four large states, including Germany, France, and Italy).

42. Wolfgang Merkel, "After the Golden Age: is Social Democracy Doomed to Decline" in *The Crisis of Social Democracy in Europe*, eds., Christiane Lemke and Gary Marks (Durham, 1992).

43. The return to "core values" may be less likely in the British Labour Party than in the German SPD, given the centripetal force of the UK's "first-past-the-post" electoral system.

44. Paterson and Sloam (see note 8).

45. Lawson and Merkl (see note 8).

46. Opposition to increasingly authoritarian leadership in the SPD was the main reason for a mini-revolt against Müntefering in October 2005, when he was unable to gain support

in the party executive for his favored candidate for General Secretary (Kajo Wasser-hövel), who was defeated by left-wing candidate Andrea Nahles. Müntefering subsequently announced his intention to resign as SPD chairman.

47. Karlheinz Blessing, ed., *SPD 2000: die Modernisierung der SPD* (Bonn, 1993); Matthias Machnig, "Vom Tanker zur Flotte," in *Der Rasende Tanker: Analyse und Konzepte zur Modernisierung der sozialdemokratischen Organisation*, eds., Hans-Peter Bartels and Matthias Machnig (Göttingen, 2001), 101-117.

48. Sigmar Gabriel, "So kommt die SPD wieder in die Mitte der Gesellschaft," *Berliner Republik* 1 (2010), available at http://www.b-republik.de/aktuelleausgabe/so kommt-die-spd-wieder-in-die-mitte-der-gesellschaft; accessed February 2010.

49. Machnig (see note 39).

50. Gabriel (see note 48).

51. Fortunately for the SPD leadership, the Federal Constitutional Court ruled (in February 2010) that the Hartz IV laws were unconstitutional, which will provide an easy opportunity for the SPD to modify its stance.

52. An amendment to the German constitution agreed in 2009 stipulates that the federal government must reduce net spending to 0.35 percent of GDP by 2016. The CDU/CSU-FDP government has, thus, committed itself to huge reductions in public spending starting from 2011.

53. We would speculate that the mercurial talents of Gabriel would be better suited to chancellor candidate than party chair.

54. Unlike Brandt, Schröder did not invest any time in building up the future generation of SPD leaders.

55. Charles Lees, "The SPD's Coalition Moment?," *Policy Network Essay*, 26 May 2010, available at http://www.policy-network.org/uploadedFiles/Publications/Publications/Charles%20Lees(1).pdf; accessed May 2010.

56. Alister Miskimmon, William Paterson, and James Sloam, "Germany at a Crossroads: The Gathering Crisis Sharpens," *Comparative European Politics* (forthcoming 2010).

57. The 2008 Obama campaign in the U.S. showed in an innovative way how political socialization might be achieved through the use of the new media.

58. Lees (see note 55).

Chapter 5

Coalition Governance under Chancellor Merkel's Grand Coalition

A Comparison of the Cabinets Merkel I and Merkel II

Thomas Saalfeld[1]

Introduction

Chancellor Angela Merkel has headed federal governments in two different political settings. From 22 November 2005 to 27 October 2009, she was federal chancellor of a so-called "grand" coalition of Christian Democrats (CDU/CSU) and Social Democrats (SPD). After the voters had strengthened the liberal FDP in the election of 27 September 2009, Merkel was able to form her second cabinet with the CDU/CSU's preferred partner, the FDP. A comparison of the two Merkel cabinets presents an interesting puzzle. In 2005, the main center-right and center-left competitors for government leadership, CDU/CSU, and SPD, entered the grand coalition reluctantly, because no other two-party majority coalition was numerically feasible. After the election of 27 September 2009, there was a sense amongst many in the political class that German politics could now return to "normality"–to a two-party coalition of one of the catch-all parties (in this case, the CDU/CSU) with a smaller partner (the FDP). Hence, the CDU/CSU-FDP coalition could have been expected to work far more harmoniously than its predecessor, the Grand Coalition. In reality, however, the first 100 days of the second Merkel cabinet were the most conflictive and acrimonious ever observed in the Federal Republic's history, whereas the Grand Coalition seemed to have managed conflicts relatively efficiently.

This chapter compares some of the underlying dynamics of party competition and patterns of portfolio allocation that have influenced the occurrence and management of inter-party conflict in the cabinets Merkel I (2005-2009) and Merkel II (2009-). It starts from the observation that coalition bargaining is an ongoing process that does not stop with the party leaders' signature on the coalition agreement and the election of the federal government by the Bundestag. Coalition bargaining is taken to consist of two main phases: a "pre-agreement stage" covering inter-party and intra-party negotiations before the ratification of the coalition agreement, and a "post-agreement stage" following the election of the chancellor. A strong interest in this post-agreement stage of coalition bargaining distinguishes this chapter from traditional formal models of coalition formation and situates it in an emerging body of scholarship that shares Lanny Martin's view that

> [m]ost studies of multiparty government have focused only on the "birth" or "death" of coalitions–dealing with such questions as who gets into government, which ministries each party controls, and how long the government will last ... Very little attention has been devoted to understanding the "life" of a coalition, even though it is during this period that policy making actually takes place.[2]

Building on agency models of coalition governance[3] and Michael Laver and Kenneth Shepsle's portfolio-allocation model,[4] this chapter develops elements of an analytic framework with a focus on institutional rules and ministerial discretion at the post-agreement stage of coalition bargaining. It uses some readily available data to explore a number of structural and strategic reasons for the seemingly paradoxical differences in overt post-agreement conflict between the cabinets Merkel I and Merkel II. In substantive terms, I argue that the differences in inter-party frictions are, at least partially, the result of very different post-agreement bargaining environments facing the different partners in 2005 and 2009. The strong initial inter-party frictions characterizing the early months of the cabinet Merkel II can be said to be the consequence of a distribution of portfolios that made it hard for the FDP to deliver on its key manifesto pledges in the area of tax reform. Many compromises in the coalition agreement of 2009 tended to be vague and "implicit,"[5] postponing contentious policy decisions to the stage of post-agreement bargaining.[6] Although the 2009 coalition agreement was not significantly less precise than its predecessor document of 2005, the Christian Democrats were now able to rely on crucial institutional features of the post-agreement bargaining environment– the pattern of portfolio allocation and their strong presence in the Bundesrat–to limit the extent to which FDP ministers were swiftly able to achieve radical legislative changes especially in tax policy. Realizing its weak position at the post-agreement stage, the FDP initially resorted to relatively "noisy" tactics in the public arena. The balance of power in the

Grand Coalition of 2005-2009, by contrast, had been far more equal both at the pre-agreement and post-agreement stage of coalition bargaining producing lower levels of publicized conflict.

Why Merkel II Should Have Been Less Conflictive Than Merkel I: Office and Policy Payoffs

As far as coalition payoffs are concerned, the 2009 coalition offered a much better deal to the coalition parties than the 2005 agreement, although both the 2005 and the 2009 cabinets were in equilibrium. Formal theories of coalition formation assume that parties will form coalitions that maximize their expected utility, although there is no absolute agreement what the "currency" of their expected utility is. William Riker's well-known theory[7] is based on the notion of minimal-winning coalitions[8] and the assumption that political parties seek to maximize office payoffs.

Table 1: Expected Office Payoffs for All Possible Minimal-Winning Coalitions 2005-2009

Minimal-winning coalition	Govt. majority (≥308)	Number of seats held by coalition parties in the Bundestag (N)					Contribution of each coalition party to the government majority (= hypothetical share of cabinet positions under a proportional allocation norm (%)				
		CDU/CSU	SPD	FDP	PDS	Greens	CDU/CSU	SPD	FDP	PDS	Greens
CDU/CSU-SPD	448	226	222	0	0	0	50.4	49.6	0.0	0.0	0.0
CDU/CSU-FDP-Greens	338	226	0	61	0	51	66.9	0.0	18.0	0.0	15.1
CDU/CSU-FDP-PDS	341	226	0	61	54	0	66.3	0.0	17.9	15.8	0.0
CDU/CSU-Greens-PDS	331	226	0	0	54	51	68.3	0.0	0.0	16.3	15.4
SPD-FDP-Greens	334	0	222	61	0	51	0.0	66.5	18.3	0.0	15.3
SPD-FDP-PDS	337	0	222	61	54	0	0.0	65.9	18.1	16.0	0.0
SPD-Greens-PDS	327	0	222	0	54	51	0.0	67.9	0.0	16.5	15.6

Sources: Calculated from data provided by the Bundestag (www.bundestag.de) and the Federal Government (www.bundesregierung.de)

Table 2: Expected Office Payoffs for all Possible Minimal-winning
Coalitions 2009

Minimal-winning coalition	Govt. majority (≥312)	Number of seats held by coalition parties in the Bundestag (N)				Contribution of each coalition party to the government majority (= hypothetical share of cabinet positions under a proportional allocation norm (%)			
		CDU/CSU	SPD	FDP	Left Party	CDU/CSU	SPD	FDP	Left Party
CDU/CSU-FDP	332	239	0	93	0	72.0	0	28.0	0
CDU/CSU-SPD	385	239	146	0	0	62.1	37.9	0	0
CDU/CSU-Left Party	315	239	0	0	76	75.9	0	0	24.1
SPD-FDP-Left party	315	0	146	93	76	0	46.3	29.5	24.1

Sources: Calculated from data provided by the Bundestag (www.bundestag.de) and the Federal
Government (www.bundesregierung.de)

Tables 1 and 2 provide information on the office payoffs arising from all
possible minimal-winning coalitions in 2005 and 2009. Based on the norm
of proportional portfolio allocation used in Germany[9] and elsewhere,[10] the
CDU/CSU could expect–and did receive–its fair share of cabinet positions
under the proportionality rule in 2005, giving it half of the portfolios
(including the federal chancellorship). An improvement in its office benefits would have been possible in three alternative coalitions (CDU/CSU-FDP-
Greens, CDU/CSU-FDP-PDS or CDU/CSU-Greens-PDS), none of which was
politically viable, if policy motivations are accounted for as well (see
below). In 2009, the Christian Democrats were able to increase their share
of portfolios in the new coalition with the Liberals to 68.75 percent,
although the Union remained slightly below a strictly proportional allocation, which would have given it 72 percent of the seats around the cabinet
table. As frequently observed in empirical studies, the proportionality of
portfolio allocation tends to be violated slightly in favor of smaller coalition partners.[11] Only one minimal-winning coalition, however, would
have offered a better payoff to the CDU/CSU in 2009: a coalition with the
Left Party, which was politically not viable given the marked ideological
differences between the two parties. The FDP had its first office payoff of
more than zero since 1998 and could not have reached a more favorable
deal under any other politically viable minimal-winning coalition.

Table 3: Weighted Ideological Distances between the Bundestag Parties 2005 and 2009 (averages)

Row party	FDP	CDU/CSU	SPD	Grüne	Linke
FDP	0	18	62	83	99
CDU/CSU	15	0	47	74	87
SPD	60	47	0	29	41
Grüne	84	72	30	0	22
Linke	99	84	40	25	0

Explanation: The values in the table reflect the column-parties' perceived (overall) ideological distance from the row-parties' perspective. The distances are based on estimates for five policy areas (employment and social affairs; economy and environment; home affairs and justice; education and science; foreign affairs and defense). For example, the FDP perceived its distance to the CDU/CSU across these five policy areas as 18, compared to 62 for the SPD.

Source: Franz Urban Pappi, Michael Frank Stoffel, and Nicole Michaela Seher, "Regierungsbildungen im fragmentierten deutschen Parteiensystem," Working Paper No. 129, Mannheimer Zentrum für Europäische Sozialforschung (Mannheim, 2009), 17.

If parties are modeled as being motivated by policy goals as well as office considerations, the comparative attractiveness of the CDU/CSU-FDP coalition becomes even more apparent. Table 3 reports data on ideological distances estimated by Franz Urban Pappi, Michael Frank Stoffel, and Nicole Michaela Seher on the basis of automated quantitative content analyses of election manifestoes using the Wordfish program.[12] The values in the table reflect the column-parties' perceived ideological distance from the row parties across five broad policy areas (employment and social affairs; economy and environment; home affairs and justice; education and science; foreign affairs and defense). These distances are weighted for the party-specific saliency each of these policy areas has for the row parties. Finally, the weighted differences were averaged for 2005 and 2009. For example, in the period 2005-2009, the FDP perceived its weighted distance to the CDU/CSU across these five policy areas as totaling eighteen out of 100 index points, compared to sixty-two in relation the SPD. Table 3 demonstrates that the CDU/CSU-FDP coalition was by far the most attractive minimal-winning coalition of which either the Christian Democrats or the Liberals could have been a member.

The puzzle, then, is why inter-party conflicts during the first 100 days of the CDU/CSU-FDP coalition were so acrimonious despite the apparent advantages the coalition had for the partners both in office and policy terms, and how the Grand Coalition managed to run relatively smoothly. These differences cannot be reduced to personality traits of some of the leaders, some FDP ministers' lack of government experience or Merkel's allegedly indecisive leadership, which occasionally was said to be more suited to a mediator's role in a grand coalition than to a leader's role in a coalition with a junior partner. Although these factors are likely to have played a role, it will be argued here that (a) there are structural and strategic reasons for the differences relating to the nature of party competition and (b) the vague coalition agreement of 2009 shifted inter-party bargaining to the post-agreement phase, where the Liberals found themselves in a weaker position than the Social Democrats had been in 2005-2009.

Policies and Rules: The Coalition Agreements of 2005 and 2009

Coalition agreements represent the publicized results of coalition bargaining. They are usually incomplete contracts lacking external enforcement mechanisms. Moreover, they do not specify rules for every possible unanticipated political, economic or other change in the coalition's policy environment at the post-agreement stage, are often vague and do not necessarily mention all of the deals agreed between the coalition partners. Nevertheless, they are signed by the leaders and ratified by special delegate conferences of all parties involved, thus allowing the government parties to commit credibly to a coalition.[13]

Figure 1: Word Length of German Coalition Agreements, 1949-2009

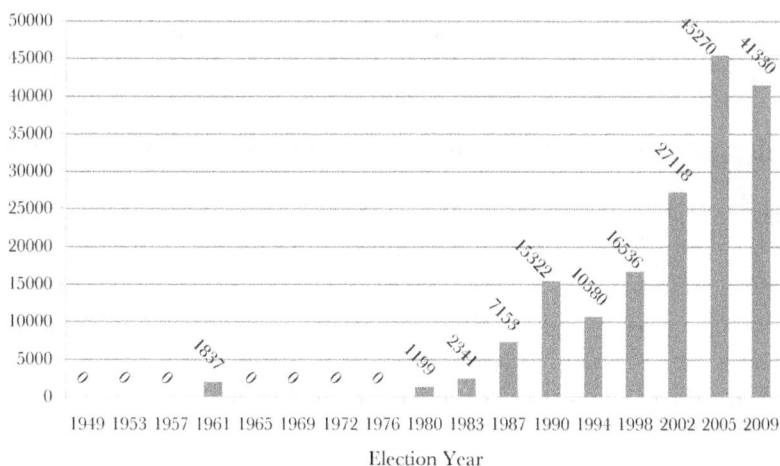

Source: Coalition Agreements 1961-2009

The coalition agreement signed by the three party leaders and ratified by party conventions in 2009 was over 41,000 words long, just marginally shorter than the 45,000 word agreement (without appendices) of 2005, the latter being the longest in the Federal Republic's history. Figure 1 graphs the growing length of German coalition agreements across time, demonstrating that written and publicized coalition agreements were hardly used before 1980, but have grown in length at an exponential rate since. This suggests an increasing formalization of negotiations and a growing level of the parties' accountability vis-à-vis the media, party activists, and voters. Although they are largely policy documents, coalition agreements typically also set out the governance structure of German coalitions. In the 2009 document, the CDU/CSU and FDP formulated a set of rules for the management of the post-agreement phase. These rules include the norm to establish consensus over each policy decision taken by the government. In practice, this means that the parties would introduce legislation jointly and refrain from voting on opposite sides in the Bundestag and other bodies (e.g., the Bundesrat). A coalition committee was to be established, meeting at the beginning of each week when the Bundestag is in session, discussing issues of fundamental importance and seeking agreed solutions in emerging areas of inter-party divergence. The coalition committee was to consist of the three party leaders, the leaders of the parliamentary party groups, the parties' general secretaries and chief whips, the chief of the Federal Chancellor's Office, the Finance Minister and one further person nominated by the FDP.[14] The rules in the 2009 agreement were largely identical with the rules written down in the 2005 agreement (they have become standard for nearly all coalition governments in Germany), except that the latter specified a slightly smaller coalition committee (the chief of the Federal Chancellor's Office, the parties' chief whips and the finance minister were—at least initially—not members of the 2005 committee) and that fewer meetings of this body were held (meetings were to be held only once a month or whenever one of the coalition parties demanded one).[15] In other words, the governance structure set out in both coalition agreements is unlikely to be the main cause of the difficulties experienced in the cabinet Merkel II.

The nature of policy compromises in the coalition agreement might be another source of the differences. Both the 2005 and the 2009 coalition agreements were overwhelmingly policy documents (98.9 and 99.2 percent of the entire text, respectively). Both were found to be relatively vague where the coalition partners' policy preferences diverged.[16] There have been a number of attempts at classifying compromises in coalition agreements.[17] For the purposes of this chapter, I will rely on Gregory Luebbert's distinction between "explicit" and "implicit" compromises that parties can formulate when their preferences diverge. "Explicit" compromises arise when one or more parties agree to adopt a non-preferred policy as "as a quid pro quo for participation in a coalition."[18] Luebbert argues that party leaders engaged in coalition negotiations have incentives to avoid such explicit compromises, because they tend to cost leaders support amongst ideologically committed activists and core voters. If compromises cannot be avoided altogether (which Luebbert believes to be the party leaders' top preference), leaders will seek to reach at least "implicit" compromises, that is, compromises where parties:

> ... are willing to agree to disagree. They might agree that the government will ignore the disagreement by having no policy on the point of contention. They might–as parties often do–further agree that if the issue arises in the legislature, they reserve the right of a free vote. Another option is for the parties to announce that they have agreed to place a moratorium on the matter for a certain length of time, after which the parties will be free to reconsider their participation in the government in light of the preferences that exist at that time. Yet another option is for the parties to agree to a period of cabinet or committee study. Or the parties might agree to the issuance of a statement of such ambiguity that each is able to interpret it as not violating its preferences.[19]

While implicit compromises reduce the intra-party costs of coalition formation for party leaders in the short run, they may create agency problems in the longer term as they merely postpone the resolution of inter-party differences to the post-agreement stage. At this stage, departmental ministers are at a particular advantage, if their party controls the median legislator on the relevant policy dimension (see below).

Luebbert suggests that the prospects for coalitions are best, if the partners' preferences are "convergent" or "tangential." Tangential constellations occur when policy agreements over several dimensions "address different issues and are sufficiently unrelated that party leaders do not consider them to be incompatible."[20] In effect, parties are using different preference intensities (or issue saliencies) to engage in some kind of logrolling. Such constellations are preferred to convergent ones, where "the two parties are concerned with the same issues and advocate principles of direction that tend toward each other." Luebbert reasons that leaders seek to:

> ... preserve the distinctiveness of their parties in a normally crowded multi-party field. ... Insofar parties who advocate the same preferences tend to compete for the support of the same poll of voters, cooperation based on convergent preferences will require that the formateur's party give one of its most menacing competitors access to governmental resources and will

enhance the competitor's image as a legitimate alternative recipient of electoral support.[21]

In other words, party leaders seek to avoid compromises. If compromises cannot be avoided, they will seek to settle on implicit compromises. Yet, even the latter are less attractive than coalition agreements based on convergent or, ideally, tangential preferences. Both the 2005 and the 2009 coalition agreements confirm Luebbert's general theoretical expectations–in both cases, explicit compromises were rare.[22] Thus, the vagueness of policy compromises in the coalition agreements cannot be considered to be the main explanation for the difficulties in the Merkel II cabinet in comparison to Merkel I. In both the 2005 Grand Coalition and the 2009 Christian Democrat-Liberal coalition the frequency of implicit compromises in the coalition agreement shifted the emphasis of coalition bargaining to the post-agreement stage. The crucial difference between the two coalitions is the balance of power between the coalition parties at the post-agreement stage: whereas inter-party relations remained relatively balanced under the Grand Coalition, they were unfavorable for the FDP under Merkel II. This is reflected in the patterns of portfolio allocation (see below). In addition, the parties under the CDU/CSU-FDP coalition did not succeed in exploiting their tangential preferences but sought direct confrontation over tax and health policy.

Portfolio Allocation and Patterns of Party Competition in the Policy Space: The Example of Health-Care Policy

One of the first attempts at incorporating institutional information on the post-agreement phase of coalition politics is Laver and Shepsle's portfolio allocation model, which is based on the assumption that actors are driven by the desire to achieve their policy goals. These policy goals are conceived of as points in an n-dimensional ideological space. Given the de facto control Laver and Shepsle assume ministers to have over the formulation, passage and implementation of policies and given the incompleteness of coalition contracts found by other authors,[23] Laver and Shepsle effectively treat the allocation of cabinet portfolios as the only credible commitment coalition partners are able to offer to each other in coalition negotiations.[24] The agenda control exercised by ministers and the informational advantages they enjoy guarantee, so the argument goes, that the party controlling a portfolio will also control policy in that area. This approach resonates with the German *Ressortprinzip* enshrined in Article 65 of the Basic Law, i.e., the legal norm that each minister has responsibility for his or her department (although the same article constrains her or him through mechanisms of collective responsibility in the "cabinet principle" and the "chancellor principle").[25]

Laver and Shepsle develop two game-theoretic solution concepts that avert the risk of "cycling" in social choice situations with several players competing against each other across multiple policy dimensions (i.e., unstable decision making in changing voting coalitions). Firstly, the so-called "dimension-by-dimension median" (DDM) cabinet is one where each key portfolio is given to the median party on the policy dimension(s) under the jurisdiction of the portfolio concerned. They prove formally that only this particular portfolio allocation can be such that no legislative majority prefers some alternative cabinet. Secondly, a "strong party" is one that is involved in, and therefore able to veto, every cabinet some legislative majority prefers to the cabinet in which the strong party takes all key portfolios. If such a strong party has an ideal point at the DDM position and no alternative portfolio allocation is preferred by a legislative majority, then it can be called a "very strong" party, which is in such a powerful position that it should be able to control all key policy portfolios without sharing power with any other party, even if it does not control a majority of seats in parliament.[26]

The DDM solution concept is helpful to illuminate differences in the dynamics of post-agreement bargaining and the different problems facing the 2005 and 2009 Merkel cabinets. This is illustrated in a brief case study of health care policy, which has been particularly controversial for both Merkel-led coalitions. The Grand Coalition made it one of its priorities to contain the costs of public health care and move the funding of health insurance towards a more sustainable model. After prolonged negotiations, the parties introduced a number of reforms including the so-called Health Fund (*Gesundheitsfonds*).[27] The main aims of the reform were to ensure the financial sustainability of the health insurance system, to increase equity in statutory health insurance, to stabilize or reduce wage related costs and hence increase employment, and to promote competition between health insurance companies by urging them to operate efficiently. Commencing in January 2009, a new entity, the Health Fund, was created to pool and allocate funds within the statutory health insurance system. The government set a uniform contribution rate. Drawing on taxes as well as employer and employee contributions, the Health Fund pays out a risk-adjusted amount for each insured person to each sickness fund. The aim of the government subsidies from taxation was to enable the health fund to cover the costs for children's health insurance. This model represented a compromise between the CDU/CSU and SPD, but could serve as a stepping stone for further reforms. With the change in government in 2009, Social Democratic Health Minister Ulla Schmidt was replaced by the Liberal Philip Rösler. Rösler, a medical doctor by training, had an ambitious reform agenda with a much larger role for the private sector. His plans, however, ran into fierce resistance from the Christian-social wing of the CDU/CSU, especially former federal health minister, Horst Seehofer, who had become CSU leader and state premier of Bavaria in 2008.[28]

There are currently no readily available data capturing information purely on the parties' position on matters of health policy. Nevertheless, the data based on hand-coded content analyses of election manifestoes conducted by the Comparative Manifesto Project do contain two items that include health policy: per504 (welfare state expansion: positive) and per505 (welfare state limitation: positive').[29] The left-right scale in Figure 2 was calculated by deducting the percentage value for per505 (i.e., the word length of statements in this category as a share of the entire manifesto's word length) from the value for per504. The higher the value in Figure 2, the stronger is the preponderance of statements containing positive evaluations of welfare-state expansion (which was taken to be a proxy of a left-wing position on matters of health care). All five Bundestag parties have at least a slight preponderance of statements favoring welfare-

Figure 2: Welfare State and Health in German Party Competition – 2005 and 2009

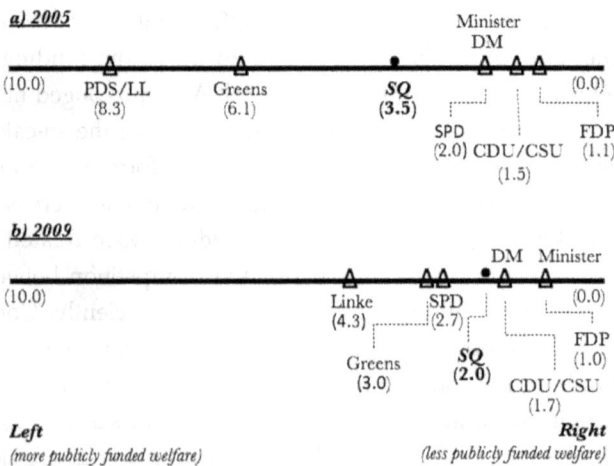

Left
(more publicly funded welfare)

Right
(less publicly funded welfare)

Source: Comparative Manifesto Project (per504 minus per505; http://www.wzb.eu/zkd/dsl/download-marpor.de.htm)

state expansion. Figure 2 provides a left-right ordering of the five Bundestag parties in 2005 and 2009 on this one-dimensional continuum. In 2005 and 2009, the PDS/LL and the Left Party, respectively, constituted the most left-wing parties, although even the Left Party—arguably under the impact of the global financial crisis—reduced its predecessor's emphasis on welfare-state expansion sharply during this period. This is reflected in a decline of the index value in Figure 2 from 8.3 for the PDS/LL in 2005 to 4.3 for the Left Party four years later. Crucially for the purposes of this chapter, the FDP consistently held the most "right-wing" (i.e., pro free market) position on this dimension, which is reflected in index values of 1.1 (2005) and 1.0 (2009), respectively.

The upper pane (a) represents the situation in the 2005 Bundestag. The status quo is assumed to be the SPD's position in the (previous) 2002-2005 Bundestag (3.5).[30] In 2005, the SPD included the median legislator on this dimension and controlled the Health Ministry (as predicted as equilibrium bargaining result by the portfolio-allocation model). Based on their election manifestoes, both government parties—CDU/CSU and SPD—wanted to move welfare policy (including health) to the right. For the CDU/CSU (1.5), the SPD's 2005 manifesto position (2.0) was considerably closer to its own ideal point than the status quo (3.5). If bargaining breakdown was to be avoided (i.e., if the status quo at 3.5 was to be changed at all), the CDU/CSU had strong incentives to agree to the SPD's ideal point at 2.0.

The lower pane (b) suggests that the situation was very different in 2009. Due to the SPD's electoral losses, the CDU/CSU now controlled the median legislator on this policy dimension. The grand coalition had already moved the status quo to the right in the previous Bundestag. The health portfolio, however, was now allocated to the FDP, which had the most pro-market position on welfare issues. In other words, there would have been a clear, ideologically connected alternative majority (of CDU/CSU and SPD) in this policy area without the FDP minister's party. If the legislative status quo in 2009 is assumed to be the SPD's ideal point during the 2005-2009 Bundestag (2.0), the CDU/CSU's ideal point was extremely close to this point (1.8), whereas the FDP health minister wanted to move the policy even further to the right (to 1.0), i.e., well outside the CDU/CSU's indifference curve of 0.2 scale points left and right of its own ideal point (with an ideal point of 1.8 and a status quo of 2.0, the Christian Democrats would be indifferent, if the policy were moved to 1.6, but would reject any policy above 2.0 and below 1.6).[31] Although CDU/CSU and FDP were not very far apart in absolute terms, events during the first 100 days of Merkel's cabinet—especially the public altercations between the FDP health minister Rösler on the one side and the CSU state premier Seehofer and the Bavarian Health Minister Markus Söder on the other—corroborate the predictions generated by the portfolio-allocation model. Relative to the other parties, the FDP was a preference outlier on this policy dimension and found it difficult to move the policy to the point it had pledged in its 2009 manifesto. If we assume that the party controlling the median legislator determines the policy, an explicit agreement would have fixed health policy at the CDU/CSU's ideal point of 1.8. This would have allowed FDP health minister Rösler to utilize his agenda powers and informational advantage as departmental minister to shift policy marginally to 1.6 in the legislative process, the point at which the CDU/CSU would have been indifferent compared to the status quo of 2.0. This "ministerial drift," however, fell short of the FDP's pre-electoral commitments.

How Does Portfolio Allocation Affect Post-Agreement Conflict?

Due to the CDU/CSU's centrality in the socioeconomic policy dimension and the proximity of the status quo to the Christian Democrats' position, there was little scope for significant ministerial drift in health and other welfare

Table 4: Sharing of Ministerial Jurisdictions in the Cabinets Merkel I and Merkel II, 2005 and 2009

Broad policy area	Merkel I		Merkel II	
	CDU/CSU	SPD	CDU/CSU	FDP
Economy, Finance	Economic Affairs	Finance	Finance	Economic Affairs
Foreign Affairs, Defense	Defense	Foreign Affairs; International Cooperation and Development	Defense	Foreign Affairs; International Cooperation and Development
Home Affairs, Justice	Home Affairs	Justice	Home Affairs	Justice
Social Welfare	Family, Women, Senior Citizens and Young Persons; Education and Research	Employment and Social Affairs; Health	Employment and Social Affairs; Family, Women, Senior Citizens and Young Persons; Education and Research	Health

policies. In other policy areas, the conditions were even less favorable. A comparison between the cabinets Merkel I and Merkel II illustrates how the pattern of portfolio allocation provided an unfavorable post-agreement bargaining environment for the FDP. Table 4 shows that, in the "Grand" and the Christian Democrat-Liberal coalition, government parties shared ministerial jurisdictions in broad policy areas. In the Grand Coalition 2005-2009, the Christian Democrats held the portfolios for economic affairs, whereas the Finance Minister was a Social Democrat; in external affairs, Defense was controlled by the CDU/CSU, the Foreign Office and International Cooperation and Development were held by Social Democrats; in home affairs, the CDU controlled the Home Office, the SPD the Ministry of Justice; in the area of social welfare, the two catch-all parties divided responsibilities almost equally and in such a way that both parties were able to retain a credible profile among core supporters and voters (e.g., through the allocation of the ministry in charge of families to the Christian Democrats and the ministry responsible for employment to the Social Democrats).

Superficially, the Christian Democrat-Liberal coalition of 2009 followed a similar pattern. The big difference between the 2005-2009 Grand Coalition and the 2009 Christian Democrat-Liberal coalition was, firstly, an imbalance in the allocation of portfolios due to the proportional allocation norm. Governing was no longer a (reluctant) partnership of two near-equals, but one between the CDU/CSU as experienced senior partner and the FDP very much in the role of a less experienced junior partner. The second major difference was the allocation of the finance ministry, which effectively has a veto over all departmental expenditures. Whereas the government parties of the Grand Coalition shared the federal chancellorship and the finance ministry between them, both of these key portfolios were controlled by the CDU in the Christian Democrat-Liberal coalition. The 2009 coalition agreement stated explicitly that all government policies were subject to financial feasibility,[32] further strengthening the finance minister's hand in tax policy. Given the fact that the Ministry of Economic Affairs, which was controlled by the FDP, does not have jurisdiction over taxation, the Liberals simply did not control the portfolio essential to deliver on their key election pledge (tax reductions) and had conceded a relatively large amount of discretion to the cautious CDU finance minister (Wolfgang Schäuble) in this area. Third, the distribution of portfolios in 2009 pitted CDU/CSU ministers as defender of the welfare state against the FDP whose only portfolio in the area of social welfare was health.

The CDU/CSU's dominance resulting from the patterns of portfolio allocation was compounded by their strong position in the Bundesrat (at least until the May 2010 Land elections in North Rhine Westphalia), which is another important institutional feature of Germany's post-agreement bargaining environment. The Christian Democrats led twelve out of the sixteen state governments, of which only seven were ruled (or were about to be ruled) by Christian Democrat-Liberal coalitions at the time the cabinet Merkel II was formed (Baden-Württemberg, Bavaria, Hesse, Lower Saxony, North Rhine Westphalia, Saxony and Schleswig-Holstein). The CDU continued to govern in coalitions with the Social Democrats in four states (Brandenburg until November 2009, Mecklenburg West Pomerania, Saxony-Anhalt and Thuringia), with the Greens in Hamburg and without any coalition partner in Saarland (until November 2009). Especially the CDU minister presidents in states without "parallel" coalitions were unlikely to be easily disciplined by Berlin. Whatever the coalition they headed, the CDU and CSU state premiers played a major role in coalition governance from the beginning. For example, the FDP's tax plans were strongly criticized and resisted by the premiers of Schleswig-Holstein, Lower Saxony and North Rhine Westphalia in 2009-2010. Following the defeat of the Christian Democrat-Liberal coalition in North Rhine Westphalia in the Land election of May 2010, the federal government lost its majority in the Bundesrat. Since the election outcome in the most populous German state was widely seen as an electoral penalty for the Berlin government's handling of the EURO crisis and its poor public image, Chancellor Merkel came under even more pressure from Christian Democratic state premiers such as Roland Koch (Hesse), Stefan Mappus (Baden-Württemberg), Christian Wulf (Lower Saxony) and Horst Seehofer (Bavaria). To the frustration of the FDP leadership, Merkel was now able to postpone significant tax cuts until at least 2012, without running into any serious resistance from her smaller coalition partner.

The Failure to Exploit Tangential Preferences

Given the CDU/CSU's median position on the economic policy dimension, the FDP was always likely to lose stand-offs in this area. While the Christian Democrats and Social Democrats managed to exploit tangential preferences in the Grand Coalition (e.g., the CDU/CSU's aim of supporting families was "tangential" in Luebbert's terms to the SPD's concern for employees and workers), the FDP focused strongly on tax and welfare reforms, a policy dimension where its extreme location in the policy space produces an unfavorable bargaining position, which was made even more difficult by the precarious economic and fiscal climate prevailing in 2009/2010. This constellation differed from previous federal governments with FDP participation where the Liberals found it easier to occupy the center ground in at least one other salient policy dimension. The data encapsulated in Figure 3 seek to illustrate this problem.

Figure 3: Party Positions in Economic Policy, Social Issues and Immigration 2002

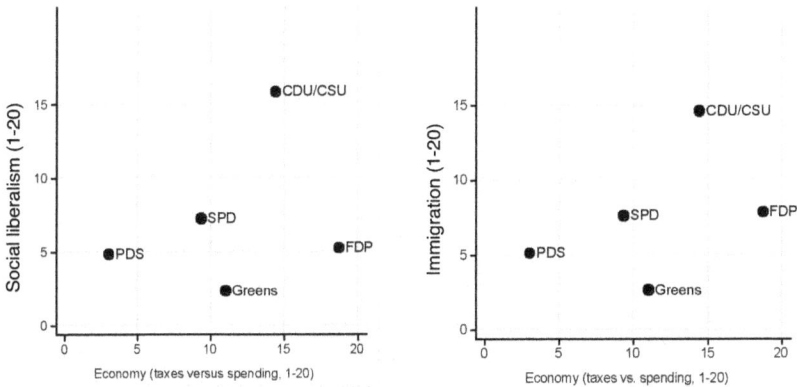

Source: Dataset provided by Kenneth Benoit and Michael Laver, *Party Policy in Modern Democracies* (London, 2006).

Figure 3 is based on Kenneth Benoit and Laver's data on the parties' policy positions generated from expert interviews (conducted in 2002).[33] The parties' economic policy positions (as perceived by experts) are captured by a question on their attitude to taxation and public spending. This item is particularly suited to assess longer-term inter-party differences in the contentious area of tax reform, which remained a major bone of contention between CDU/CSU and FDP. With a value of 14.40 out of twenty, the CDU/CSU is perceived to be located in the median position between the FDP to its right (18.71) and the SPD to its left (9.32), with a slightly stronger affinity to the FDP. The vertical axes on the left pane of Figure 4 map the parties' attitudes along the dimension of "social liberalism" such as abortion and gay rights and are designed to capture the authoritarian-libertarian dimension Herbert Kitschelt and others believe to be of particular significance in advanced postindustrial societies.[34] The right pane of Figure 3 uses the parties' attitudes to immigration as an indicator of their position on the "nationalist-internationalist" dimension Hanspeter Kriesi and his co-authors have identified as an increasingly important dimension of inter-party conflict in the age of globalization.[35] On both dimensions, the CDU/CSU is relatively far to the right (north on the vertical axis), whereas the FDP is much closer to the position of the median party on these dimensions. Indeed, in 2009 it included the median legislator on the "cosmopolitanism-nationalism" dimension. This could have opened up opportunities to establish a set of complementary (or "tangential") policy positions, thus sharpening their own profile while avoiding costly clashes with the CDU/CSU over taxation and welfare-state retrenchment. Yet, the Liberals' election campaign and post-electoral appearance was strongly dominated by economic policy, where was in a much weaker bargaining position.

Conclusions

A comparison of the 2005-2009 cabinet Merkel I and the cabinet Merkel II formed in 2009 presents an interesting puzzle. Political commentators and coalition theorists alike would have expected a conflictive appearance of the CDU/CSU-SPD coalition 2005-2009. an alliance characterized by stalemate and tactical maneuvers—and a more consensual relationship between the government parties in the CDU/CSU-FDP coalition formed in 2009. Yet, based on the Christian Democrat-Liberal coalition's public appearance in the first months after its formation, relations in this coalition were relatively conflictive with sharp public controversies in some areas (e.g., health policy). The Grand Coalition, by contrast, did not only govern relatively smoothly, it also achieved a number of significant policy reforms: the constitutional reform of German federalism; welfare programs to support families; the funding of pensions and the raising of the retirement age; the reduction of business taxes; and a relatively coherent and successful policy in the face of the global financial crisis dominating the policy agenda since 2008.[36]

This chapter concedes that there may have been some situational factors affecting inter-party relations in the two coalitions. Nevertheless, it could be shown that these seemingly paradoxical differences between the two coalitions can be explained with the help of a principal-agent model that goes beyond traditional game-theoretic models of coalition formation—one that largely focuses on the expected policy and office payoffs at the time of cabinet formation. The key argument is that both the 2005 and the 2009 coalition agreements were relatively vague and postponed contentious questions to the phase of post-agreement bargaining. Vague coalition agreements produce relatively generous levels of discretion to ministers at the post-agreement stage. Post-agreement policy bargaining is influenced by the patterns of government portfolio allocation, the parties' role in the legislative institutions of the Bundestag and their position in the Bundesrat. In all these respects, the 2005-2009 Grand Coalition was characterized by a balance of power between Christian Democrats and Social Democrats. Moreover, Christian Democrats and Social Democrats managed to exploit "tangential" preferences in the coalition agreement and portfolio allocation—which allowed both parties to maintain a credible profile vis-à-vis core supporters without competing on each other's turf. The parties in the Christian Democrat-Liberal coalition formed in 2009, by contrast, faced an asymmetric situation as far as post-agreement bargaining is concerned. The CDU/CSU controlled the finance ministry; its (much larger) parliamentary party had a more developed infrastructure supporting the work of Bundestag legislative committees; and Christian Democratic state premiers had a strong presence in the Bundesrat. These factors made it likely that any discretion offered by the coalition agreement would be exploited primarily by CDU/CSU ministers, especially in areas of high saliency for the FDP. Moreover, the FDP's bargaining position was undermined by its strong emphasis on relatively extreme policy proposals in the area of tax and welfare state reform. Conflicts were exacerbated by competition between Christian Democrats and Liberals on the socioeconomic policy dimension(s). Policy areas where the Liberals occupied a more centrist position and had better chances of policy success were not prioritized and, given the importance of the recession (and then the Greek debt and EURO crises), perhaps could not be prioritized.

Notes

1. I owe thanks to Andrea Volkens who granted me early access to the German manifesto data for 2005 and 2009, which were collected for the Comparative Manifesto Project.
2. Lanny W. Martin, "The Government Agenda in Parliamentary Democracies," *American Journal of Political Science* 48 (2004): 445-446.
3. Martin (see note 2); Lanny W. Martin and Georg Vanberg, "Policing the Bargain: Coalition Government and Parliamentary Scrutiny," *American Journal of Political Science* 48 (2004): 13-27; Lanny W. Martin and Georg Vanberg, "Coalition Policymaking and Legislative Review," *American Political Science Review* 99 (2005): 93-106.
4. Michael Laver and Kenneth A. Shepsle, *Making and Breaking Governments: Cabinets and Legislatures in Parliamentary Democracies* (Cambridge, 1996).

5. Gregory M. Luebbert, *Comparative Democracy: Policymaking and Governing Coalitions in Europe and Israel* (New York, 1986).

6. Thomas Saalfeld, "Regierungsbildung 2009: Merkel II und ein höchst unvollständiger Koalitionsvertrag," *Zeitschrift für Parlamentsfragen* 41 (2010): 181-206.

7. William H. Riker, *The Theory of Political Coalitions* (New Haven, 1962).

8. John von Neumann and Oskar Morgenstern, *Theory of Games and Economic Behavior* (Princeton, 1953).

9. Eric Linhart, Franz Urban Pappi and Ralf Schmitt, "Die proportionale Ministerienaufteilung in deutschen Koalitionsregierungen: akzeptierte Norm oder das Ausnutzen strategischer Vorteile?" *Politische Vierteljahresschrift* 49 (2008): 46-67.

10. Luca Verzichelli, "Portfolio Allocation," in *Cabinets and Coalition Bargaining: The Democratic Life Cycle in Western Europe*, eds., Kaare Strøm, Wolfgang C. Müller and Torbjörn Bergman (Oxford, 2008), 237-267.

11. Ibid. It should be noted, however, that the CDU was compensated for its low share of cabinet seats through an over proportional allocation of junior ministerial positions below the cabinet level (Parlamentarische Staatssekretäre); See Saalfeld (see note 6), 194.

12. Franz Urban Pappi, Michael Frank Stoffel and Nicole Michaela Seher, "Regierungsbildungen im fragmentierten deutschen Parteiensystem," Working Paper No. 129, Mannheimer Zentrum für Europäische Sozialforschung (2009). Wordfish was developed by Jonathan B. Slapin and Sven-Oliver Proksch. Based on the open-source statistics software R, Wordfish provides a scaling algorithm to estimate policy positions based on word frequencies in texts such as election manifestos. For further information see Jonathan B. Slapin and Sven-Oliver Proksch, "A Scaling Model for Estimating Time-Series Party Positions from Texts," *American Journal of Political Science* 52 (2008): 705–722.

13. Kaare Strøm and Wolfgang C. Müller, "The Keys to Togetherness: Coalition Agreements in Parliamentary Democracies," *Journal of Legislative Studies* 5 (1999): 255-283.

14. "Wachstum. Bildung. Zusammenhalt: Koalitionsvertrag zwischen CDU, CSU und FDP. 17. Legislaturperiode," (Berlin, 2009).

15. "Mit Mut und Menschlichkeit: Koalitionsvertrag zwischen CDU, CSU und SPD," (Berlin, 2005), 141.

16. Uwe Thaysen, "Regierungsbildung 2005: Merkel, Merkel I, Merkel II?" *Zeitschrift für Parlamentsfragen* 37 (2006): 582-610; Saalfeld (see note 6).

17. Luebbert (see note 5); Saalfeld (see note 6); Thaysen (note 16); Arco Timmermans and Catherine Moury, "Coalition Governance in Belgium and The Netherlands: Rising Government Stability Against All Electoral Odds," *Acta Politica* 41 (2008): 389-407.

18. Luebbert (note 5), 63.

19. Ibid.

20. Ibid.

21. Ibid., 63-64.

22. Saalfeld (see note 6); Thaysen (note 16).

23. See Luebbert (see note 5).

24. Michael Laver and Kenneth A. Shepsle, "Coalitions and Cabinet Government," *American Political Science Review* 84 (1990): 873-890.

25. See, above all, Laver and Shepsle (see note 4).

26. Michael Laver, "Models of Government Formation," *Annual Review of Political Science* 1 (1998): 1-25.

27. Nils C. Bandelow, "Health Governance in the Aftermath of Traditional Corporatism: One Small Step for the Legislator, One Giant Leap for the Subsystem?" *German Policy Studies* 5 (2009): 45-63.

28. See the media interviews given by Seehofer in the daily newspaper *Die Welt* and Rösler on the television show "Beckmann." "Ich wünsche Herrn Rösler viel Freude dabei," interview with Horst Seehofer, *Die Welt* 8 December 2009; available at www.welt.de/

die-welt/politik/article5460416/Ich-wuensche-Herrn-Roesler-viel-Freude-dabei.html; accessed 23 May 2010; "Rösler: Kopf durch die Wand," *Süddeutsche Zeitung* 2 February 2010; available at www.sueddeutsche.de/medien/713/501953/text/9/; accessed 23 May 2010.

29. Hans-Dieter Klingemann et al., *Mapping Policy Preferences II: Estimates for Parties, Electors, and Governments in Eastern Europe, European Union and OECD 1990-2003* (Oxford, 2006).

30. In spatial models, it has usually been difficult to establish the location of the legislative status quo. For the purposes of this chapter (and in line with the portfolio-allocation model) I assume the position of the health minister's party in the previous government to represent the legislative status quo (i.e., the SPD's ideal point in 2002 and 2005, respectively).

31. The CDU/CSU would prefer any point $2.0 > x > 1.6$ to the status quo of 2.0 and would be expected to reject any point $2.0 < x < 1.6$.

32. Koalitionsvereinbarung 2009 (see note 14).

33. Kenneth Benoit and Michael Laver, *Party Policy in Modern Democracies* (London, 2006).

34. Herbert Kitschelt, "Citizens, politicians, and party cartellization: Political representation and state failure in post-industrial democracies," *European Journal of Political Research* 37 (2000): 149-179.

35. Hanspeter Kriesi et al., *West European Politics in the Age of Globalization* (Cambridge, 2008).

36. Reimut Zohlnhöfer, "Große Koalition: Durchregiert oder im institutionellen Dickicht verheddert?" *Aus Politik und Zeitgeschichte* B38 (2009): 9-14.

Chapter 6

COALITIONS AND CAMPS
IN THE GERMAN PARTY SYSTEM AFTER THE
2009 BUNDESTAG ELECTION

• • • • • • • • • • • • • •

Frank Decker

and

Jared Sonnicksen

Introduction

When the interior designers of the Reichstag building were planning the conference rooms of the parliamentary groups back in the mid 1990s, they could not have yet anticipated the transformation of the party landscape that was to occur about a decade later. By now, the difference in size between the smallest major party, the Social Democrats (SPD), and the largest small party, the Free Democrats (FDP), has become so narrow that there is a gaping void in the last few rows of the SPD parliamentary conference room. At the same time, the FDP now needs a larger space because its parliamentary group has almost doubled in size. Also, a large number of staff and parliamentary group members from the major parties had to vacate their offices in order to make room for the staff of the small parties. These logistical challenges imposed by the results of the 2009 Bundestag election provide a clear reflection of the "seismic shift"[1] within and between political parties in Germany.

On the whole, there are five aspects of the election that warrant particular consideration and analysis in view of the developments in the German party system. *First,* the 2009 election has stabilized the five-party structure that has been developing since 2005 when the Left Party established itself firmly at federal level.[2] *Second,* the election has reinforced the bipolar structure of the party system with two opposing ideological camps in electoral and coalition terms. *Third*, the election has generated a shift in relative strength within both the "left" and "right" camps in favor of the smaller parties. *Fourth*, the election has resulted in a structural asymmetry between the two major parties in favor of the Conservatives, that is, the Christian Democratic Union (CDU) and the Bavarian Christian Social Union (CSU), or the Union parties. *Finally*, the election has refuted the assumption that "small" two-party majority coalitions (i.e., consisting of one major party and one smaller party) were no longer possible in the five-party system.

Consolidation of the Five-Party System

The consolidation of the five-party system comes as no surprise given the electoral and political developments that have occurred in a number of Länder since 2005.[3] In the first six months following the inauguration of the Grand Coalition of the CDU/CSU and SPD, it appeared as if the Left Party did not stand much of a chance at significant electoral success in the western Länder. Its poor electoral results at the regional level in spring 2006 (e.g., in Baden-Wurttemberg and Rhineland Palatinate) were mainly a reflection of the Grand Coalition's overall positive standing in the electorate at the time, even though the Union parties were able to benefit more from this than the SPD.[4] The regional elections in Bremen (May 2007) as well as in Hesse, Lower Saxony, and Hamburg (January/February 2008), however, reversed that trend,[5] with the Left Party entering parliaments in western German Länder for the first time. In light of this growing competition, the SPD saw no choice but to change its strategy, which admittedly was carried out in an uncoordinated, if not chaotic manner. Especially in Hesse, the SPD suffered a massive loss of confidence among voters by reneging on an explicit campaign promise when it sought to cooperate with the Left Party after the election in order to form a government.[6] The internal power struggle and tensions that ensued within the party proved not only fatal to the career of Andrea Ypsilanti, SPD candidate for minister president in Hesse, but also eventually led to the resignation of SPD chairman Kurt Beck.

In the first months of the financial and economic crisis, the public's focus naturally turned to the national government, whose crisis management was viewed positively on the whole. Although the Left Party's critique of the system of international financial capitalism turned out to have some merit, this did not translate directly into more support for their party. On the contrary, in addition to the governing Grand Coalition, the

Figure 1: Results for the Left Party in Western Länder Elections, 2006-2009 (in percent)

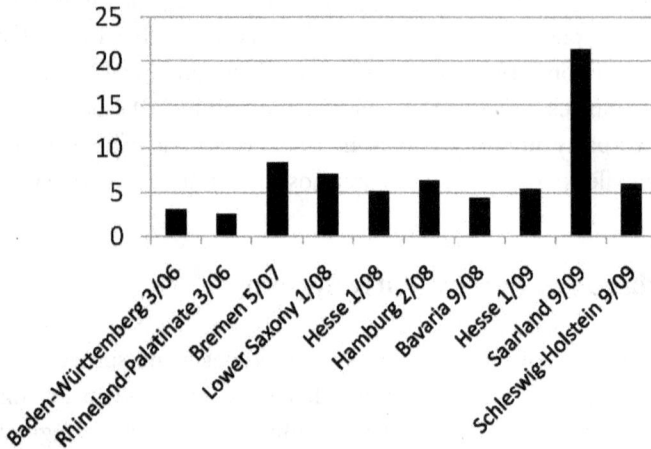

Source: official election data

liberal, market-friendly FDP gained the most support of all the parties from the crisis, managing skillfully to distinguish itself through its warnings against too much state interventionism. Because the liberal-conservative parties generally are credited with more competence in economic issues by the public, they were able to benefit from the change in agenda by 2008-2009, which now centered on financial security issues, limiting damages, and maintaining the status quo. Still, this only temporarily marginalized or postponed the issue of social justice in political debate. Thus, in this context, the SPD was able to play down its weak results in the European elections in June 2009, claiming that at least it did not lose additional votes to the Left Party and hence authority on social issues. However, on the national election night of 27 September, it once again had to face the painful reality of losing more than one million votes to Oskar Lafontaine and Gregor Gysi's Left Party. Thus, the financial and economic crisis had only momentarily delayed the rise of the Left Party.

The "Center-Right" and "Left" Camps

Political scientists occasionally challenge the concept of two political camps in the German party system, not least because of the disputable terminology of "liberal-conservative" or "center-right" versus "left." Nonetheless, the run-up to the election and its results in 2009 provide another testament to the existence of these camps.[7] Both the electoral dimension, i.e., shifts in voter behavior, as well as the partisan dimension, i.e., coalition patterns, attest to the party system's bipolarity.

According to polling center Infratest dimap, the bulk of the voters who voted differently in 2009 than in the 2005 elections stayed within the same camp or preferred not to vote over voting for a party from the other camp. This effect has been demonstrated in a particularly impressive way among the voters of the Union parties, since approximately one million voters abstained and another one million voters switched to the FDP, whereas there was hardly any crossover to the parties on the left. With traditional SPD voters as well, the number shifting within the left camp and abstaining altogether was much higher than those switching to the opposing camp. Over 3 million of those who voted SPD in 2005 either stayed home or voted for the Left Party (1,110,000) or the Green Party (860,000)–more than 1 million crossed camp and voted CDU/CSU or FDP (520,000 of them surprisingly chose the FDP). Together with the nonvoters, the voters who switched camps decided the election in favor of the center-right parties.

Figure 2: Analysis of Voting Transfer (CDU/CSU–SPD)

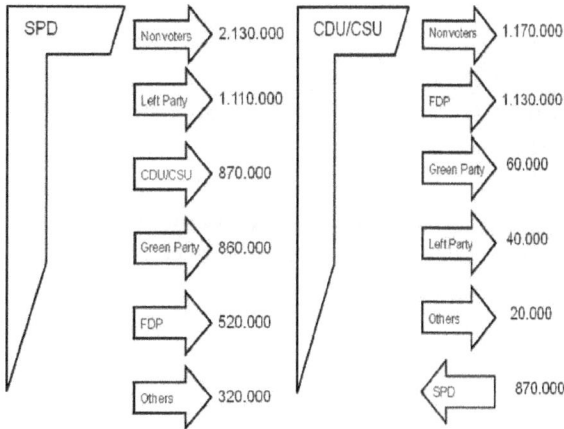

Source: Infratest Dimap

Comparing the percentages of the vote, the pivotal relevance of the cross-camp swing voters becomes evident. In 2005 the three left parties together garnered 51 percent of the vote, thus exceeding the Union parties' and FDP's total 45.1 percent. This time, the relation reversed in favor of the center-right parties (48.4 percent compared to 45.5 percent for the three left parties). Thus, the two camps are separated by a slim margin. It is also important to note the surprising 2 percent of the vote gained by the Pirate Party, which were most likely lost by the parties on the left.[8] It would only require winning back a relatively small number of swing voters and non-voters from the center-right camp to reverse the majority situation again.

Figure 3: Center-right and Left Camps' Percentage of the Vote in National Elections

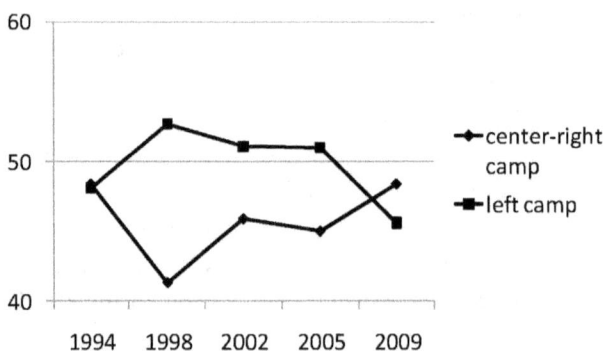

Source: own calculations

Nevertheless, taking the coalitional behavior of the parties into account, we need to make some restrictions to the thesis of the two opposing camps.[9]

The future development of the party system (and therefore of the coalition and government formation options) also will depend on whether these restraints will continue to apply. While the Union parties and the FDP can continue their political cooperation, the three leftist parties face a difficult path to mutual opening and rapprochement, which could begin with coalitions on the Länder level and ultimately lead to a coalitional majority option in the Bundestag elections in 2013. Breaking the taboo in Hesse prepared the way for a possible coalition of the SPD with the Left Party even before the 2009 election. The Social Democrats did take this opportunity assertively during the elections in Saarland and Thuringia in the hopes of being able to form the new governments in those two states.[10] Nevertheless, the national party's unanimous support for this change in strategy is surprising, even more so considering the lack of opposition one would have expected from the conservative wing of the SPD. This sea change in the SPD is even more evident given that the head of the party in Thuringia, Christoph Matschie, faced massive criticism for his decision to form a coalition with the CDU instead of with the Left Party, the option clearly preferred by most SPD partisans.

The Rise of the Small Parties

One of the most dramatic effects of the 2009 elections was the change in the relative strength among the large and small parties.[11] Union and SPD together only received 58 percent of all votes (compared to 69 percent in 2005), which constitutes an historical low point. (In the first Bundestag election in 1949, which still stood in the multi-party tradition of the Weimar Republic, they together managed to gain 60 percent.) These figures are even more impressive in relation to the electorate as a whole. Because voter participation declined dramatically (from 77.6 to 70.8 percent), the former *Volksparteien* or catch-all parties were supported by only 40 percent of all eligible voters. When support for the two major parties was at its peak in the early and mid 1970s, the support level, at 80 percent, was twice as high.

At which point–at which percentage of the vote–does a party cease to be a catch-all party? Commentators have posed this question, sometimes with bitter irony, sometimes with serious concern, and primarily with the SPD in mind.[12] On 27 September, the latter had to cope with its worst result ever in Bundestag elections, whereas the Union parties (at 33.8 percent) placed only slightly above their historic low point from 1949 (31 percent). As important as it may be to address the long-term factors behind the decline in voter participation, it is equally correct to attribute the main reason for the significant drop in support for the major parties in 2009 to the Grand Coalition that the Union parties and the SPD had entered in 2005. On the one hand, grand coalitions always lead to rising support for the small oppositional parties at the next election.[13] On the other hand, in this election there was an additional incentive to support the small parties on account of the coalitional preferences and options expressed by the Grand Coalition parties. Voters from the center-right camp may have had it easier. CDU and CSU voters who wanted to prevent another grand coalition were proverbially driven into the arms of the liberal FDP.[14] Conversely, the Social Democrats had their hands tied after the FDP forcefully rejected the option of an SPD-Green-FDP coalition and thus lacked any realistic chance to bring about a change in government. Bereft of a viable alternative to another grand coalition, in the end the SPD electoral campaign could only focus on the objective of preventing a CDU/CSU-FDP coalition.

Figure 4: Combined Percentage of the Vote for CDU/CSU and SPD in Relation to Total Number of Eligible Voters in National Elections

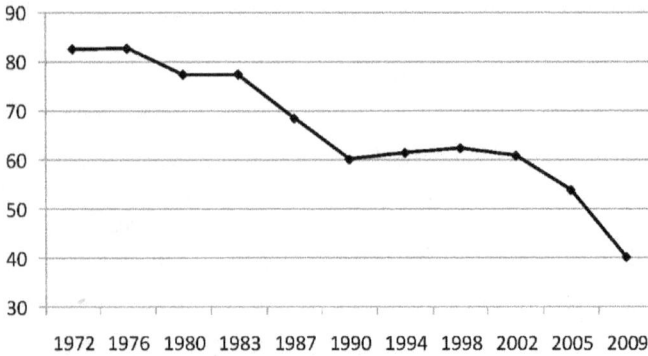

Source: own calculations

The relevance of the governmental constellation for the results of the large and small parties could prove effective in the next elections at the Länder level. The German party system's normal state consists of dualism of government and opposition, at least gauging by its sixty-year history with the exceptions of two grand coalitions (1966-1969, 2005-2009). Should the party system return to these conditions, the sanctioning effect often spawned by "midterm elections" may be revived,[15] which usually means losses to the parties governing at federal level and wins for those in the opposition. Accordingly, there was good reason why the CDU/CSU and FDP almost immediately were concerned about the elections in North Rhine Westphalia on 9 May 2010. The electoral defeat for the incumbent CDU-FDP government there meant a loss of the CDU/CSU-FDP majority in the second chamber (Bundesrat). Taking into account the normal pattern of midterm elections, the largest governing party, the CDU above all other parties bore the risk of being penalized for unpopular political measures taken at the federal level (for example the bailout of Greece and a support fund for other wobbly Eurozone members), while the junior partner is usually spared.

In the case of the present coalition, this could turn out differently. It was the FDP which, in contrast to the CDU, announced lofty plans and long-ranging proposals in its election campaign. With the party in a particularly delicate situation facing the reality in government, the FDP thus has more to lose. One can safely assume that FDP voters will not let the party off the hook for falling through on their campaign promises. The SPD on the other side, which is the largest party in the opposition with the Left Party and Greens, will have the chance to benefit most from its opposition status.

Additionally, the SPD can take advantage of breaking with its recent pre-election strategy and open up to the Left Party in trying to form coalitions at the Länder level, making it possible to vote out CDU/CSU-FDP coalitions there. One of the most interesting issues in the next legislative period will be how the relations and competition of the SPD vis-à-vis the Left Party will develop on account of including the Left Party in government coalitions at subnational levels and how this in turn will affect election results.[16]

It is one of the paradoxes in the development of the German party system that the SPD's situation is now even more difficult, percentage-wise, in the eastern parts of Germany than in the western regions.[17] In recent years, the Social Democrats noticeably dropped behind the Left Party in eastern Germany–it was only in Berlin where SPD and the PDS-successor party turned out to be neck-and-neck in the 2009 Bundestag election. If this proves to be a pattern in the upcoming Länder elections, it might be easier to form a coalition in the western Länder than in the eastern in the future. The attempt of the Thuringian SPD to include the Left Party as a junior partner, although the latter had even gained more seats in the 2009 Land election, illustrates this dilemma.

At the same time it would be appropriate to include the Left Party in government in order to trim the party back to a normal size. It is symptomatic that the former PDS in past Länder elections was the weakest whenever it was directly or indirectly part of government before (as illustrated in Saxony-Anhalt, Mecklenburg West Pomerania and Berlin).[18] Including the unloved competitor would not only put the SPD in position to win majorities again, it would also provide a means for dealing with the Left Party.

Rivalry at federal level with the Left Party is no less delicate for the SPD. Already in the 1980s, the SPD had to learn the lesson that competition coming from within the own camp can probably be even more unpleasant in an opposition role than in government, when the Greens immensely challenged the SPD in the parliamentary arena.[19] The same thing could happen again today. It remains to be seen whether Frank-Walter Steinmeier, the 2009 chancellor candidate of the SPD, made a wise decision in proclaiming himself leader of the opposition on election night, seeing that until now he has had no experience as a sitting member of parliament and has not yet shown any noticeable talent for polarizing. In order to withstand the competition among the Left Party leader Gregor Gysi, as well as Renate Künast and Jürgen Trittin of the Greens, it may have been a better tactical move to have Sigmar Gabriel appointed party group leader in the Bundestag–instead of party chairman as he has now become–and then,

vice-versa, making Steinmeier head of the party instead of the parliamentary party group. Having to share the stage in the Bundestag with the
rhetorically eloquent Sigmar Gabriel could put Steinmeier in a more negative light among the party leadership.

Another important question concerns the future of the party's program
or its political substance. Certainly, the new dual leadership arrangement
would not indicate a forthcoming shift to the left. With such a strategy the
party would be ill-advised anyway and for two fundamental reasons. On
the one hand, that would endanger the SPD's potential to attract voters of
the broad middle class. Considering the fact that around three million former SPD-voters refused to visit the ballot boxes or even voted for CDU/CSU
or FDP, it is doubtful that these citizens could be brought back into the
camp via a political program one-sidedly geared toward the recipients of
social welfare benefits or other unprivileged societal groups.[20] On the
other hand, a programmatic shift to the left would be counterproductive
in view of coalition options because this would prevent the Left Party on
its part from orienting further towards the center and more pragmatic
views. It is precisely this point—aside from personnel and historic incompatibilities—that constitutes the main obstacle to future collaboration. This
problem is also reflected in the chaotic conditions found with a number of
the Länder or regional Left Party organizations. The SPD would never
stand a chance in a populist competition to outbid this rival.

The New Hegemony of CDU/CSU

The SPD's rapprochement toward the Left Party as a possible coalition
partner has been made necessary by broader changes in the German five-
party system in general,[21] but also more acutely by the hegemonic position that the CDU/CSU has gained in this constellation. This likewise
represents a noteworthy shift among the parties. In previous national elections, the SPD and CDU/CSU shared quite similar percentages of the vote,
with the SPD either tied or closely behind the Union parties—in 1998 the
SPD was even ahead of the CDU/CSU. This led political scientists and party
experts to conclude that Germany demonstrated a structural symmetry in
its party landscape.[22] Today this symmetry can only apply in reference to
the two camps, but not with regard to the two catch-all parties.

Figure 5: Comparing CDU/CSU and SPD National Election Results

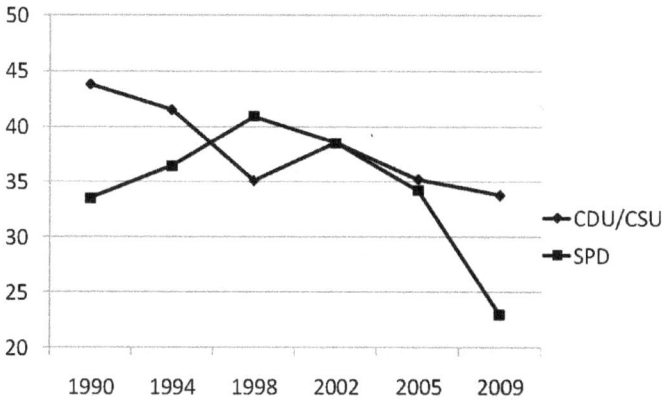

Source: official election data

Because the CDU/CSU only faces one, while SPD faces two competitors within their own camps, the latter must surely be worried about falling into a minority position in relation to the other catch-all party in the long run. Being the strongest party, the CDU/CSU enjoys a dual strategic edge. For one, this puts the party in the position of being able to form small two-partner coalitions on the federal and Länder level, with the added bonus that not only the FDP, but also the Green Party as of recently, represent possible coalition partners. Moreover, if it is arithmetically impossible to do so, the CDU/CSU may find it easier than the SPD to form a grand coalition in which the party can claim the office of head of government. In contrast, the SPD's only chance to attain a parliamentary majority appears to be a three-party coalition, either including the Left Party and the Green Party or—crossing camp boundaries—including the FDP and Green Party.

Because both of these coalitions were not realistic options for the 2009 elections, the Social Democrats suffered from an immense competitive disadvantage against CDU/CSU and FDP. But this alone cannot explain the defection of former SPD voters to the liberal-conservative camp. That shift is also a result of the clever repositioning of the CDU under the leadership of Angela Merkel, which was ultimately a correction to the disastrous election campaign mistakes made in 2005,[23] the strategy now being to deprive the SPD of any target to attack in the campaign. Merkel used the period of the Grand Coalition to cleanse her party from overly conservative and neoliberal dead weight. In pushing through a modernization of family policy and warding off all proposals for a radical reform in the social and

labor market policy areas, the chancellor thus managed to occupy otherwise social democratic terrain. Her strategy was so successful that the
SPD's attempt to stirs fears of an impending "social ice age" under a CDU-
FDP government merely fell flat in the campaign. The Union parties also
had an additional boost from its "chancellor bonus" generated by the
widely popular incumbent. Admittedly, the CDU/CSU strategy drove a lot
of voters to the normally less-preferred liberals. Nonetheless, the adherence of the FDP to an "anti-social democratic" agenda, with a mantra-like
repetition of their demands for tax cuts, led to a broad coalition of voters
in the end, ensuring a clear majority for the center-right parties.

Conclusion: Bipolar or Multipolar Party Competition?

Thus emerges the next critical question. How will the party landscape
develop in Germany in the future? After the landmark 2005 Bundestag
elections, most journalists and social scientists assumed that the era of
catch-all party dualism, which had been the foundation for the small two-
party coalitions, had come to an irreversible end. Two future scenarios
were depicted: one positive and one negative. Either a grand coalition
would be perpetuated, as in the case of Austria, or a party landscape
would emerge that allows for multiple coalitions similar to the Scandina-
vian countries, where cross-camp three-party-coalitions would become the
dominant pattern.[24]

Both scenarios have not come true. The Green Party has indeed opened
up toward the CDU and allowed for the first Conservative-Green coalition at
Länder level since 2008 in the city-state of Hamburg.[25] But, faced with substantial pressure from the party base in the run-up to the national elections,
the Green leadership still had to rule out the option of a CDU-FDP-Green
coalition–nicknamed the "Jamaica Coalition" because of the colors black
for the Conservatives, yellow for the Liberals and green, of course, for the
Greens. Interestingly, after the series of 2009 elections, just such a coalition
has been realized for the first time at the Länder level in Saarland. The FDP
seems even more hermetic in its resistance to a possible SPD-Green Party-
FDP coalition, or "Traffic Light Coalition" (red, yellow and green), a resistance the Liberals continue to uphold even at the Länder level, as coalition
negotiations in North Rhine Westphalia in May 2010 attest.[26]

Against the background of the three-party coalitions that, by and large,
have not yet come to fruition, it is noteworthy that grand coalitions also
have lost attractiveness as an alternative governing model. Whereas up to

the elections in August and September 2009, there were grand coalitions of SPD and CDU in five Länder, there are now only three such coalitions. Adding together the CDU-Green coalition in Hamburg and the new Jamaica coalition in Saarland, a total of only five camp-crossing coalitions stand against eleven of the more classic type of coalition of either conservative-liberal parties or leftist coalitions (with the SPD-governed Rhineland-Palatinate being a lonely exception).

It would seem that the party system is returning to a bipolar structure. If the SPD, Greens and Left Party manage to overcome their mutual antipathy, Germany may again see a dualism of two equally strong and discernible camps competing for government power. The situation, therefore, would be similar to the 1980s, except that the left camp will consist of three instead of two parts. What makes it difficult to determine the likelihood of that scenario actually happening is the uncertainty about how exactly the relationship between SPD, Greens and Left Party will develop. For one thing, a mutual interest in winning majorities and thus government power does not guarantee that these parties will overcome personnel and programmatic incompatibilities. For another, the individual parties' various coalition options mean that their strategic interests might not always be congruent. Especially the Greens might resist absorption into the left camp. If the Greens manage to stay open to coalitions within both camps, they might be able to take on the pivotal role in coalition-building formerly played by the FDP. Why should the Green Party deliberately give up this advantage?

In the Länder elections in Schleswig-Holstein and Saarland, keeping their coalition options open did not harm the Greens at the ballot box. The problem is–if anywhere–a problem of the party base, which clearly leans more to the left compared to both party leadership and the electorate. Nevertheless, the Greens' state convention in Saarland voted with a clear majority to form a Jamaica coalition, which shows that delegates as well as members can be convinced to shift to the conservative-liberal or center camp if such a move is well prepared and communicated by the party leadership.

Nevertheless, a complete bipolarization will not and cannot be possible, if anything, due to the federal make-up of the country.[27] It is not uncommon for politicians on the Länder level to pursue a different coalition strategy than the one taken by their party at federal level and for various reasons. The examples of the failed attempt of the Hessian SPD to form an SPD-Green minority government tolerated by the Left Party or the recent coalition negotiations in Thuringia, where the Left Party top candidate's decision not to pursue the office of head of the state government caused as much aggravation in his own party as the decision taken by the Thuringia state committee of the SPD to form a grand coalition with the CDU rather than with the Left Party–all serve to illustrate this point. As soon as parties that are in opposition to one another at federal level collaborate on the Länder level, the antagonistic model reaches its limits. The existence of two easily discernible, opposing camps might be preferred from a democratic perspective, in the sense that such conditions provide the voter with a clear choice. One may doubt, however, that such model can fit with the actual decision-making needs and alternatives of the complex reality of governing in Germany's federal republic.

Taking these necessities into account, the time for cross-camp coalitions in German politics is not over yet. Certainly, a model with multiple coalition options would be more demanding than the past and present persistence of a political camp mentality, as it would require a fundamental change in behavior of both parties and voters. The former would have to learn to moderate their confrontational tendencies against one another and deal with each other more sensibly; the latter would have to accept that, in the end, it is not their votes, but rather the parties and party leaderships that determine coalition governments. The clear electoral victory in 2009 of CDU/CSU and FDP cannot reverse the transforming framework of the five-party system, but it might impede the transition to a more consensus-oriented system. The Länder elections in the next few years will give some indication of whether the return to bipolarity currently foreshadowed in fact will become definitive of the future model of party competition in Germany. For German politics, that would be a rather bad omen.

Notes

1. Roger Cohen, "Germany Unbound," *International Herald Tribune,* 1 October 2009, 7.
2. David P. Conradt, "The Tipping Point: The 2005 Election and the Deconsolidation of the German Party System?" in *Launching the Grand Coalition: The 2005 Bundestag Elections and the Future of German Politics,* ed., Eric Langenbacher (New York, 2006), 13-28.
3. Michelle H. Williams, "Kirchheimer Revisited: Party Polarisation, Party Convergence, or Party Decline in the German Party System" in *German Politics* 17, no. 2 (2008): 105-123; Hermann Schmitt and Andreas Wüst, "The Extraordinary Bundestag Election of

2005: The Interplay of Long-term Trends and Short-term Factors" in Langenbacher (see note 2), 29-48.

4. Bernd Schlipphak and Ulrich Eith, "Die baden-württembergische Landtagswahl 2006 im Einflussfeld der Bundespolitik: Auswirkungen und Rückwirkungen" and Sigrid Koch-Baumgarten, "Die Landtagswahl in Rheinland-Pfalz 2006 und ihre bundespolitische Bedeutung" in *100 Tage Schonfrist*, eds., Jens Tescher and Helge Blatt (Wiesbaden, 2008), 139-154, 155-175.

5. Sören Messinger and Jonas Rugenstein, "Der Erfolg der Partei die Linke. Sammlung im programmatischen Nebel" in *Patt oder Gezeitenwechsel? Deutschland 2009*, eds., Felix Butzlaff, Stine Harm, and Franz Walter (Wiesbaden, 2009), 67-93.

6. Wolfgang Schroeder, Florian Albert, and Arijana Neumann, "Die hessische Landtagswahl 2008" in *Parteien und Parteiensystem in Hessen. Vom Vier- zum Fünfparteiensystem?*, ed,. Wolfgang Schroeder (Wiesbaden, 2008), 27-55.

7. Oskar Niedermayer, ed., *Die Parteien nach der Bundestagswahl 2005* (Wiesbaden, 2008).

8. Marcel Solar, "Klarmachen zum Ändern? Aufstieg und Perspektiven der deutschen Piratenpartei" in *Mitteilungen des Instituts für Parteienrecht und Parteienforschung* (MIP) 16 (2010): 108-111.

9. For coalition formation in the German Länder, see chapters in Uwe Jun, Melanie Haas, and Oskar Niedermayer, eds., *Parteien und Parteiensysteme in den deutschen Ländern* (Wiesbaden, 2008); as well as chapters in Kerstin Völkl, Kai-Uwe Schnapp, Everhard Holtmann, and Oscar W. Gabriel, eds., *Wähler und Landtagswahlen in der Bundesrepublik Deutschland* (Baden-Baden, 2008).

10. Frank Decker, "Koalitionsaussagen und Koalitionsbildung," *Aus Politik und Zeitgeschichte* 51 (2009): 20-26.

11. Such "dramatic" changes of course were well underway in the previous election. See: Eric Langenbacher, "The Drama of 2005 and the Future of German Politics" in Langenbacher (see note 2), 1-12.

12. Peter Lösche, "Ende der Volksparteien,", *Aus Politik und Zeitgeschichte* 51 (2009): 6-12; Franz Walter, "Vor dem großen Umbruch: Die SPD" in *Volksparteien: Erfolgsmodell für die Zukunft?*, eds., Volker Kronenberg, Tilman Mayer (Freiburg/Breisgau, 2009), 101-126.

13. Melanie Haas, "Auswirkungen der Großen Koalition auf das Parteiensystem," *Aus Politik und Zeitgeschichte* 35-36 (2007): 18-26.

14. This effect was supported by the German two ballot electoral system, which allows voters to strategically split their votes. See Bernhard Weßels, "Splitting sichert den Wechsel", in *WZB-Mitteilungen* 126 (2009): 33-35.

15. For an overview on the effect of midterm elections (*Zwischenwahlen*), see Frank Decker and Marcel Lewandowsky, "Landtagswahlen als bundespolitische Zwischenwahlen. Der vermeintliche Sonderfall Hessen" in *Parteien und Parteiensystem in Hessen. Vom Vier- zum Fünfparteiensystem?*, ed., Wolfgang Schroeder (Wiesbaden, 2008), 259-283, especially 261-267; Jens Hainmüller and Holger Lutz Kern, "Electoral Balancing, Divided Government, and Midterm Loss in German Elections" in *Journal of Legislative Studies* 12, no. 2 (2006): 127-149.

16. Chances for collaboration may improve after the resignation of Left Party chairman Oskar Lafontaine in January 2010 due to health reasons. Lafontaine, who had been a member of the Social Democrats (and their former party chairman) until he joined the Left Party in 2005, was regarded by many SPD officials as the main obstacle to a rapprochement.

17. Frank Decker and Anne-Kathrin Oeltzen, "Mitgliederpartei oder professionelle Wählerpartei: ein Widerspruch?" in *Neuanfang statt Niedergang–Die Zukunft der Mitgliederparteien*, eds., Fabian Schalt et al. (Berlin, 2009), 258-272, especially 266-270.

18. Jonathan Olsen and Dan Hough, "Don't Think Twice, It's Alright: SPD-Left Party/PDS Coalitions in the Eastern German Länder," *German Politics and Society* 25, no. 3 (2007): 1-24.

19. Daniel Hough, Michael Koß, and Jonathan Olsen, *The Left Party in Contemporary German Politics* (Basingstoke, 2007), especially Ch. 4 "Haven't We Been Here Before?," 66-83.
20. Marcel Lewandowsky, "Wir waren schon einmal weiter," *Berliner Republik* 10, no. 6 (2008): 72-77.
21. Kimmo Elo, "The Left Party and the Long-Term Developments of the German Party System," *German Politics and Society* 26, no. 3 (2008): 50-68.
22. Oskar Niedermayer, "Die Entwicklung des bundesdeutschen Parteiensystems" in *Handbuch der deutschen Parteien*, eds., Frank Decker and Viola Neu (Wiesbaden, 2007), 128.
23. Volker Best, "Die Strategie der kommunizierten Ehrlichkeit im CDU/CSU-Bundestagswahlkampf 2005," *Zeitschrift für Parlamentsfragen* 40, no. 3 (2009): 579-602.
24. Geoffrey K. Roberts, "The German Bundestag Election 2005," *Parliamentary Affairs* 59, no. 4 (2006): 668-681.
25. Patrick Horst, "Die Wahl zur Hamburger Bürgerschaft vom 24. Februar 2008: Wahlsieger Ole von Beust bildet die erste schwarz-grüne Koalition auf Landesebene," *Zeitschrift für Parlamentsfragen* 39, no. 3 (2008): 509-527.
26. Frank Decker and Volker Best, "Looking for Mr. Right? A Comparative Analysis of Parties' Coalition Statements prior to the Federal Elections of 2005 and 2009," in *German Politics* 19 no. 2 (2010): 164-182.
27. Klaus Detterbeck and Wolfgang Renzsch, "Multi-Level Electoral Competition: The German Case," *European Urban and Regional Studies* 10, no. 3 (2003): 257-269.

$\mathcal{C}$OALITION DYNAMICS AND THE CHANGING GERMAN PARTY SYSTEM

• • • • • • • • • • • • • •

Charles Lees

Introduction

The outcome of the 2009 federal election is already familiar to students of German politics. In nominal terms, the distribution of party weights in the seventeenth Bundestag saw a shift in legislative power towards the smaller parties: with the FDP winning ninety-three seats (up from sixty-one in 2005), the Left Party seventy-six seats (up from fifty-four in 2005) and the Greens sixty-eight (up from fifty-one in 2005). As a result, the small parties now control 237 seats (or just over 38 percent) of the 622 seat Bundestag. By contrast, the combined seat share of just under 62 percent for the two *Volksparteien* can be interpreted as indicative of the emergence of what Oskar Niedermayer calls a "fluid party system,"[1] in which the process of dealignment[2] associated with late capitalism has eroded the certainties of the past.

Christian Democratic Union/Christian Social Union (CDU/CSU) strategists would point out, however, that—despite only winning 33.8 percent of the vote, down 1.4 percent on the 2005 election—their combined seat share actually rose from 226 to 239 seats; representing a rise in their percentage share of legislative seats from 36.8 percent to 38.4 percent. Indeed, it is the Social Democratic Party (SPD)—with 23 percent of the vote, down 11.2 percent from 2005—that was the main loser of the 2009 election: ending up with just 146 seats, down from 222 and representing a drop in their share from 36.2 to 23.5 percent. For the SPD, this was indeed an electoral debacle of historic proportions.

Leaving the comparative performances of the CDU/CSU and SPD to one side, however, it is clear that the 2009 federal election does crystallize and throw into relief some of the changes that undoubtedly have taken place within the German party system, especially over the last thirty years. Clearly, there has been a shift in the role and status of the *Volksparteien* and there would appear to be little possibility of their combined share of the vote returning to the 80 percent or more that they enjoyed over the eight elections from 1961 through to 1987. Nevertheless, in their programmatic and organizational features, the CDU/CSU and SPD remain true catch-all parties,[3] and in coalition terms, the only two parties within the German party system that have the legislative weight to act as *formateur* in the coalition game. This gives them a configuration of resources that the other smaller parties lack. These resources are both numerical (in terms of their shares of party weights within the legislature) and ideological (in terms of their programmatic profiles).

This chapter argues that, because of these two sets of resources, it is perhaps a little early to talk about a crisis of the *Volksparteien*. Drawing upon a long-term analysis of the German party system, I argue that many of the changes that have taken place in recent years have actually enhanced the strategic position of the *Volksparteien* in terms of the coalition game.[4] It is undeniable that the normative role of the *Volksparteien* as integrators and aggregators of societal interests has been weakened by their reduced electoral and legislative shares. But, even at the height of their powers in the 1960s and 1970s, this role was problematized by the fact that they were nearly always forced to bargain with the FDP, which, despite its relative electoral weakness, acted as the perpetual "kingmaker" within the party system. Moreover, given the almost continual participation of the FDP in coalitions that formed, any notion of responsible party government was difficult to sustain. By contrast, I argue that the emergence of the Greens and the PDS (after 2005 the Left Party) and their consolidation within the German party system means that in most coalition games, the distribution of party weights allows no single small party to act as kingmaker in the manner previously enjoyed by the FDP. In addition, because of their relative positions in ideological space, it is at present difficult to conceive of circumstances in which the small parties would be able to act in concert to extract concessions from the *Volksparteien*. Thus, even in the context of the 2009 federal election, when all of the smaller parties performed well and the FDP may even had expected to exercise the kind of leverage it enjoyed in previous coalition negotiations with which it was involved, it was the CDU/CSU–as *formateur*–that enjoyed strategic ascendancy. This is because both *Volksparteien* are in principle less vulnerable to threats of a decisive defection by small parties to alternative coalitions than they were in the past.

The rest of this chapter is structured as follows. First, I review the coalition literature in the light of the numerical and ideological dimensions noted above in order to yield six analytical insights for the analysis of changing coalition dynamics in Germany. Second, I use these insights to assess the impact of party system change on the numerical and ideological dimensions of the coalition game and the changes in the strategic environment that can be inferred from this. Finally, I review the arguments made and come to some conclusions about the impact of party system change on coalition dynamics.

Analyzing Coalition Formation

The coalition theory literature is conceptually diverse and many of the more important models within the genre are to some extent contradictory. In addition, theorists take different aspects of coalition behavior as their starting point, with the bulk of the early literature concerned exclusively with the process of coalition formation rather than coalition maintenance. Drawing upon formal theories of politics,[5] much of the early modeling relied upon a strictly game-theoretical approach and the majority of it took an "office-seeking" perspective that either ignored or down-graded the policy dimension as a formation criterion. Thus, although the assumptions and logic that underpin their work are not identical, scholars such as William Riker,[6] William Gamson,[7] or Michael Leiserson[8] argue that political parties are rational office-seeking actors and that it is therefore possible to construct formal and predictive models of coalition formation. This process takes place in an environment that is both "constant sum" (limited in size and scope) and "zero-sum" (one player's gain diminishes the potential utility of all other players). Each player in the coalition game is assigned a weight based upon the resources that he/she brings to any potential coalition and, as office-seeking rather than policy is assumed to be the central formation criterion, these resources take the form of parliamentary seats. Riker predicts that players will try to create coalitions that are only as large as they believe will ensure winning. In its pure theoretical form, such a "minimal winning" coalition would be so small as to maximize the payoffs to each coalition member. With repeated plays of the bargaining game there would be a tendency towards the smallest subset of potential minimal winning coalitions, a "minimum winning" coalition of 50 percent plus one vote. Gamson also argues that repeated plays will result in a minimum winner but adds that, all things being equal, parties will favor the "cheapest winning" coalition, in which they are the larger partner in a coalition, even when the office-seeking payoffs of any alternative are broadly comparable. Leiserson, by contrast, does not predict an automatic *reductio* towards the arithmetical minimum winner, but rather argues that players will favor coalitions with the smallest number of partners. This is Leiserson's so-called "bargaining proposition" and is based on the assumption that the ease with which coalitions can form and be maintained is in inverse proportion to the number of players within them. This assumption supports the argument made in this chapter about the collective action problems that junior coalition partners would face in trying to co-ordinate pressure on the *formateur*.

The kind of office-seeking approaches discussed above privilege the seat share each player brings to the coalition game. The bargaining power that these shares generate is captured by power indices (PIs) such as the normalized Banzhaf index.[9] The Banzhaf PI is derived from a legislature's decision rules, and in its simplest form, assumes a binary decision rule in which players have two choices—yes and no. Binary decision rules must fulfill three criteria: (1) When all/a majority votes yes, the result must be positive and the proposition passes; (2) When all/a majority vote no, the result must be negative and the proposition is blocked; and (3) If a vote has a positive outcome and sufficient voters transfer from yes to no or vice versa, the result of the proposition changes. In a coalition game, this last quality is known as "swing" and this can be "negative" (where a player's withdrawal of support turns a winning coalition into a losing coalition) or "positive" (where a party's support turns a losing coalition into a winning coalition) The extent of swing a players possesses is an indicator of its real voting power and parties with no swing are dummy players, irrespective of the number of seats they hold. Again, this notion of swing is highly relevant to my analysis of coalition dynamics in Germany[10].

Despite their obvious parsimony and elegance, all of the approaches discussed above have been criticized for being "policy blind" and therefore unrealistic.[11] This observation led more inductive scholars[12] to openly reject them as useful tools for analyzing real-world politics, while adherents of formal approaches to politics reacted to this criticism by introducing a policy dimension to the coalition game. Two of the most cited examples of this turn towards ideology are the work of Robert Axelrod[13] and Abram de Swaan.[14] Axelrod assumes that while office-seeking remains the central strategic goal of all players, the members of the successful coalition will ideally be adjacent to one another along a single Downsian left-right ideological dimension. The "minimal connected winning" (MCW) coalitions that are assumed to arise from this coalition logic are as large as necessary to secure a majority in the legislature, and as adjacent as possible to minimize the potential for conflicts of interest within the coalition. De Swaan builds upon Axelrod's assumptions and introduces the notion of ideological distance as well as adjacency. Thus, rather than just preferring MCWs, de Swaan assumes that players will prefer to be members of MCWs with the smallest ideological range and that players' preferences are assumed to be Euclidian and informed by their relative proximities to the median or "Mparty." De Swaan's theory is referred to as the median legislator (ML) model because it is based on the assumption that the party that controls the median legislator is decisive because it blocks the axis along which any majority connected winning coalition must form. If a party is Mparty, and crucially, a majority coalition is required, then it must be included in the coalition. If a party also controls the median legislator in the coalition, it is "MpartyK" and in cases of majority rule it is theoretically decisive in determining the coalition's potential composition, program, and stability.

The assumptions that underpin the ML model seem reasonable and, in de Swaan's own statistical tests, the model convincingly outperformed pure office-seeking accounts of coalition formation.[15] It can, however, be criticized for retaining a single left-right dimension. The modeling of multidimensional policy spaces, through the use of "core theory"[16] or the calculation of dimension-by-dimension medians (DDMs)[17] has yielded many useful insights. As Keith Krehbiel points out, however, "simply expanding the choice space from one to two has profoundly disequilibriating consequences"[18] because there will always be an alternative coalition package that can block any potential winning coalition.[19] In the context of this analysis, an emphasis upon the left-right dimension, albeit cross-cut by a weaker libertarian-authoritarian dimension, is consistent with empirical understandings of the German party system.[20] Therefore, the ML model remains a useful organizing framework.

To sum up this section, the *tour d'horizon* of the coalition literature has yielded six analytical insights that can illuminate analysis of the changing coalition dynamics within the German party system. In terms of the numerical dimension, this chapter 1) retains the notion of some sort of numerical formation criteria, based upon Leiserson's bargaining proposition; 2) emphasizes the notion of swing; and 3) acknowledges the use of the Banzhaf PI in comparing changes in voting power over time. In terms of the ideological dimension, I 1) modify the numerical formation criteria through the recognition of ideological adjacency and the MCW (thus problematizing a trade-off between the utility functions associated with the smallest number of parties and the smallest ideological range); 2) emphasize the importance of ideological distance; and 3) assume that the location of the Mparty and MpartyK is of significance. Equipped, as it were, with this analytical toolkit, I now move on to the empirical portion.

Numerical and ideological dimensions of party system change in Germany

Figure 1 sets out the number of MCWs and coalitions with swing following German federal elections over the period 1949 to 2009. As already discussed, coalitions with swing are those coalitions in which a party is able to transform a winning into a losing coalition by its defection from a coalition (or vice-versa). Figure 1 reflects the extent to which the German party system was consolidated over the postwar period. Thus, following the first Bundestag election in 1949, there were twenty-six minimal connected winning coalitions and 197 coalitions with swing yet, by 1961, this had been reduced to three MCWs and three coalitions with swing: the classic triangular party system of the Pappi model.[21]

Figure 1. MCWs and Coalitions with Swing Following Federal Elections, 1949-2009

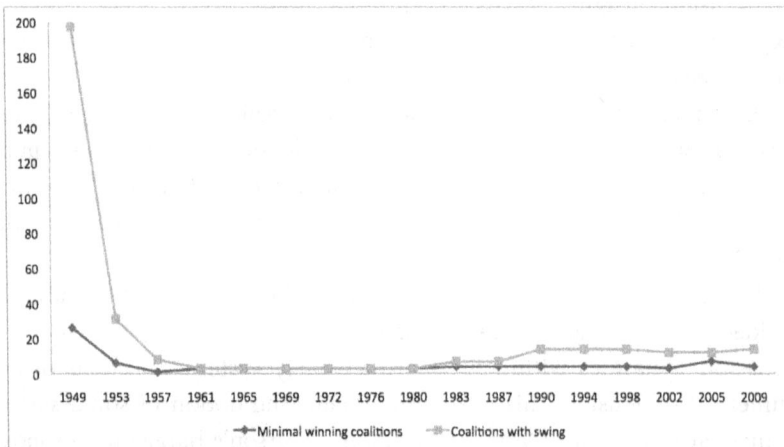

Source: calculated from data sourced at http://www.wahlrecht.de

Figure 1 also demonstrates, however, that the emergence of the Greens and subsequently the PDS undermined the FDP's kingmaker role. The arrival of the Greens in 1983 increased the number of MCWs to four and the number of coalitions with swing to seven, while the emergence of the PDS further fragmented the party system: with four MCWs and fourteen coalitions with swing following the first all-German election in 1990 (a pattern that was repeated in the 1994 and 1998 elections). Interestingly, the 2002 federal election reduced the number of MCWs to three and the number of coalitions with swing to twelve, but in 2005, the number of MCWs increased to seven, even though the number of coalitions with swing remained at twelve. Following the 2009 election, the number of MCWs was reduced to four, but the number of coalitions with swing increased to fourteen.

The picture today, therefore, is one of a party system in which the number of potential MCW outcomes is only slightly higher than during the period of the triangular party system but the number of coalitions with swing has increased more than 400 percent. The limited number of MCWs reduces the potential discriminatory power of Leiserson's bargaining proposition, but the argument made earlier about how this proposition illustrates the collective action problems faced by junior coalition partners still stands. In addition, the role of the *formateur* is also enhanced by the fact that, given the number of potential coalitions and the dispersal of swing across the party system, it is impossible for one single small party to act as kingmaker.

Table 1. Normalized Banzhaf Scores for the Main Political Parties, Following Federal Elections, 1949-2009

Year	Party				
	CDU/CSU	**SPD**	**FDP**	**Greens**	**PDS/Left Party**
1949	0.3082	0.2594	0.2373		
1953	0.75	0.05	0.05		
1957	0.1	0.1	0.1		
1961	0.3333	0.3333	0.3333		
1965	0.3333	0.3333	0.3333		
1969	0.3333	0.3333	0.3333		
1972	0.3333	0.3333	0.3333		
1976	0.3333	0.3333	0.3333		
1980	0.3333	0.3333	0.3333		
1983	0.5	0.1667	0.1667	0.1667	
1987	0.5	0.1667	0.1667	0.1667	
1990	0.5	0.1667	0.1667	0	0.1667
1994	0.5	0.1667	0.1667	0.1667	0
1998	0.1667	0.5	0.1667	0.1667	0
2002	0.3333	0.3333	0	0.3333	0
2005	0.5	0.5	0.25	0.25	0.25
2009	0.5	0.1667	0.1667	0	0.1667

Source: calculated from data sourced at http://www.wahlrecht.de

Table 1 sets out the normalized Banzhaf scores for the CDU/CSU, SPD, and FDP over the same period of time. Again, as discussed above, the Banzhaf PI measures potential voting power in terms of the coalitions that can form, given the distribution of party weights in a given legislature. The table vividly demonstrates the extent to which, despite its modest electoral performances over the period up until the 1980s, the FDP increased its voting power and, from the 1960s until the 1980s, enjoyed the same Banzhaf score as the CDU/CSU, and SPD (0.3333 out of 1). But, as with the analysis of MCWs and coalitions with swing, Table 1 demonstrates that the period since 1983 has seen the Banzhaf indices of the CDU/CSU, SPD, and FDP shift in the new strategic environment generated by the erosion of the triangular party system. Thus, with the entry of the Greens in 1983, the CDU/CSU's score rose to 0.5, while those of the SPD and FDP fell to 0.1667 (the same score as the Greens). These Banzhaf PIs were reproduced following the 1987 and 1994 federal elections but the overall pattern since 1983 has been one of trendless fluctuation. There are instances in which either the CDU/CSU (after the four successive Bundestag elections between 1983 and 1994, as well as after the 2009 election) or the SPD (after the 1998 election) enjoyed a higher PI than its *Volkspartei* competitor, as well as others (after the 2002 and 2005 elections) in which their PIs were identical. What is important for this analysis, however, is that since the 1990s both *Volksparteien* have enjoyed Banzhaf PIs of up to 0.5–far higher than during the period of the triangular party system.

The PIs following the 2009 elections are CDU/CSU 0.5, SPD 0.1667, FDP 0.1667, Greens 0, and Left Party 0.1667. Under conditions of majority rule, the Greens score of 0 makes it a dummy player, just as the PDS was in the 1994, 1998, and 2002 elections. These observations are central to the argument that as a result of the changes in the distribution of party weights that have taken place no small party has enjoyed the extent or stability of bargaining power enjoyed by the FDP in the period of the triangular party system. In numerical terms, even the FDP has had to endure dummy status following one federal election (2002). Thus, in a strict interpretation of the normalized Banzhaf PI scores, the impact of party system change has been to generate a strategic environment in which the smaller parties must operate under conditions of uncertainty about the future distribution of party weights, thus reducing their capacity for strategic action in the run-up to federal elections and, arguably, limiting their subsequent utility functions after them. This constraint on the small parties' individual and collective strategic calculi, which for obvious reasons strengthens the position of the *Volkspartei* acting as *formateur*, has become apparent since the emergence of the Greens in 1983 but has been particularly evident since unification in 1990.

A closer analysis of coalition outcomes since 1983 re-enforces the argument that party system change has buttressed the strategic positions of the *Volksparteien*. Table 2 sets out the real-world coalition outcomes following federal elections over the period, as well as the minimum winners, the relevance of the bargaining proposition, the Mparties and the MpartiesK. In terms of numerical formation criteria, without the bargaining proposition there were no minimum winners and only two minimal winners (the Black-Yellow coalitions formed by the CDU/CSU and FDP after the 1994 and 2009 elections). If I apply the bargaining proposition, then five out of eight coalition outcomes fulfill the criteria. The exceptions are the Black-Yellow coalition formed after the 1987 election (which represents a surplus majority coalition compared with a so-called Jamaica coalition made up of the CDU/CSU and Greens), the Red-Green Coalition after 2002 (again, a surplus majority compared with Jamaica), and the current Black-Yellow coalition (a surplus majority coalition compared with a CDU/CSU-Left Party alternative).

A skeptic of strict numerical interpretations would point out that, because of ideological distance or disconnection, most of the minimal winners in Table 2 are highly unlikely combinations and some (most notably the SPD-FDP-PDS coalition in 1990) are to all intents and purposes flights of theoretical fancy. Thus, a look at the ideological dimension is necessary. Here, the table demonstrates that all of the coalition outcomes were ideologically adjacent and six out of eight real-world outcomes where MCWs with the smallest ideological range (the exceptions being the Black-Yellow coalition formed after the 1983 election and the Grand Coalition formed after 2005). In addition, the table demonstrates that the Mparty is, as predicted, included in all coalition outcomes. Crucially for the arguments made in this chapter, the table also demonstrates that, although the FDP remained Mparty after the 1983, 1987, 1990, and 1994 elections, it lost this position following the 1998 federal election, which brought Gerhard Schröder's Red-Green coalition to power.[22] Since then one of the two *Volksparteien* has been Mparty (the SPD following the 1998, 2002, and 2005 elections, and the CDU/CSU following the 2009 elections). The crucial change, however, is that throughout its many years in government, the relatively small FDP never controlled the median legislator within the coalition and thus was never MpartyK. This role was always fulfilled by the *Volkspartei* acting as *formateur*, because of its relative legislative weight. Since 1998, however, when the FDP lost its Mparty status, on three occasions

Table 2. Coalition Outcomes Following German Federal Elections, 1983-2009

Election:	06/03/83	25/01/87	02/12/90	16/10/94	27/09/98	22/09/02	18/09/05	27/09/09
Seats in Bundestag								
CDU/CSU	244	223	319	294	245	248	226	239
SPD	193	186	239	252	298	251	222	146
FDP	34	46	79	47	44	47	61	93
Greens	27	42	8	49	47	55	51	68
PDS/Left Party	--	--	17	30	35	02	54	76
Total Seats	498	497	662	672	669	603	614	622
Decision rule	250	249	332	337	335	302	308	312
Coalition	CDU/CSU-FDP	CDU/CSU-FDP	CDU/CSU-FDP	CDU/CSU-FDP	SPD-Greens	SPD-Greens	CDU/CSU-SPD	CDU/CSU-FDP
Degree of Change	None	None	None	None	Total	None	Partial	Partial
Minimum Winner?	No	No	No	No	No	No	No	No
Minimal Winner	SPD-FDP-Greens	CDU/CSU-Greens	SPD-FDP-PDS	CDU/CSU-FDP	CDU/CSU-FDP-Greens	CDU/CDU-Greens	SPD-Left Party-Greens	CDU/CSU-Left Party
Bargaining Proposition	CDU/CSU-FDP	CDU/CSU-Greens	CDU/CSU-FDP	CDU/CSU-FDP	SPD-Greens	CDU/CDU-Greens	CDU/CSU-SPD	CDU/CSU-Left Party
Adjacent?	Yes	Yes	Yes	Yes	Yes	Yes	Yes	Yes
MCW/Smallest ideological range	SPD-FDP-Greens	CDU/CSU-FDP	CDU/CSU-FDP	CDU/CSU-FDP	SPD-Greens	SPD-Greens	SPD-PDS/Left Party-Greens	CDU/CSU-FDP
Mparty	FDP	FDP	FDP	FDP	SPD	SPD	SPD	CDU/CSU
MpartyK	CDU/CSU	CDU/CSU	CDU/CSU	CDU/CSU	SPD	SPD	CDU/CSU	CDU/CSU

Source: Forschungsgruppe Wahlen, 1983, 1987, 1990, 1994, 1998, 2002, 2005, 2009

either the CDU/CSU or SPD has been the combined Mparty/MpartyK (the SPD in 1998 and 2002 and the CDU/CSU in 2009). Policy positions should theoretically fall within the interstices of the preference curves of the median legislator in the parliament and median legislator within the coalition, making the MpartyK decisive in intracoalition negotiations.[23] This is again evidence of the enhanced strategic positions of the two *Volksparteien.*

Conclusion

It will be recalled, then, that the above review of the coalition literature yielded six analytical tools. These were 1) a numerical formation criteria based upon Leiserson's bargaining proposition; 2) the notion of swing; 3) the Banzhaf PI; 4) the importance of ideological adjacency; 5) the importance of ideological distance; and 6) the location of the Mparty and MpartyK. The application of these analytical tools provides an organizing framework for the empirical analysis and supports the argument put forward in this chapter.

   To sum up, first, the bargaining proposition holds empirically in more than half of the cases and the logic behind it is that co-ordination problems increase with the size of coalitions. Obviously, this is a potential problem for all coalition partners, including the *formateur*, but–in the context of this chapter–it very directly supports the argument that it is much harder for multiple small parties to act in concert against the *formateur* than it would be for one small party acting as kingmaker. Second, the dispersal of swing across the party system that I have indentified reduces the possibility of any small party acquiring kingmaker status. Third, the Banzhaf analysis demonstrates that, since the decline of the triangular system, one or the other of the *Volksparteien* has always enjoyed much greater bargaining power than was the case during the period of the triangular party system and that the smaller parties have had correspondingly less power (and on occasions, none at all). Fourth, all of the coalitions since 1983 were ideologically adjacent. This factor is important in itself, but especially if the *formateur* is the Mparty and MpartyK, as will be discussed below. Fifth, the prevalence of MCWs demonstrates that political parties recognize that there is a trade-off between the utility functions associated with the smallest number of parties and the smallest ideological range. The relationship between coalition size and the collective action problems for small coalition partners has already been discussed, while the degree of ideological range between them presents similar problems when the *formateur* is Mparty and/or MpartyK. Finally, given that one or the other of the two *Volksparteien* now tend to be both Mparty and MpartyK, one would expect policy positions adopted by the coalition to be closer to the *formateur*'s ideal point, i.e., within the interstices of the preference curves of the median legislator in the parliament and median legislator within the coalition.

The message from this summary is that the *Volksparteien* have more coalition options open to them and greater ideological leverage within coalitions that form. This means that, even if the real-world outcome is a Black-Yellow coalition like the one that formed after the 2009 federal election, the FDP should not be expected to wield the same influence within the coalition that the party enjoyed in similar coalitions in the past. I argue that this has been borne out by events surrounding the formation and early months of the coalition. The FDP went into coalition negotiations with a number of strongly-held positions on revision of the tax system (suggesting EURO 35 billion of tax cuts), supply side reforms, and a reorientation of the social insurance system towards individual provision,[24] but in the course of an ill-tempered negotiation process,[25] the FDP had to accept a coalition agreement in which most of its proposals—although agreed to in principle—were framed within the agreement as vague future commitments subject to future review and its key policy plank, EURO 35 billion of tax cuts, was cut to EURO 24 billion and would be paid for by increased borrowing rather than cuts in spending.[26] Subsequent developments have seen the CDU/CSU distance itself from this proposal as well and, in early 2010, the FDP appeared very much the junior partner in a weakly reformist coalition, from which the threat of a decisive defection, partly because of the constitutional requirement for a "constructive vote of no confidence" to depose an incumbent chancellor and partly because of the FDP's own ideological disconnectedness with other coalition options, is not credible. In short, and as argued in more general terms in this chapter, events have shown that the FDP's kingmaker status is very much a thing of the past. By contrast, as has been the case since at least 1998, at present it is one of the two *Volksparteien* that currently enjoys the strategic advantage within the German party system—a reality showing that the numerous obituaries for the *Volksparteien* are premature.

Notes

1. Oskar Niedermayer, "Das Parteiensystem Deutschlands" in *Die Parteiensysteme Westeuropas*, eds, Richard Stöss, Melanie Hass, and Oskar Niedermayer (Wiesbaden, 2006), 109-34.
2. Russell Dalton, Ian McCallister, and Martin Wattenberg, "The consequences of partisan dealignment," in *Parties without partisans: electoral change in advanced industrial democracies*, eds., Russell Dalton and Martin Wattenberg (Oxford, 2002); see also Russell Dalton, *Citizen Politics: Public Opinion and Political Parties in Advanced Industrial Democracies* 2nd ed. (Chatham, 1996).
3. Otto Kirchheimer, "The Transformation of Western European Party Systems" in *Political Parties and Political Development*, eds., Joseph LaPalombara and Myron Weiner (Princeton, 1966), 177-200.
4. See Charles Lees, "The Paradoxical Impact of Party System Change in Germany," Paper presented at the APSA 100th Annual Meeting and Exhibition, Toronto, 3-6 September 2009.
5. See Anthony Downs, *An Economic Theory of Democracy* (New York, 1957); John von Neumann and Oskar Morgenstern, *Theory of Games and Economic Behaviour* (Princeton, 1947); Leonard J. Savage, *The Foundations of Statistics* (New York, 1954).
6. William Riker, *The Theory of Political Coalitions* (New Haven, 1962).
7. William Gamson, "A Theory of Coalition Formation," *American Sociological Review*, 26 (1961): 373-82.
8. Michael Leiserson, "Factions and Coalitions in One-Party Japan: An Interpretation Based on the Theory of Games," *American Political Science Review* 62, no. 3 (1968): 770-787.
9. John F. Banzhaf, III "Weighted voting doesn't work: a mathematical analysis," *Rutgers Law Review* 19 (1965): 317-343.
10. See Charles Lees and Andrew Taylor, "Explaining the 2005 coalition formation process in Germany–a comparison of Power Index and Median Legislator coalition models," *German Politics* 26, no. 3 (2006): 151-160; Charles Lees and Andrew Taylor, "Exposing norms, values, and practices in coalition formation: a comparative analysis of Germany and New Zealand," Mimeo, University of Sheffield (2009).
11. Michael Laver and Norman Schofield, *Multi-Party Government: The Politics Of Coalition In Europe* (New York, 1990), 90.
12. Geoffrey Pridham, ed., *Coalition Behaviour in Theory and Practice* (Cambridge, 1986); Klaus von Beyme, *Political parties in Western Democracies* (Aldershot, 1984); Vernon Bogdanor, ed., *Coalition Government in Western Europe* (London, 1983).
13. Robert Axelrod, *Conflict of Interest* (1970).
14. Abram de Swaan, *Coalition Theories and Cabinet Formation* (Amsterdam, 1973).
15. The Riker and Gamson models correctly predicted 8 percent of actual outcomes, while the ML model yielded a 69 percent prediction rate of actual outcomes from data on European coalition processes. Cited in Eric Browne, *Coalition Theories: A Logical And Empirical Critique* (Beverly Hills, 1973), 76.
16. See Roger A. Hanson, *Majority Rule And Policy Outcomes: A Critique Of The Calculus Of Consent*, PhD Thesis, University of Minnesota (1972); Roger A. Hanson and Peter M. Rice, "Committees, representation and policy outcomes," *Annals of the N.Y. Academy of Sciences* (1972).
17. Michael Laver and Kenneth Shepsle, "Coalitions and Cabinet Government," *American Political Science Review* 84 (1990): 873-90.
18. Keith Krehbiel, "Spatial Models of Legislative Choice," *Legislative Studies Quarterly*. 3 (1988): 259-319.
19. Michael Bacharach, *Economics and the Theory Of Games*. Basingstoke, 1976), 128.

20. Charles Lees, *Party Politics in Germany–A Comparative Politics Approach* (Basingstoke, 2005).
21. Franz-Urban Pappi, "The West German Party System," *West European Politics* 7 (1984): 7-26.
22. See Charles Lees, *The Red-Green Coalition in Germany: Politics, Personalities and Power* (Manchester, 2000).
23. de Swaan (see note 14).
24. Christine Schniedermann, "The Liberal Renaissance," AICGS Briefing Paper (Washington, 2009).
25. Charles Hawley, "Angela Merkel's 'project haze,'" *Spiegel online*, 15 October 2009; available at http://www.spiegel.de/international/germany/0,1518,655375,00.html, accessed 14 May 2010.
26. See bundesregierung.de/Webs/Breg/DE/Bundesregierung/Bundeskabinett/bundeskabinett.html; accessed 27 October 2009.

Chapter 8

𝒢ENDER QUOTA COMPLIANCE AND
CONTAGION IN THE 2009 BUNDESTAG ELECTION

• • • • • • • • • • • • • • •

Louise K. Davidson-Schmich

[1]

Introduction

The 2009 Bundestag election marks the seventh federal election in Germany since the Greens ushered in gender quotas for their electoral lists in the mid 1980s. The Greens' decision to institute party statutes promoting women on the ballot was followed by the Social Democrats (SPD) adopting a gender quota in 1988, and the Christian Democratic Union's (CDU) introduction of a "quorum" in 1996. Today's Left Party follows its PDS predecessor's quota adopted in 1990.[2] After the Greens began using quotas, the percentage of Members of the Bundestag (MdB) who were female broke the 10 percent barrier for the first time in the history of the Federal Republic, and by 2002, this figure had risen to 32.8 percent.[3] Women clearly have made great strides in German politics and, compared to other parliaments, the Bundestag contains a high percentage of female members. Today, Germany is one of only twenty-four countries worldwide with more than 30 percent women in the national legislature.[4]

Throughout the last decade, however, the unprecedented rise in women's presence in the Bundestag leveled off; of the 622 members of the seventeenth Bundestag elected on 27 September 2009, 204 or 32.8 percent were women–the same figure as earlier in the decade.[5] Because slightly more than half of the Federal Republic's population is female,[6] women continue to remain underrepresented in the German parliament and their numbers are not increasing. Indeed, the percentage of women in the Bundestag has stagnated at the level of the *lowest* quota adopted for women.

Clearly, gender quotas have been effective in increasing the number of female MdBs, but why did the recent election not bring even more women to parliament? Did parties not implement their gender quotas in this election? Or have the quotas in use simply reached the limits of their ability to bring more women into the Bundestag? This chapter addresses these issues using data on the candidates for the 2009 national election. I investigate three main questions. First, did German political parties comply with their voluntarily adopted gender quotas for their electoral lists in this election—both in terms of the numbers of women nominated and their placement on the list? Second, how did the number of women nominated by parties without quotas compare to statistic for parties with quotas? In other words, have candidate gender quotas had a "contagion effect," inspiring parties without quotas to promote women's political careers? Third, what propensity did all parties have to nominate women to run for the direct mandates awarded via the first vote, for which no gender quotas are in place? That is, have quotas had a contagion effect across Germany's dual ballot?

I find that while the German parties by and large complied with their gender quotas for electoral lists, there was only mixed evidence of quota contagion in terms of parties with no quotas. In addition, all political parties but the Left Party were unlikely to nominate female candidates to run for the direct mandates they were expected to win. In order to further increase the percentages of women serving in the Bundestag, women-friendly candidate selection rules for direct seats and for parties without quotas seem necessary. To develop these conclusions, first, I review the literature on candidate gender quotas and apply it to the German case. Second, I discuss the methodological challenges of investigating gender quota compliance in the Federal Republic. Third, I develop a new indicator to measure quota compliance, and fourth I utilize this indicator to investigate the 2009 Bundestag election. I conclude by discussing the policy ramifications of my findings.

Gender Quota Compliance in Comparative Perspective

The scholarly literature on gender quotas offers divergent perspectives on whether or not German parties could be expected to comply with their gender quotas in 2009. While one strand of this scholarship anticipates quota violations, the other is more optimistic that parties will have lived up to their promises and that a contagion effect will occur. I discuss these two viewpoints in turn.

First, while many countries have implemented what are known as "constitutional" or "legislative" quotas, which legally reserve certain seats in parliament or ballot places for women, German parties have adopted "voluntary" gender quotas.[7] While some parties have promised to place a certain percentage of women on the ballot in Germany, there is no legal sanction for non-compliance.[8] Comparative research has found that quotas without official enforcement mechanisms are less effective in increasing women's representation than constitutional or legislative quotas.[9] That being said, on average, countries with some type of quota (even voluntary ones) send more women to parliament than countries with no quotas at all.[10] Thus, this view would expect the German parties that have not adopted quotas for their party lists would be unlikely in practice to nominate many women to appear on their electoral lists. Moreover, given that gender quotas are only in place for the second part of Germany's dual ballot system (the closed list proportional representation ballot), and are not used for the "first vote" or plurality ballot, this school of thought would think it likely that few women would win directly elected seats to the Bundestag. As a result of the voluntary nature and limited scope of party gender quotas in Germany, this line of scholarship suggests that women's representation in the Bundestag would be hampered by a lack of quota compliance and by low numbers of directly elected female MdBs.

A second strand of the academic literature would be more optimistic about fulfillment of quotas in the 2009 federal election. Scholars studying the worldwide proliferation of quotas have observed a "contagion effect" whereby when one party or country adopts quotas, others are likely to follow.[11] For example, after the German Green party introduced a gender quota for its electoral lists, the Social Democrats began losing feminist voters to their postmaterialist rivals and developed a quota for women as a self-defense mechanism to stem further electoral losses.[12] Once the main parties of the left had adopted quotas, the CDU's leadership also became concerned about losing women's votes should it not also implement measures to promote female candidates. As a result, they too began to use what the party called a women's "quorum." [13]

The logic of contagion would suggest a similar pattern to the enforcement of voluntary quotas: no party has an electoral incentive to open itself to charges by opponents that it has reneged on promises to women. Once quotas are ushered in, it is electorally risky for parties not to implement them. Moreover, once quotas establish a norm of reserving ballot spots for women, including gender diversity on electoral lists will seem to party members drawing up electoral lists the "natural" thing to do. Research from Indian localities, where gender quotas were used in one election and then withdrawn, indicates that the numbers of women winning elective office there continue to remain high even after quotas are no longer in use.[14] This school of thought would thus expect a rise in women's candidacies among parties without quotas and among direct mandate candidates, as norms of gender equality diffuse across parties and electoral systems.

Methodological Drawbacks to Using Official Statistics

In order to determine which of these two expectations, or combination thereof, actually was borne out in the 2009 Bundestag election, it is necessary to obtain appropriate empirical evidence. Unfortunately, it is difficult to study gender quota compliance and contagion effects with the data that is routinely reported by the German Bundestag and the Federal Election Authority (Bundeswahlleiter). These official sources highlight either the total number of female candidates a party nominates or the total number of woman elected to the Bundestag from a certain party. Both of these statistical approaches have drawbacks for the study of quota compliance.

Analyzing the total number of women nominated by a political party to run on its electoral list has one main drawback. These lists are routinely much longer than the actual number of candidates elected from them, making it important not only to understand *whether* women appear on the list but also *where* their names can be found. To give an example, in 2009 the SPD in Baden-Württemberg entered a party list with thirty-six candidates on it; the Social Democrats only won fourteen list seats, however. Of the thirty-six candidates, fifteen (or 42 percent) were women. While this appears to be a high number of female candidates, had these women occupied the last fifteen places on the party list, none of them would have entered the Bundestag.[15] Gender quotas are designed with this reality in mind and, as a result, all German parties with quotas include placement mandates for locating female candidates on the list. For instance, the SPD's statutes require that of every five list spots, a minimum of two and a maximum of three are allotted to women–preventing the scenario described above. Thus, in order to assess quota compliance, it is important to count not only the total number of women on a party's list, but where they are on the list. While the Bundeswahlleiter makes electoral lists available so that researchers may measure this, there are no official statistics providing aggregate data about women's list placement.

Studying the total number of women a party nominates for all 299 direct mandate seats in the Bundestag–a statistic routinely kept by the

Federal Election Office—also fails to capture parties' efforts (or lack thereof) to promote female candidates because over half of Germany's constituencies (*Wahlkreise*) can be considered "safe districts," almost guaranteed to be won by a particular party. If a party nominates a woman for a "safe mandate," she is highly likely to become a MdB whereas nominating a woman for a seat a party is virtually assured of losing, i.e., designating her a "sacrificial lamb,[16]" will do nothing to build women's presence in the parliament. Hence, more meaningful information can be gleaned by examining not the percentage of female candidates for all direct mandates, but the number of female nominees for winnable seats. Again, however, government agencies do not perform such calculations.

Counting the number of women who ultimately get elected to the Bundestag—as is routinely done by the parliament—is also of limited utility when attempting to study quota compliance and contagion effects. As opinion pollsters know, it is difficult to accurately predict the outcome of an election in advance. Parties may *a priori* consider certain direct mandates or list places to be safe (or risky) only to be surprised with a less-than (or better-than) expected showing on election night. As a result, a party may ultimately send more (or fewer) women to the Bundestag than it planned. Consider two states' CDU party lists, each with six candidates and an anticipated win of three seats: one state's list with women placed according to the party's quorum (in places three and six) and the other with the women shunted to the bottom (places five and six). The former list fulfills the party's quorum and placement mandate, whereas the latter does not. Yet, were the CDU to have a worse than expected result in the first state and win only two seats, while scoring an unexpectedly good result in the second state, winning six seats, the percentages of women sent to the Bundestag would be 0 percent and 33 percent, respectively, erroneously suggesting that the latter party had fulfilled its quorum and the former had not.

The drawbacks to studying who wins as a measure of a party's desire to promote female candidates also can be witnessed when applied to direct mandates. A surprise victory by a female "sacrificial lamb" nominated by a party for a long-shot direct mandate would make her party seem sympathetic to female candidates, while a party that suffers an unanticipated loss by a woman they had promoted for what they believed to be a safe seat would seem hostile to female candidacies. Although the former party sent a woman to Berlin and the latter did not, the latter actually had more female-friendly intentions.

A New Measure of Quota Compliance and Contagion

Thus, rather than studying who wins in order to determine quota compliance, it is more productive to study who was nominated for what appeared *a priori* to be a safe list spot or a safe direct mandate. To do so requires making four determinations. First, scholars must ascertain what party statutes specify in terms of placement mandates. Second, they must establish which list places are considered safe. Third, they must verify the sexes of the candidates in each of the safe list places, and finally, they must determine which *Wahlkreise* count as safe seats for which party and record the sexes of the nominees for these seats. I elaborate on the logistics of this process before going on to present its results.

Electoral Lists

All of the German parties publish their statutes in which, among other procedures, rules for selecting candidates (such as gender quotas) are set out. The Greens' "Frauenstatut" calls for all of the odd-numbered list places to go to women while allowing even numbered places to be occupied by females as well. If no woman can be found to occupy an odd-numbered place, a man may fill that ballot slot–but only if all women present agree to give it to him.[17] The SPD's "Wahlordnung" gives protections to both men and women during the creation of the party list. Once the lead candidate (*Spitzenkandidat*) has been selected, the next candidate on the list must be of the opposite sex; the two sexes then alternate for the third and fourth spots, while the fifth list place may be awarded to either a man or a woman. This procedure then continues down the list.[18] The SPD's rules do not specify what happens if this procedure is not followed. The CDU's party statute requires at least one woman among every three list candidates, without identifying which of the three spots a woman must receive. Nevertheless, if the party leaders who put together the list do not comply with this quorum, they need simply "justify" their decision to the assembled party members, who may in turn approve a list without women in the requisite places.[19] The Left Party's statute requires one of the top two list places to be granted a female candidate. Beginning with the third list place, every odd-numbered slot must be reserved for a woman, as long as acceptable female candidates can be found; the Left Party's rules allow unqualified female candidates to be turned down. Their even-numbered ballot spots may be occupied by either males or females.[20] The other two parties winning seats in the Bundestag–the Christian Social

Union (CSU) and Free Democratic Party (FDP)–do not specify any candidate quotas for women, although the CSU's "Satzung" does include a vague reminder that women should be "taken into consideration."[21]

Thus, to measure quota compliance for the Greens and the Left Party, a scholar must study candidate placement in even-numbered list intervals. To study Social Democratic quota observance, units divisible by five must be used, and for the Christian Democrats increments dividable by three. For ease of comparison across parties, I coded party lists in intervals of six for the Greens, Left Party, and CDU, and of five for the SPD.[22] Although the CSU and FDP have no quotas for female candidates, I nevertheless examined the placement of women in six-unit ballot intervals to determine how their lists compared to those of parties with quotas.

Ideally, the researcher would also have access to information about the candidate selection meeting for, technically, if a violation of the Green quota had been approved by all of the women present at a nominating meeting, if no qualified woman had been found for a "female" Left Party list place, and if the CDU party leadership had justified a lack of quota adherence, these parties would not have violated the letter of their quotas. Obtaining such data for a large-N study such as this, however, would be virtually impossible. As a result, what are coded here as transgressions against these three parties' quotas, may actually have been authorized. As will be seen below, however, such occurrences were so rare in practice as to lead to the conclusion that quota lapses are rare, even using this measure biased toward over-counting quota violations.

After establishing the list intervals for measuring quota compliance, a scholar must then determine how far down the party's list to gather data. As the list of candidates is virtually always longer than the number of seats won, adhering to a party quota near the bottom of the list is, in practical terms at least, meaningless. What counts is whether a party sticks to its quota for the winnable list spots. To calculate the latter, I took the number of list seats each party won in each Land in 2005 and 2009 and rounded the highest number of seats obtained up to the nearest number divisible by six (five for the Social Democrats). For example, in both elections, the Left Party won three list seats in Mecklenburg West Pomerania, so I analyzed the placement of women among the Left Party's top six list candidates. Rounding up, rather than down, was chosen for three reasons. First, dual candidacies are common and those individuals who win a constituency seat are then removed from the list and lower-ranking candidates are bumped up after the election. Second, this method allowed for the inclusion of a greater number of cases. In twenty-one of the eighty party lists analyzed in

2009 rounding down would have excluded these state party organizations from the analysis because less than six (five) candidates were elected from the list. Third, rounding up also allows for the possibility of an unexpectedly poor showing—party leaders bent on winning an election likely overestimate the number of seats they may win, making their *a priori* assessment of safe list places larger than the *de facto* number of safe spots.

The final step which needs to be completed before determining whether a party has adhered to its gender quota is to determine the sex of the candidate in each safe space on the list. Given German's stringent naming laws, which require babies born in Germany to be given sex-specific names, this is by and large a relatively straightforward task. A scholar fluent in German can readily identify most nominees as either male or female simply by reading the names on the lists of candidates which are available on-line from the Bundeswahlleiter.[23] These records also indicate the person's profession using gendered nouns (for example, *Jurist* or *Juristin*), which can confirm the sex of those individuals with foreign or otherwise gender-ambiguous names.[24]

Direct Mandates

By thus determining placement mandates, safe list spots, and candidate sexes, a researcher is in a position to assess gender quota compliance for the second vote in a given election. Before I report the results of the 2009 Bundestag election, however, I will discuss my approach to studying direct mandates. None of the political parties utilizing quotas for the second vote have ushered in any kind of gender-based rules for selecting nominees for the first vote. Indeed, the Greens', Left Party's, and SPD's statutes are completely silent about this portion of the ballot. In contrast, the Christian Democrats' statute calls on party leaders to "work toward the sufficient participation of women in direct candidacies" such as those used in Bundestag elections.[25] However, the document specifies neither precisely what "sufficient" participation is nor how exactly party members should "work toward" this goal, making this provision relatively meaningless in practical terms. Thus, it is not possible to speak of gender quota compliance in terms of the first vote as there are no quotas in place.

Instead, a researcher can assess a party's propensity to nominate women for seats it is likely to win. Political science scholarship conventionally defines a safe seat for a plurality election in a two-party system as one in which the incumbent political party won 60 percent or more of the vote in the previous election.[26] Because Germany has a multiparty system, making it unlikely that any single party could receive over 60 percent of the votes cast, I instead used a 10 percent margin of victory over the nearest competitor in the past election to define a safe seat. In order to confirm that such a margin was a useful definition, I also investigated whether parties winning 10 percent or more than their nearest competitor in 2005 also won that particular *Wahlkreis* in 2002.[27] The latter was the case in every instance. Moreover, of the seats designated *a priori* as safe in 2009 using this method, 93 percent were indeed retained by the incumbent party. These controls confirm that this measure is appropriate for a multiparty system. Of the 299 direct seats contested in 2009, 168 fell into the "safe" category–sixty-nine of these districts were won by the SPD, fifty-eight by the CDU, thirty-eight by the CSU, two by the Left Party, and one by the Greens.[28] An additional three districts fit this description in 2005, but 2009 redistricting changed these constituencies' boundaries enough that I excluded them from analysis here.

Once I identified these safe seats, I then recorded the sex of the dominant party's candidate as well as the sex of the 2009 nominee from the party that came in second in 2005. In most instances the runner-up party had been either the CDU, SPD, or the Left Party, although in five districts it was the FDP or the Greens. The candidates nominated by these second-place parties are the "sacrificial lambs" discussed in the analysis below.[29] For both the safe seat nominees and the long-shot candidates, sex was determined in the manner used for studying party lists. I now turn to the results of my investigation.

Quota Adherence in 2009

By way of comparison, I report not only the measures described above, but also discuss the evidence provided by official statistics. Looking first at the total number of list candidates fielded across the Federal Republic, women make up less than 50 percent of all parties' lists (see Table 1).[30] With the exception of the CDU, which slightly exceeded its 33 percent quorum and fielded party lists containing 35.5 percent female candidates, the parties with quotas had (slightly) lower overall percentages of women on their lists than called for by their statutes. The Greens approximated their 50 percent quota, giving 49.5 percent of all list places to women, whereas the SPD fell slightly below its minimum 40 percent rule, filling 37.2 percent of its slots with female nominees. The Left Party dipped significantly below its 50 percent quota, as only 39.2 percent of its list candidates were women. Thus, this measure from the Bundeswahlleiter suggests only a mixed record of quota compliance. While the Christian Democrats surpassed their 33 percent mark and the Greens' met their 50 percent goal, the Social Democrats and especially the Left Party fell below their promises to women.

Table 1: Percent of Women on Party Lists in 2009 (in percent)

Percent of women in...	Green	Left	SPD	CDU	FDP	CSU
... all list places	49.5	39.2	37.2	35.5	22.5	31.7
... *a priori* safe list places	49.6	51.5	45	32.5	25.3	50
... winning list places	57.8	55.6	42.7	42.9	25.8	N/A

Source: See text for details. Figures represent the sum of candidates in all sixteen Länder (for the Union, fifteen Länder for the CDU and Bavaria for the CSU).

While the overall number of women on some parties' lists may have been below quota levels, studying the percentage of female candidates in winnable list places paints quite a different picture (see Table 1). This measure finds more consistent evidence of gender quota compliance in 2009 than do the official statistics discussed above. All parties of the left ran higher percentages of women in seemingly safe list places than they did overall. In contrast, the CDU had a slightly lower percentage here, but still in keeping with its quorum. The SPD exceeded its 40 percent quota, giving women 45 percent of what *a priori* could be considered good list places— the same was true for the Left Party which, with 51.5 percent women in safe spots, exceeded its 50 percent quota. If one rounds to the nearest decimal, the Greens and CDU also met their targets, allotting 49.6 percent and 32.5 percent of *a priori* safe list places to female candidates. Although the Social Democrats and the Left Party may have not nominated enough overall female candidates to meet their quotas, these parties did seem to fulfill their quotas where it matters—in list places which appear winnable.

Indeed, there were only three instances in which state party groups did not place enough women on the ballot to fill their quotas. In Hamburg, the CDU's six-member party list contained no women at all, while the quorum required at least two. In the Saarland, only one of the Left Party's candidates was a woman, despite a quota requirement of at least three, and in Thuringia the Green's six-person list contained only two, rather than the requisite three, female candidates. In the remaining fifteen (fourteen for the CDU) Länder, however, all these parties nominated at least enough women to fill their quotas and the Social Democrats did so in all sixteen Länder. Eleven state party groups actually exceeded the minimum number of women specified by their quota or quorum: six of these instances involved the SPD, three the Left Party, and one each the CDU and Greens. On balance, then, this indicator suggests that, although they are voluntary, German political party gender quotas were adhered to in the 2009 federal election.

To confirm that this is indeed the case, the placement of female candidates among the safe spots on electoral lists must be examined. Table 2 depicts the total number of safe list places (the denominator) and the number of those slots that were filled in accordance with a particular party's quota (the numerator). For example, the top eighteen spots on the Green list in Baden-Württemberg were considered promising spots and, within this subset of the overall list, the party's "zipper" system with women in odd and men in even numbered spaces was indeed applied. This indicator confirms that parties complied with their placement mandates in fifty-one of sixty-three cases. Moreover, five of the twelve violations of placement mandates occurred when female candidates appear to have been bumped up the list and men pushed down (marked in the table with **). Thus, of the CDU's top six list places in Brandenburg, two were occupied by women. Rather than placing one woman among the top three candidates and the other among the next three nominees, which would have fulfilled the quorum, the party placed the two women among the top three contenders and the following three were all male.[31]

Table 2: Placement Mandate Compliance in 2009

State	Green	Left	SPD	CDU
Baden-Württemberg	18/18	12/12	18/20	6/6
Bavaria	18/18	12/12	25/25	n/a
Berlin	6/6	6/6	5/5	6/6
Brandenburg	4/5*	10/10	5/5	5/6**
Bremen	4/4	6/6	5/5	6/6
Hamburg	5/5	6/6	5/5	4/6*
Hesse	12/12	6/6	14/15**	12/12
Mecklenburg West Pomerania	5/6*	4/5*	5/5	6/6
Lower Saxony	12/12	10/10	15/15	17/18**
North Rhine Westphalia	18/18	18/18	20/20	24/24
Rhineland-Palatinate	6/6	6/6	14/15**	6/6
Saarland	2/5*	3/5*	5/5	5/6**
Saxony	6/6	12/12	5/5	6/6
Saxony-Anhalt	6/6	10/10	5/5	6/6
Schleswig-Holstein	6/6	6/6	5/5	6/6
Thuringia	5/6*	6/6	5/5	6/6
Sum	133/139	133/136	156/160	121/126
Total percent of safe seats complying with quota	95.7	97.8	97.5	96.0

The denominator is the total number of safe list places; the numerator is the number of these seats in which candidates were placed according to the quota/quorum.

* represents violations with men in higher places than allotted by quota

** represents quota violations with lower numbers of women than required in lower positions, but women over minimum representation in higher spots.

Source: See note 24; see text for further details.

Quota transgressions were most common in states with very short electoral lists such as Brandenburg, Mecklenburg West Pomerania, and Saarland, a finding in keeping with some political science literature indicating that larger district magnitudes are associated with higher women's representation.[32] When only a few good places are available, even parties such as the Greens and the Left sometimes delegate these scarce resources to men. Furthermore, Table 2 offers some evidence of a "reverse contagion" effect. Half of the placement mandate breeches occurred in states where at least one other party failed to adhere to its gender quota, suggesting that when one political group breaks its voluntary quota, others feel more secure in reneging on their promises as well. For example, in Mecklenburg West Pomerania both the Left Party and the Social Democrats disregarded their placement mandates and the Free Democrats included no women at all on their seven-member electoral list. Overall, however, compliance with placement mandates was extremely high, especially given that German quotas are voluntary and are not backed by the force of electoral law—over 95 percent of promising list positions were filled correctly in 2009.

An examination of the percent of women winning seats via party lists (calculated with data available on the Bundestag's webpage) indicates that placement mandates successfully elevate women to electable ballot slots (see Table 1).[33] By this measure, all parties *exceeded* their quotas: 57.8 percent of the Greens and 55.6 percent of the Left Party's winning list candidates were female—above their 50 percent quota mark. The CDU also came in far above its 33 percent quorum with 42.9 percent women elected via party lists, whereas the SPD also was slightly above its 40 percent quota with 42.7 percent women among its winning list members. Comparing these results to those derived from the measure developed above shows the usefulness of the latter indicator. Although the SPD and CDU both featured 43 percent women among their winning list candidates, the SPD arrived at this result by placing many women among its promising list candidates, whereas the high percentage of women within the CDU *Fraktion* can be attributed to the large number of direct mandates won by this party, rather than to its exceeding the quorum among *a priori* promising list places. As will be shown below, the vast majority of the Christian Democrats' winning constituency candidates were men who ran on both halves of the ballot; as these successful first vote getters moved off the list, many CDU women in turn moved up the list into the Bundestag. Both the CDU and the SPD, however, as well as the Greens and the Left Party, complied with their voluntary gender quotas in the 2009 election. Now I turn to the major German parties with no gender quotas.

Parties without Quotas in 2009

In this section, I discuss the CSU and FDP's 2009 lists for the second vote (see Table 1) in search of evidence of quota contagion. Overall, the quota-less CSU's ballot looked similar to its quorum-adopting sister party, the CDU, featuring 31.7 percent women. This figure also resembles that of other parties with quotas when one considers the gender make-up of the various political groups' rank and file (see Table 3). In all parties, women make up a minority of members, ranging from 18 percent in the CSU to 38 percent within the Left Party.[34] Among the four parties adopting quotas, the average quota is 10.75 percent higher than the percentage of female party members. Compared to the CSU's overall membership which is only 18 percent female, then its 31.7 percent female list represents a better list-to-members ratio than all parties with quotas. The evidence for contagion is not consistent, however. In contrast to the CSU, the quota-less FDP ran with lists totaling only 22.5 percent women–considerably below all other political parties and only approximating its overall female membership (23 percent).

Table 3: Percentages of Women in German Parties and Party Quotas in 2009

Party	Percent members female	Quota: Percent candidates female	Difference: Members – Minimum Quota
Left Party	38	≥ 50	-12
Greens	37	≥ 50	-13
Social Democrats (SPD)	31	40 - 60	-9
Christian Democrats (CDU)	25	33	-8
Free Democrats (FDP)	23	None	N/A
Christian Social Union (CSU)	19	None	N/A

Source: See note 34.

Examining the percentage of female candidates in winnable list slots also provides mixed evidence of gender quota contagion in the 2009 Bundestag election. The quota-less CSU's party list resembled that of the Greens and the Left Party: 50 percent of the top candidates were women, up from 33 percent in 2005. Although the CSU had no quota, a lower overall percentage of women on its electoral list than most other parties, and the lowest percentage of female members of all German parties, the Christian Social Union seems to have felt compelled to promote women into visible list places. (The top five candidates on a party's list appear on the ballot.)

In contrast, however, the FDP's lack of gender quotas was evident in the 25.3 percent of women among its top list places. Although the FDP placed comparatively few women in promising electoral list slots, the party's campaign materials prominently featured female faces. Silvana Koch-Mehrin, member of the European Parliament and that body's vice president, adorned many of the FDP's brochures and posters in the fall of 2009 although she was not actually a candidate for the Bundestag. This suggests that this party too—while it did not actually run very many female candidates—felt pressured to at least appear as if it did. Like the CSU, the FDP did also take steps to place the few women they did have in visible positions—half of the FDP's Bundestag leadership is now female.[35] Thus, quotas may be pressuring the FDP to act *as if* it has many female candidates, even if this did not prompt the party to actually nominate large percentages of women for their top list places in 2009.

Unsurprisingly given its list described above, the quota-less FDP elected far fewer women than the parties adopting quotas—only 25.8 percent of the Liberals' parliamentarians are women. This figure was nonetheless double that of the FDP's party group in the eleventh Bundestag (1987-1990).[36] The CSU won no party list mandates at all, making their promotion of women to top slots irrelevant in practice. One might therefore argue that the quota-less CSU's use of gender parity at the top of its party list does not indicate contagion as party leaders did not actually anticipate any of the list candidates winning. In past federal elections, however, the CSU did send five or more list members to the Bundestag, suggesting that these top placements for female candidates were more than simply symbolic. While an examination of the party's list (*WahlkreisbewerberInnen*) for the 2008 Bavarian state elections finds a far lower percentage of women on the list than for the Bundestag—a mere 26.9 percent, much like the FDP's federal list[37]—this figure is nevertheless 9 percent above the CSU's percentage of female members, akin to the CDU's member to quota ratio, indicating that the former party does practice positive discrimination toward women on its electoral lists.[38]

In sum, there is mixed evidence of contagion across party lists. While the quota-less CSU acts roughly similar to the quorum-adopting CDU, the same is not true of the FDP, although it now sends more women to the Bundestag than it did in the past and places them in visible positions. Were the Bundestag to consist solely of MdBs elected through the second vote, it would contain 43.4 percent women, making Germany the fourth-highest ranked country in the world in terms of descriptive representation for women in the lower house.[39] Voluntary gender quotas have been met or exceeded for parties that have them and appear to have exerted some pressure on the CSU to promote female candidates. As will be shown below, the real hurdle to women's equal participation in the Bundestag lies in the first part of Germany's dual ballot.

Party Nominations in Promising Constituencies

While voluntary quota compliance in the proportional representation (second vote) portion of the ballot is high, and while there is some evidence of quota contagion to parties without quotas, the evidence from the plurality (first vote) portion of the ballot finds hardly any contagion effect (see Table 4). Regardless of how it is measured, the proportion of direct mandate nominations awarded to women in Germany was very low in the 2009 election and can account for the stagnation of the number of women in the Bundestag.

Table 4: Percent of Women Nominated for Direct Mandates

Percent Female Candidates for	Green	Left	SPD	CDU	CSU	FDP
... *all* direct mandates	35.8	28.3	35.8	21.6	13.3	16.4
	(N = 296)	(N = 297)	(N = 299)	(N = 254)	(N = 45)	(N = 299)
... *safe* seats	0	100	23.2	8.6	13.1	N/A
	(N = 1)	(N = 2)	(N = 16)	(N = 58)	(N= 38)	
... "sacrificial lambs"	0	52	39.7	30	N/A	0
	(N = 2)	(N = 21)	(N = 78)	(N=59)		(N = 3)
... all direct mandate winners	0	43.7	29.7	25.4	13.3	N/A
	(N = 1)	(N = 16)	(N = 64)	(N = 173)	(N = 45)	

Source: See text for details.

I first discuss the total number of women nominated as direct candidates, the official statistic reported by the Bundeswahlleiter (see Table 4). While the Greens and the Left Party pledged one half of their list spots to women, and while both fulfilled their promises, these parties gave only 35.8 percent and 28.3 percent of their direct seat candidacies to women, respectively. The Christian Democrats also had a great discrepancy— although they surpassed their list quorum of 33 percent, only 21.6 percent of CDU direct candidates were women. The Social Democrats came closer to their 40 percent quota, allotting 35.8 percent of constituency nominations to women. The quota-less FDP and CSU trailed with 16.4 percent and 13.3 percent women, respectively.

In the SPD, CDU, and CSU these figures dropped even more conspicuously in constituencies where they parties were virtually assured electoral victory. In these safe seats, only 23.2 percent, 8.6 percent, and 13.1 percent, respectively, of the direct mandate candidates were women. Not only were these figures below quota levels for the Christian and Social Democrats, they were also far below the percentages of female members in these parties (compare to Table 3). These numbers also stand in sharp contrast to these parties' propensity to nominate women in electoral districts where a sacrificial lamb is called for. The CDU and SPD were much more likely to approximate their gender quotas among constituencies they were likely to lose than in districts they were likely to win; in the former *Wahlkreise*, 39.7 percent of the Social Democratic candidates were women and 30 percent of the Christian Democratic nominees were female. The CSU's dominant position in Bavaria meant that nowhere did they face an opponent enjoying a safe seat, making it impossible to measure their behavior under such circumstances.

This gendered direct mandate nomination pattern clearly manifests itself when the sexes of those who win direct mandates for the SPD and the Union are examined (see Table 4). Only 29.7 percent of all the Social Democratic *Wahlkreis* winners were women and this figure fell to 25.4 percent for the CDU and 13.3 percent for the CSU. Admittedly, these numbers do represent an increase from the twelfth electoral period (1990-1994) when quotas were introduced–then only 16.5 percent of the SPD's direct seat winners and 10.6 percent of the Union's constituency holders were female.[40] Nevertheless, the discrepancy between the gender make-up of the *Volksparteien*'s list and sacrificial lamb candidates and their nominees for (safe) direct seats suggests only a limited contagion effect across electoral systems.

For the Greens and the FDP, direct candidacies are largely symbolic because it is virtually impossible for these narrowly focused parties to win in a plurality election. Indeed, the Greens did not even run a candidate in every constituency in 2009. The Greens' only direct mandate–won in Berlin/Friedrichshain-Kreuzberg–is classified as a safe seat according to the methodology described above. This seat has been held by Hans-Christian Ströbele since his election in 2002. Despite the party's policy of leading their electoral list with a woman, and their earlier commitment to term limits for elective offices, the Greens have continued to nominate Ströbele for this safe seat. The Free Democrats won no direct mandates in 2005 or 2009.

The Left Party is the only party that evinces a degree of contagion across electoral systems (see Table 4). Although only 28.3 percent of its overall direct mandate candidates were women, compared with 52 percent of its sacrificial lambs, 43.7 percent of the Left Party's directly elected MdB were female. This latter figure approximates (but still falls below) the party's 50 percent quota for women. Both of the Left's safe seats–*Wahlkreis* 86, Berlin-Marzahn-Hellersdorf and Wahlkreis 87, Berlin-Lichtenberg– were returned to the women who have held them for much of the past decade (Petra Pau and Gesine Lötzsch, respectively).

Overall, however, there is little evidence that gender quotas have inspired German political parties to nominate more women for auspicious electoral districts. Some parties only approximate their quotas for women when it comes for constituencies the party is likely to lose, whereas other parties do not even select many female sacrificial lambs. The numbers of women on this portion of the ballot fall below the already low percentage of women among German political parties' members. If the seventeenth Bundestag were comprised solely of directly elected members, only 22.4 percent would be women–up only 10 percent in the two decades since quotas were introduced[41]–ranking Germany forty-eighth worldwide in terms of women in the lower house of the legislative branch, immediately below the United Arab Emirates.[42]

Concluding Thoughts and Policy Recommendations

The evidence presented here shows that, although they are voluntary, German political parties' candidate gender quotas for electoral lists were indeed enforced in the 2009 federal election. Although some lists did not contain as many women as promised overall, women did appear in *a priori* safe list places and *ex post* elected list places in accordance with the Green, Left, SPD, and CDU quotas. In the vast majority of cases placement mandates were followed.

Mixed evidence of a contagion effect was found in terms of parties without gender quotas. On the one hand, the Christian Social Union appears to be under pressure to increase the percentage of female candidates it places in the visible part of its party list– the CSU's overall list also had higher percentages of women than its rank and file did. On the other hand, the Free Democrats' 2009 Bundestag delegation has only 5.5 percent more women than did its 1990 Bundestag *Fraktion*. The Liberals placed only a slightly higher percentage of women in top list spots than the party has female members, and this figure was far lower than for any other major German party. While the FDP's top list spots contained a quarter women, the Greens' and Left Party's lists featured gender parity.

Perhaps the difference between the CDU and the FDP stems from the two parties' contrasting electoral fortunes. While the CSU has been losing ground in Bavaria, especially among younger, postmaterialist voters, the FDP's appeal has been on the rise. In order to modernize its image and attract a new generation of Bavarian voters, the Christian Social Union has, without adopting quotas, begun to run electoral lists which resemble Angela Merkel's Christian Democrats' rather than traditional Bavarian male-dominated slates the CSU has run in the past. The FDP, led by openly gay *Spitzenkandidat* Guido Westerwelle and Vietnamese-German Phillipp Rösler, and riding a wave of popularity in the face of the global economic crisis, did not face as intense pressure to modernize its image by nominating large numbers of female candidates.

Finally, there was little if any evidence to suggest contagion of quota norms from the second to the first portion of Germany's dual ballot. The vast majority of all parties' total nominees for direct mandates was male, as were the individuals selected to contest each party's safe seats. Only where victory was unlikely did some (but not all) parties choose to run female candidates in numbers close to the party's quota. As a result, almost 80 percent of direct mandate winners were male in 2009. The exception to this pattern was the Left Party, which awarded its two safe seat nominations to female candidates and saw 43.7 percent of its *Wahlkreis* victories go to women. Even this figure was below the party's list quota, however, and the party's "sacrificial lambs" were disproportionately female.

These findings make several contributions to the literature on gender quotas and suggest some policy recommendations for the German case. First, at least in Germany, voluntary gender quotas for party lists have been implemented, despite the lack of official sanctions. Such quotas have ensured that the Bundestag has one of the highest percentages of women among national legislatures worldwide. In a few states where one party failed to follow its placement mandate, however, others followed, highlighting the danger of a "reverse contagion effect." Second, this case finds some evidence of a contagion effect to parties without quotas, but hardly any evidence of contagion across electoral systems.

German quotas appear to have reached the limits of their ability to increase the percent of women in the Bundestag. Additional changes to current political practices would be necessary to achieve gender parity. One extreme possibility would be to abolish the dual electoral system in favor of one based solely on proportional representation lists, such as that used in Saarland Land elections and many local contests in Germany. Were the federal electoral system to remain the same and parties to continue to implement their quotas, an increase in the Social or Christian Democrats' minimum quota (quorum) requirement for female candidates would likely raise the percentage of female MdBs somewhat, as would the FDP's adoption of a quota or the CSU's winning candidates through the second vote.

One factor that also may be hampering the overall number of women on Bundestag electoral lists is the low percentage of females among the rank and file membership of political parties. Were there more women in political parties, it might follow that more women get nominated. For example, by all measures, the gender make-up of the FDP's party lists mirror the sex of its party's members. Thus, if more women joined the Liberals, they might send more women to the Bundestag. Increasing political parties' attraction to German women, however, would require significant changes to a deeply entrenched masculine party culture.[43]

Even if parties contained more women, given the current gap between parties' memberships and their direct mandate candidates, specific gender-based candidate selection procedures for direct mandates would likely still be needed to improve women's chances of getting elected at the federal level. While such rules are rare in plurality electoral systems, they are possible. For example, the British Labour Party used "twinning" rules for paired constituencies in which they have similar electoral prospects—a process that requires one electoral district's candidate to be female and the other male.[44] Labour has also utilized "all female shortlists" for constituency seats, allowing only women to contest a particular seat, although these measures proved legally controversial.[45] Other parliaments, primarily in the developing world, contain "reserved seats," which only women are permitted to contest.[46] Were any of these measures to be adopted in Germany, future Bundestag elections would likely result in a gender composition of parliament that would more closely resemble that of the population as a whole.

Notes

1. I would like to thank Grant Blumberg for invaluable research assistance.
2. Louise K. Davidson-Schmich, "The Implementation of Political Party Gender Quotas: Evidence from the German *Länder* 1990-2000," *Party Politics* 12, no. 2 (2006): 211-232.
3. Peter Schindler, *Datenhandbuch zur Geschichte des Deutschen Bundestages 1949-1999: Band I* (Baden Baden, 1999); Louise K. Davidson-Schmich, "Ahead of Her Time: Eva Kolinsky and the Limits of German Gender Quotas," *German Politics* 16, no. 3 (2007): 391-407.
4. "Women in National Parliaments," available at http://www.ipu.org/wmn-e/classif.htm, accessed 8 January 2010.
5. Author's calculations based on http://www.bundestag.de/bundestag/abgeordnete17/index.jsp, accessed 25 January 2010; see also http://www.ipu.org/wmn-e/classif.htm, accessed 25 January 2010.
6. See http://www.destatis.de/jetspeed/portal/cms/Sites/destatis/Internet/DE/Content/Statistiken/Bevoelkerung/Bevoelkerungsstand/Tabellen/Content50/Geschlecht Staatsangehoerigkeit,templateId=renderPrint.psml, accessed 25 January 2010.
7. See http://quotaproject.org/aboutQuotas.cfm, accessed 25 January 2010.

8. Technically, individuals could take their parties to court and charge them with failing to comply with party statutes, but to my knowledge no one in Germany has ever made use of this option. Since political parties ultimately control candidate nominations and party organizations would be highly unlikely to nominate an individual who took them to court, it would seem to be career suicide for an aspiring candidate to legally challenge her party for failing to adhere to its quota.

9. Richard E. Matland, "Electoral Quotas: Frequency and Effectiveness" in *Women, Quotas and Politics*, ed., Drude Dahlerup (New York, 2006); "Gender Quotas Around the World," available at http://www.quotaproject.org/, accessed 20 January 2010; for evidence of failed voluntary quotas see Mala N. Htun and Mark P. Jones, "Engendering the Right to Participate in Decision-Making: Electoral Quotas and Women's Leadership in Latin America," in *Gender and the Politics of Rights and Democracy in Latin America*, eds., Nikki Craske and Maxine Molyneux (New York, 2002), 32-56; for evidence of inconsistent quota enforcement in Germany see Davidson-Schmich (see note 2).

10. Aili Mari Tripp and Alice Kang, "The Global Impact of Quotas: On the Fast Track to Increased Female Legislative Representation," *Comparative Political Studies* 41, no. 3 (2008): 338-361; Miki Caul Kittilson, *Challenging Parties, Changing Parliaments: Women in Elective Office in Contemporary Western Europe* (Columbus, 2006).

11. Richard E. Matland and Donley T. Studlar, "The Contagion of Women Candidates in Single-Member District and Proportional Representation Electoral Systems: Canada and Norway," *The Journal of Politics* 58 (1996): 707-33. Kittilson (see note 10) refers to this process as "diffusion." Mona Krook also agrees that contagion is a variable which can help explain quota adoption. Mona Lena Krook, *Quotas for Women in Politics: Candidate Selection Reform Worldwide* (Oxford, 2009).

12. Eva Kolinsky, *Women in West Germany: Life, Work, and Politics* (New York, 1989), 236-237.

13. Eva Kolinsky, "Party Change and Women's Representation in Unified Germany" in *Gender and Party Politics*, eds., Joni Lovenduski and Pippa Norris (Thousand Oaks, 1993), 132; Sarah Elise Wiliarty, "Bringing Women into the Party: The Christian Democratic Union as a Corporatist Catch-All Party," PhD. Dissertation, University of California, Berkeley (2002), UMI Dissertation Number 3082460, 174, 182; Sarah E. Wiliarty, *Bringing Women to the Party: The CDU and the Politics of Gender in Germany* (Cambridge, 2010).

14. Rikhil R. Bhavnani, "Do Electoral Quotas Work after They Are Withdrawn? Evidence from a Natural Experiment in India," *American Political Science Review* 103, no. 1 (2009): 23-35.

15. As it was, these women were actually bunched up toward the top of the list occupying seven of the top fourteen spots resulting in gender parity.

16. Cornelia Schmalz-Jacobsen, *Klimawechsel: Berichte aus dem politischen Parterre* (Reinbek, 1981).

17. See http://www.gruene.de/fileadmin/user_upload/Dokumente/Beschl%C3% percent-BCsse/090508_-_satzung_bundesverband.pdf, Part I, Paragraph 1, accessed 25 January 2010.

18. See http://www.spd.de/de/pdf/rechtliches/071026_spd-statut.pdf, 49-50; accessed 25 January 2010.

19. See http://www.cdu.de/doc/pdfc/080121-CDU-statut.pdf, 11-12; accessed 25 January 2010.

20. See http://die-linke.de/partei/dokumente/bundessatzung_der_partei_die_linke/2_die_basis_der_partei/10_geschlechterdemokratie/, accessed 25 January 2010.

21. See http://www.csu.de/dateien/partei/partei/satzung/080718_satzung.pdf, 35, accessed 29 January 2010. The FDP's "Bundessatzung" makes no mention of women at all and uses only male forms of nouns (e.g., *Bewerber, Kandidat*); see http://www.fdp-bundespartei.de/files/363/Geschaeftsordnung.pdf, accessed 29 January 2010.

22. In some small states such as Bremen and Hamburg, party lists contained only five candidates and in such cases I simply coded all available candidates.

23. See http://www.bundeswahlleiter.de/de/bundestagswahlen/BTW_BUND_09/ wahlbewerber/land/, accessed 29 January 2010.
24. One drawback to this method is that it may categorize inaccurately transgendered individuals whose lived gender does not match their legal names.
25. See http://www.cdu.de/doc/pdfc/080121-CDU-statut.pdf, 11; accessed 25 January 2010.
26. Gary C. Jacobson, "The Marginals Never Vanished: Incumbency and Competition in Elections to the U.S. House of Representatives, 1952-82," *American Journal of Political Science*, 31, no. 1 (1987): 126-141.
27. For results of the 2005 Bundestag election see http://www.bundeswahlleiter.de/de/ bundestagswahlen/BTW_BUND_05/ergebnisse/wahlkreisergebnisse/, accessed 1 February 2010. Results from 2002 can be calculated from the data available here about vote losses or gains.
28. A complete list of these *Wahlkreise* is available from the author upon request.
29. Subsequent analysis does not discuss the results for the FDP and Greens because, with only one exception, all of these parties' direct candidates can be considered sacrificial lambs, providing a more meaningful statistic than these five cases. In all five instances, however, the candidate was male.
30. See http://www.bundeswahlleiter.de/de/bundestagswahlen/BTW_BUND_09/ wahlbewerber/wahlbewerber/tab04.pdf, accessed 29 January 2010.
31. This action still remains a quorum violation, however. Were two women to be selected for the top three candidates, the correct action would have been to include a third woman on the top of the list, placing her among the second trio of candidates–hence the classification of this list as containing one quorum violation.
32. For a review of this literature see Leslie A. Schwindt-Bayer, "The incumbency disadvantage and women's election to legislative office" *Electoral Studies* 24, no. 2 (2005): 227-244. Research on Germany has found only mixed evidence of a district magnitude effect, however. See Richard E. Matland and Kathleen A. Montgomery, *Women's Access to Political Power in Post-Communist Europe* (Oxford, 2003), 72-75.
33. See Bundestag (see note 5). Interestingly, in previous legislative periods, the Bundestag reported the exact percentage of women within its ranks on its website. Now that the FDP is in government, however, this figure does not appear for the seventeenth electoral period and must be derived from other data.
34. See http://www.bpb.de/themen/YX2B5Z,0,0,Parteien_in_Deutschland.html, accessed 30 January 2010. The "Zahlen und Fakten" section for each party provides party membership broken down by sex.
35. See http://www.liberale.de/Frauen-sind-die-Gewinner/3759c7059i1p104/index.html, accessed 29 January 2010.
36. See Schindler (see note 3), 636.
37. Author's calculations based on http://www.statistik.bayern.de/wahlen/landtagswahlen/, accessed 21 May, 2010.
38. The percentage of women in the CSU's Bundestag Fraktion has fluctuated considerably over the past two decades–ranging from 10 percent to 24.1 percent–and this variance corresponds to the number of list places the party won, which ranged from zero to fourteen. See Melanie Kintz, *Data on the Members of the German Bundestag 1994-2006* (Chemnitz 2009); accessed 21 May 2010.
39. See Interparliamentary Union (see note 4).
40. See Schindler (see note 3), 638.
41. Ibid.
42. See Interparliamentary Union (see note 4).
43. For a discussion of the extensive feminist literature on this point, see Davidson-Schmich (see note 3). A change in the gendered household division of labor in Germany would likely be necessary as well.

44. See Alice Brown, "Taking their Place in the New House: Women and the Scottish Parliament" in *Women and Contemporary Scottish Politics: An Anthology*, eds., Esther Breitenbach and Fiona Mackay (Edinburgh, 2001), 241-248 and Joni Lovenduski, *Feminizing Politics* (Malden, 2005).

45. Pippa Norris, "Breaking the Barriers: Positive Discrimination Policies for Women" in *Has Liberalism Failed Women? Parity, Quotas and Political Representation*, eds., Jytte Klausen and Charles S. Maier (New York, 2001).

46. See note 7.

Chapter 9

THE INTERNET, POLITICAL PARTICIPATION AND ELECTION TURNOUT

A Case Study of Germany's www.abgeordnetenwatch.de

● ● ● ● ● ● ● ● ● ● ● ● ● ● ● ●

Hartwig Pautz

Introduction[1]

Germany's representative democracy, based on strong political parties with an active membership, and legitimized through regular elections with high turnouts in the past, is said to be in crisis.[2] Both *Volksparteien* (people's or catch-all parties)–the Social Democratic Party (SPD) and the Christian Democratic Party (CDU/CSU)–have lost members.[3] The SPD's membership declined from 755,000 in 1999 to 530,000 in 2008, when the CDU for the first time exceeded the SPD's membership count, albeit only because of a less dramatic decrease in its own rank-and-file.[4] Moreover, even after twenty years, neither these bigger parties nor the smaller parties have managed to build a significant membership base in eastern Germany–bar the Left Party.[5] Identification and linkage with parties is waning and electoral volatility is increasing.[6] Four months before the 2009 federal elections, for instance, over 70 percent of citizens stated that they had not decided for which party to cast their vote.[7] Voters and even party members increasingly perceive parties as mere electoral vehicles for office-seeking, career politicians, rather than as associations with programmatic principles, and see them as interchangeable in terms of their respective programmatic principles.[8] Voters' faith in parties to solve political problems is also low. In 2008, 82 percent answered "no" to the question whether they trusted political parties to be problem solvers.[9]

Thus, there is arguably "party decline in the party state"[10] while parties, nonetheless, continue to serve as central actors in the political system.[11]

This has effects at the ballot box with election turnout decreasing at municipal, Länder, and federal levels. At the 2009 Bundestag election, just under 71 percent of voters turned out compared to close to 78 percent in 2005. This was an all-time low for elections on this level with especially the SPD suffering by losing over 2 million votes to the growing portion of non-voters.[12] According to pollsters, the reputation of politicians in Germany is at an all-time low: while in the early 1970s, 27 percent of West Germans said that politicians deserve their highest respect out of all professions, whereas today only 6 percent of Germans in both the East and West say so.[13]

At the same time, some claim that Germans are more interested in politics than in the 1990s, overwhelmingly support democracy, and are keen on participating– particularly in local political decision making.[14] Citizens seem to be turning away from representative democracy, while not losing their interest in participating in politics in a different sense. Certainly civil society activities have increased in the 2000s so that by 2004, 34 percent of the population over fourteen years of age was committed to civic engagement (with party politics being only a minor field of activity).[15] Concomitant to these developments, Stephen Coleman and Josephine Spiller argue that today's politics is characterized by a "post-deferential culture, where institutions and individuals are expected to earn the respect" of citizens.[16] Clearly, Germany's politicians and political institutions have yet to find ways to live up to these expectations.

Inspired by such or a similar diagnosis of the state of (representative) democracy in Germany, the internet website www.abgeordnetenwatch.de (representative watch, AW) was set up in 2004 by supporters of a more personalized proportional electoral system then debated in and for the city state of Hamburg–one of Germany's sixteen federal Länder. The specific situation that stimulated the establishment of the website was that political activists were dissatisfied with the public debate about the proposed changes to electoral law. At the same time, they were concerned that if the new personalized system was put into place, voters would find it difficult to actually know what the candidates stood for, to communicate with them, and to evaluate their voting behavior in the legislature. Consequently, the website was set up to allow citizens with little effort to put questions directly to politicians standing for election to the Hamburg regional parliament. These questions and the politicians' answers were to be made publicly accessible and archived online. The new website received (initially reluctant) support from all political parties and obtained limited public funding from the Landeszentrale für politische Bildung, the state political education authority. In the following years, AW expanded to further Länder, municipal levels and even to the European Union Parliament—more on this expansion later.

Academics and others have long debated the potential of information and communication technologies (ICT) to increase electoral turnout and political participation and to address other "democratic deficits" in representative democracy. The actual spread and availability of, and thus access to, the internet as the latest innovation in ICT, is a far more recent phenomenon and its usage is still spread unevenly. In 2009, only 67 percent of Germans stated they used the internet "occasionally," while of all those who use the internet 71 percent are online on a daily basis. Women, with the exception of the youngest age group, use the internet considerably less and in different ways than men. Only 27 percent of all people over sixty use the internet "occasionally" compared to 96 percent of all between fourteen and twenty-nine. The internet has become the preferred source for political information for internet users and thus leaves television and other traditional news sources behind.[17]

Just like the internet, AW is also a relatively recent phenomenon. This chapter uses the 2009 federal elections as a prompt for discussing AW as an e-democracy instrument that has thus far received considerable media attention, but that has not been analyzed extensively from an academic perspective. The aims are of this chapter are to describe the emergence of AW, to discuss its potential effects on voters, the elected, and the representative system, and to discuss AW within the context of the 2009 Bundestag election. After an initial discussion of the different understandings of the meaning of ICT for the future of democracy, which is helpful to understand the motivation behind the establishment of AW, the history of AW is described in some depth to contextualize the case study approach pursued later where I discuss the potential effects of AW. Methodologically this is done by looking at it through the lens of existing research on e-democracy following the example of James Thurman's and Urs Gasser's analysis of the Swiss "Smartvote" electronic voting aid application (VAA).[18] Thus, this chapter makes several *a priori* judgments on the effects of AW, which are largely based on such existing research results. Therefore, the findings reported here are of a preliminary nature. The justification for this approach is that AW does not systematically gather its own user data and that it was not possible to generate data single-handedly. Only some data could be obtained from AW directly, from material published on its website or in the media. My hope is that this chapter stimulates (comparative) empirical research about AW and similar e-democracy instruments existing in other countries—for example, the UK's www.writetothem.com,

Ireland's www.kildarestreet.com, Austria's www.meinparlament.at, France's www.nosdeputes.fr, and the European Parliament's www.euprofiler.eu.

The Potentials and Pitfalls of E-democracy

The internet has found several political purposes. First, it has become a tool for what is termed "e-government" and is used, for example, to improve service quality delivery, to reduce costs, and to renew administrative processes.[19] Rachel Silcock defines e-government as "the use of technology to enhance the access to delivery of government services to benefit citizen, business partners and employees."[20] Second, ICT has been understood and employed as means to enhance democratic practices and processes. Here, the term e-democracy refers to democratic practices in the public sphere of "cyberspace." The public sphere consists of the "vital channels in civil society in which individuals and groups can become informed about issues, discuss and debate these issues autonomously and ultimately have an impact on policy agendas."[21] In another concept of e-democracy less concerned with the public sphere, Ken Hacker and Jan van Dick define it as:

> the use of ICTs and computer-mediated communication to enhance active participation of citizens and to support the collaboration between actors for policy-making purposes without the limits of time, space and other physical conditions in democratic communication.[22]

In similar vein, Rosa Tsagarousianou et al. define e-democracy as having three sub-fields: information provision, deliberation, and participation in decision-making.[23] Others refute this separation of e-government and e-democracy, arguing that the former already includes the potential to make processes of administration more transparent and opens up potential opportunities for citizens to engage in decision-making processes.[24]

Within the academic literature, there are a number of differing understandings of the consequences of ICT for representative democracy. Scott Wright identifies three schools of thought.[25] The first and oldest suggests that the internet—the "largest and most democratic system that human beings have ever created"[26]—will revolutionize politics as it has removed the "technical difficulties that until now have made it impossible for large numbers of citizens to participate in policy making."[27] Thus, the internet can reinvigorate civil society as it is an "integral tool of strategies to revitalize governance and renew democratic culture."[28] Advances in ICT, an inherently democratizing technology according to this account, would "allow a much more substantive implementation of the democratic ideals described by Abraham Lincoln: the government of the people, by the people, and for the people."[29] As early as 1980, Alwin Toffler voiced the hope that ICT could remove time and space barriers and, as a result of this, direct democracy would become possible.[30] In these accounts, representative democracy is seen as only a developmental stage towards full direct democracy. The internet provides the necessary last push finally to realize direct democracy in large, complex and heterogeneous communities.[31]

A second perspective is also critical of representative democracy and hopes that ICT can provide a remedy for its flaws. Proponents of this school of deliberative or participative democracy, however, criticize supporters of direct e-democracy for promoting nothing more than a "push button democracy."[32] They argue that the internet would make possible the free and equal participation of citizens in the debates preceding decision-making.[33] Thus, ICT would contribute to the development of the good citizen as an active and well-informed member of the community.[34] Proponents of this position have come to see "cyberspace as a medium for implementing the public sphere"[35]–as described by Jürgen Habermas[36]–in which prejudices and obstacles hindering equal participation do not exist[37] and argue that the internet "is incontestably the most important public sphere available today."[38] A related but much weaker version of deliberative democracy can be found in the model of contestatory democracy in which, according to Jeroen van den Hoven, ICT can play a fundamental role.[39] Employing Michael Schudson's idea of the "monitorial citizen,"[40] he argues that in a contestatory democracy, individuals have the means to call into question public decisions and to trigger an appeal in an impartial forum. In such a system, information is crucial so that ICT can be the means to allow everyone to become a monitorial citizen–not a well-informed citizen in the maximal sense but "more like a vigilant reader of headlines."[41]

These two optimistic beliefs in the power of technology for developing democracy have given way to more skeptical views: the third school of thought suggests that "politics will normalize the internet into its established structures, having limited impact." Politicians will actively incorporate the internet into the existing representative system and tame its revolutionary potential so that little change towards a deliberative or plebiscitary democracy should be expected.[42] Skeptics also point out that development of new technologies does not mean the same as their use, and that technological determinism should be avoided–a pessimism harkening back to the enthusiasm that met the introduction of television with regards to its supposedly democratizing and educative powers.[43]

What is www.abgeordnetenwatch.de?

In 2004, Gregor Hackmack and Boris Hekele from the charitable civic association Mehr Demokratie e.V. established AW to facilitate direct contact between voters and members of the Hamburg Landtag. The British charity MySociety.org and its website www.WriteToThem.com, established only shortly before AW and building on the project FaxYourMP, served as the inspiration and model for AW. After the successful start in Hamburg, a similar website for the 2005 Bundestag election was set up. This site remains live, so that not only during the election campaign were voters able to communicate with candidates and incumbents, but also throughout the four year parliamentary period.

Operating according to the same principle on all electoral levels, candidates to and incumbents of a seat in the Bundestag have a basic profile page set up by AW whether or not they wish to participate. Those members of the Bundestag (mdbs) who want to make a more active use of it can pay euro 200 to AW for uploading a photo, statements on their political objectives, and links to Twitter and RSS feeds. The main purpose of aw, however, is not monodirectional self-presentation of mdbs on just another website, but for citizens to put questions to candidates and incumbents. A group of silent moderators vets all contributions made by users—candidates, representatives, and citizens—for abusive or racist content before they are published for everyone to see. A further censoring occurs as monitors only post contributions that they have identified as questions or as requests for positions on particular issues. Thus, AW does not provide space for online deliberation of policy or politics through its question-and-answer function. Nevertheless, it is possible anonymously to post general comments not directly aimed at specific representatives or candidates elsewhere on the website. Not surprisingly, politicians can rarely be found engaging with this part of aw. Monitors also refuse posting an inappropriate number of questions by a single participant to a single politician on the same issue[44] because "a politician who doesn't give a clear answer after two questions is likely to never give a clear answer. Our approach is to show to electors how politicians deal with public questions," says a member of aw.[45] If questions are rejected, users can appeal to aw's board. Politicians can also be sanctioned. For example, all candidates from the extreme-right National Democratic Party standing for the 2009 Land election in Thuringia were banned from AW because many questions to them were submitted from the same computer.[46] To allow AW to act as a "collective memory,"[47] all responses are archived and can be easily juxtaposed to incumbents' voting records, which are also registered on aw. Combined, these data allow for monitoring of the representative's positions over time to check for congruence between voting behavior and pre-election statements. Lastly, membership in parliamentary committees and additional activities–for example, positions on company boards or in voluntary organizations–are registered to make AW a fully fledged parliamentary informatics system with the VAA function at its center.

After the 2005 elections, it became clear that permanently maintaining the site for Hamburg and the Bundestag, as well as establishing sites for the remaining fifteen Länder, the European Parliament, and the local level would necessitate professionalization and could not be continued on a voluntary basis. External sponsors had to be found for financing staff and infrastructure. BonVenture Ltd–a social venture capital fund focused on environmental and social projects–helped AW through a financial advance. AW also established the charity Parliamentwatch e.V. to gather donations and sponsorship contributions. Furthermore, in 2009, one of AW's founders became a fellow of the Ashoka network of entrepreneurs with a social conscience.[48] Additional sources of income include fees for upgraded online individual profiles, the sale of franchise rights for AW's internet code base, and online advertisements. This income must cover costs of about EURO 20,000 a month. Today, AW employs five full-time staff members and one part-timer, while fifteen volunteers act as silent monitors.[49] Nevertheless, the geographical expansion of AW has been relatively slow: by 2010, Bavaria remains the only Land to have joined Hamburg with its own permanent AW site. Yet, AW set up temporary websites in the run-up to all 2009 and 2010 Länder elections and Germany's representatives in the EU Parliament also were connected for the legislative period 2005-2009.

The founders' stated intentions seem to be ambiguous, as they are not guided by a consistent understanding of what kind of democracy AW wants to support. According to Hackmack, AW "was not meant to be a pure monitoring site. The main thing was to create transparency so that trust in parliament and politicians is recreated" by building a "bridge into parliament" and by facilitating communication on the same level.[50] Going beyond this desire to support parliament and the connection between voters and their representatives, AW's makers also want to facilitate a shift "from a democracy made up of spectators to a democracy of participants"[51] thus, effectively reshaping the functioning of the representative system.

The Effects of AW

Because comprehensive data on who uses AW, why, and to what effect does not exist, analysis of AW has to remain mostly speculative and based on empirical findings from other research on the effects of ICT on voters, the elected, and the representative system. This said, a look at user statistics of AW reveals the following picture. In the six weeks before the 2005 federal election, there were 2.6 million hits on the site: 12,000 questions were put to the 2,061 candidates. Of these questions, 8,500 received responses.[52] Between 2005 and 2009, 40.000 questions were posted to MdBs of which 90 percent received a response. In the run-up to the 2009 elections, 95 percent of MdBs responded to questions.[53] The 2,195 candidates for seats in the Bundestag received a combined 7,890 questions for which 6,199 answers were posted on AW–a response rate of 79 percent.[54] In the months preceding the 2009 election, "unique visits"–the number of actual visitors–increased steadily from 260,000 in July to 500,000 in September. In August, there were 4.5 million site hits and in September 3.37 million site hits–according to AW, the overwhelming majority of these hits were related to the Bundestag election.[55] Combining all AW websites on all electoral levels, as of February 2008, candidates had responded to 81 percent of questions posed since 2004.[56] Thus, while AW has generated significant interest in the media and can boast the influential *Der Spiegel* as its media partner, overall numbers of active participants are, not surprisingly, very low. Interest in AW seems to have waned slightly if we compare the 2005 and the 2009 elections, yet the high response rates demonstrate continual commitment of representatives to responding to questions.

What conclusions can be drawn from existing research regarding, first, the represented? If the majority of research findings on e-democracy is anything to go by, it can be assumed that AW is unlikely to stimulate a significant increase of political interest or to enhance public debate beyond those who are already active and informed,[57] as only those who are already politically active "off-line" are likely to make valuable contributions to online debates.[58] The "economics of information cost" limit the effectiveness of more easily available communication channels, such as those provided by the internet, on political activity. The "anticipated effects of expanded communication are limited by the willingness and capacity of humans to engage in complex political life."[59] While the technological potential exists to allow everyone to be a well-informed and actively participating citizen, in reality this is an unattainable ideal in modern democracy. The increasing number of e-democracy tools–e-discussion forums, e-consultations, e-petitioning, e-voting, web-logs, VAAs, and parliamentary informatics systems–has not led to more citizens engaging more strongly in the political processes.[60] Certainly, British respondents in a 2003 poll were not too optimistic about the effects of the internet. When asked whether they thought that the internet had helped to bring democracy closer to citizens, less than one third responded in the affirmative while the same number said it had not.[61]

The conclusions to be drawn for AW are that it may create better citizens, but it does not promote the creation of more good citizens. In this context it is perhaps important to note that researchers have found that voters need relatively little information to vote competently in line with their existing political preferences: the overwhelming majority chooses the "correct" party or candidate despite having little concrete and detailed policy information.[62] With regards to VAAs, which match preferences with political party programs through more or less sophisticated assessments of the user's political standpoints and give direct voting advice, it has been established that only the already sophisticated voter will make more "correct" decisions at the ballot box thanks to a VAA. Moreover, VAAs have a debilitating effect on the voting accuracy of less sophisticated voters.[63] If such findings about VAAs can be extrapolated to AW–which is clearly more than a simple matching party-to-preference device–then AW cannot succeed in politically emancipating more citizens.

The literature on the internet's effect on electoral turnout paints a slightly more optimistic picture than that on ICT's impact on politicization and on levels of political information. In fact, some researchers have found a positive relationship between the two. With regard to U.S. presidential campaigns, the political parties' and candidates' usage of the internet activated citizens to register to vote.[64] Caroline Tolbert and Ramona McNeal found that access to the internet and online election news increased the probability of voting by an average of 12 percent and 7.5 percent respectively in the 2000 presidential elections, and argued that internet access of voters might have to enter the explanatory toolkit of the electoral analyst.[65] Germany's Federal Political Education Agency's "Wahl-o-Mat," a government-sponsored VAA, has been evaluated as moderately successful in terms of increasing electoral turnout.[66] Nevertheless, only very few users wanted to genuinely find information about party programs or went on the site to receive advice and orientation for their decision at the ballot box. The majority of voters, 51 percent, used it to "check" whether their political convictions correlate with those of the party they had voted for in the past and intended to vote for in the future. Only 6 percent of users stated they changed their voting intentions after using the VAA and 8 percent said they would now participate in the elections.[67] Even more so than the Wahl-o-Mat, AW is a medium that addresses those already interested and informed about politics–those likely to participate in off-line politics and through elections anyway–so that AW is unlikely to have any significant positive effect on electoral turnout as it cannot reach those disinterested in electoral politics.

The so-called digital divide' has been an important topic in the debate of e-democracy. Bharat Mehra argues that "socioeconomic status, with income, educational level, and race among other factors associated with technological attainment" contribute to this divide.[68] Others have shown that political communication depending on the internet further disadvantages the poor, illiterate, physically disabled, and technology-resistant members of the society, as well as those who live in regions where there is no or limited internet connectivity.[69] Interestingly, in rural regions even the provision of modern broadband access has not stimulated the same degree of interest in getting connected to the World Wide Web than it has in urban areas.[70] Arguably, AW is likely to contribute to the widening of the digital divide between those citizens with access to the physical internet infrastructure and with the skills to use it effectively and those who have limited access and/or limited skills. Therefore, some social groups are likely to be under-represented and others over-represented on AW. Furthermore, observers of online discussion forums have noted a strong concentration of contributions from a small core of very active users,[71] so that despite impressive numbers of site visits and contributions only a small number of participants actually make active use of a tool such as AW. AW can therefore necessarily only represent a distorted reflection of the electorate's concerns and opinions and thus potentially lead to policies to the detriment of those not using AW, i.e., those who are already likely to be marginalized. Instead of "balancing the traditional inequality of access to politics, the internet reinforces existing problems. If more and more deliberations are to be held online, only the voices of the informational avant-garde" will be heard, as Steffen Albrecht finds in a study of a German policy e-deliberation pilot.[72]

The focus of this chapter is on the represented, but ICT also have effects on the elected. As discussed above, e-democracy enthusiasts hope that the internet would facilitate the development of allegedly superior forms of democracy, namely, either direct or deliberative democracy. Research has shown that, unsurprisingly, there is a general lack of enthusiasm for e-democracy on the side of elected members. As Zahid Parvez has demonstrated, UK local councillors only very reluctantly endorse the introduction of elements of participatory and direct democracy within the representative model in which they have gained their positions.[73] Elected members associate e-democracy with the loss of power and control over their political objectives. AW might therefore also be perceived as a threat by elected representatives as it is based on the diagnosis of serious flaws of representative democracy and Germany's *Parteienstaat*,[74], on the "presumption of incompetence" of elected members,[75] and on the demand for more direct democracy. For example, one MdB has refused to answer questions via AW as she rejects AW's implicit charge that MdBs were "somewhat aloof" and only approachable under public pressure as exerted by AW.[76] Furthermore, elected members might be opposed to AW because voters could come to perceive representatives as operating according to a "tribunal system"[77] in which parliamentarians are expected to vote according to the expressed views of their constituents regardless of their own political stance and that of their party. After all, political parties are barely mentioned on AW as everything revolves around the individual elected member or candidate.

The high usage of AW indicates, however, that it has been accepted by representatives, and the fact that politicians defend party lines and their own political positions indicates that they have not changed their understanding of their own role. While representatives are unlikely to turn into tribunes, AW is also unlikely to promote a more direct or deliberative praxis of democracy. AW certainly does provide a public space for political exchange and goes beyond the one-directional communication of, for instance, politicians' or parties' websites by providing some interactivity. Nonetheless, the monitored and restricted question-and-answer structure leaves no space for policy deliberation. Voter and politician certainly do not communicate on the same level, as AW's makers claim for their project.[78] Yet, the communication that does exist via AW might address voters' complaints that their representatives do not hear them. As U.S. research shows, for the represented, it is of particular importance that their views get acknowledged by representatives while it is not so important weather the elected member agrees with their views or not[79]–perhaps Coleman and Spiller are correct in speculating that this is far more important for voters than participating directly in the actual decision-making process.[80]

Another aspect of AW is that, thanks to its monitorial features, it can be expected to have an impact on the accountability of elected members *vis-à-vis* the electorate. Paraphrasing van den Hoven, AW allows citizens to be potentially informed to realize an adequate level of accountability of elected representatives. Representatives or those wishing to get elected might be more motivated to act accountably when they know that citizens can easily gather information about voting behavior and past policy statements. Hence:

> the positive impact of the internet is not that it triggers more political involvement and participation, but that it facilitates access to information, enhances our strategies and technologies to find it when needed, and may therefore increase the responsiveness of government to the public ... without a dramatic change in citizen engagement and participation in the political process.[81]

Therefore, while most citizens have continued to keep their pre-e-democracy distance to politics and assume that, for example, journalists and watchdog NGOs will inform and warn them of political developments which may affect their lives, AW as the "collective memory"[82] may increase politicians' accountable behavior at little cost to the citizen.

There is an additional, more positive aspect to AW. The user figures demonstrate that elected members and candidates at least in their large majority have endorsed AW as one means to support them in their complex roles. It has been argued that the internet has created an opportunity to restructure communication between MdBs and their constituents. According to Parvez, many elected members "still prefer personal contact, the press and radio and television to some extent" and understand the internet as merely an electronic device to distribute material that otherwise exists on paper in the off-line world.[83] AW, as a bottom-up initiative, may contribute to compensating for such general lackluster or superficial usage of the internet by elected members themselves who barely use the internet as a two-way communicative medium,[84] let alone the social networking functions of "Web 2.0." In this sense, AW might educate representatives with regards to the value of the internet.

So far, I have discussed the potential effects of AW on the represented and the representatives, but AW also can have effects on the representative system. AW is part of the trend from "contractual" to "permanent representation."[85] In the former, the politician enters into a relationship with voters by offering a program based on their party's commitments, which voters evaluate before election day and that they re-evaluate prior to the next election. In permanent representation, campaigning and governing are fused and representatives are reflexive and reactive. In their time in office, they react to voters' demands and adapt to public opinion while constantly being monitored. The contract between voters and elected member is being constantly re-negotiated and elected members are in permanent contact with an increasingly volatile electorate.[86] AW has potentially contributed to establishing such permanent representation–but the question of actual effects on the representatives requires more thorough empirical research.

The nature of contractual representation implies that political parties are weakened because of the necessity of the individual parliamentary candidate or member to react to voters' demands rather than consistently following and supporting the agreed and programmatically codified party line. Does AW have potential effects on party democracy? Arguing with Bruce Bimber,[87] the internet, rather than providing a technological basis for digital community building will lead to "accelerated pluralism," referring to the fact that single issue groups, activists, grass roots movements, and NGOs have flourished also due to the spread of the internet. The "internet exacerbates the proliferation of special interest groups and moral factions in a globalising world of value pluralism," because the "logics and the dynamics of pluralism ... are fully accommodated by the on-line environment."[88] The "internet has fragmented and decentralised the context in which communication occurs"[89] and has created self-referential "fragmented publics."[90] Furthermore, it has contributed to the dissolution of political hierarchies in exchange for networked social structures[91] where it is the individual much more than a single organization that matters so that the individual gains competency and power. As an unintended consequence, AW may contribute to this fragmentation affecting Germany's party democracy by allowing individual citizens to directly contact representatives so that the political party as a unifier of varying interests is circumvented and pushed into the background in the mind of electors and elected. Additionally, AW is a forum for single issues and not a forum on which broader norms, values, or ideologies underlying, for example, political parties are discussed and formed. The internet indeed could redefine the relationship between legislators and electors on a systemic level.[92]

Summary and Conclusion

This chapter introduced AW and provided an analysis of what AW could mean for represented, representatives and for the system of representation itself–here in the context of the 2009 Bundestag election. To recap, AW was designed to re-establish the supposedly broken link between representatives and represented. It is underpinned by the hope that e-democracy tools can breathe new life into democracy by providing easy and direct communication channels to representatives and by remedying information deficits to help citizens make informed decisions at the ballot box. Therefore, AW is an expression of the technological determinism which characterizes the first school of thought about ICT and its potential for building a better democracy. It is also based on the political theory that posits an informed, engaged, and active citizenry as essential for the functioning of democracy. At the same time as AW wants to support the representative system of democracy, it may also undermine party democracy because it promotes what was referred to as permanent representation. AW was not designed to fulfill the hopes put forth by proponents of the second school of thought. AW's interactivity is too constrained to promote a deliberative model of decision making and is merely aimed at allowing the represented to gain a better impression of the representatives' policy positions and to increase representatives' accountability to citizens. AW supports the representative model of democracy despite AW's makers' somewhat ambiguous discourse when they speak of a desirable shift "from a democracy made up of spectators to a democracy of participants."[93] The third school has suggested that politics will normalize the internet into its established structures. AW has certainly become accepted by politicians despite some initial suspicion and is unlikely to have led to significant changes with regards to the represented, the representatives or the representative system—although these *a priori* findings require further empirical substantiation. As demonstrated above, representatives have used AW as another means of communicating with the electorate and AW is likely to have contributed to creating an informational elite. What has become clear is that, while the internet has the potential to change some democratic practices, decreasing political participation and low electoral turnouts need to be tackled through more than technological innovations.

In the 2009 federal elections, AW is unlikely to have played a significant role in terms of influencing turnout or voter preferences. The internet as a whole was not a central instrument for political actors' campaign efforts compared to the visible role it had, for example, in Barack Obama's candidacy. While politicians in Germany were present on Facebook and StudyVZ.de, and while they used Twitter and personal web pages, the degree of interactivity was low, as was the usage of the sites by voters. A combined 10,000 Facebook "supporters" were counted for Angela Merkel and her challenger for the chancellorship, Frank-Walter Steinmeier—a number that pales in comparison to Obama's 6 million.[94] The fact that Angela Merkel has never responded to any of the hundreds of question put to her on AW but instead refers to her Chancellery's www.direktzurkanzlerin.de where questions are dealt with by the public relations division, indicates that Germany's politicians and their campaign masters are wary of or not interested in the internet's interactivity and still see it as a one-way communication device. A much more effective use of the internet was made by the electoral phenomenon of the Pirate Party–a new single-issue party mostly concerned with off-line and online civic liberties–that was at able to mobilize 13 percent of first-time male voters through an almost exclusively online campaign.[95]

To conclude, e-democracy is likely to continue to grow in importance. VAAs have increased in numbers and appear to become a marketable product because of international voter dealignment trends, increasing number of floating voters, decreasing turnouts, and party ideological convergence. They are most popular in countries with fragmented party systems such as Germany and the Netherlands, and where personalized electoral systems exist, for example in Switzerland. The spread of these systems should stimulate scholarly interest in e-democracy so that AW and similar websites undergo systematic (comparative) research.

Notes

1. I would like to express my gratitude to Dr Christian Junge and to Dr Alastair Stark whose ideas and critique were extremely helpful for writing this chapter. I would also like to thank www.abgeordnetenwatch.de for providing data.
2. Claus Offe, "Repräsentative Demokratie. Reformbedarf und Reformoptionen," *WZB-Mitteilungen* 98 (2002): 28-30.
3. Oskar Niedermayer, ed., *Die Parteien nach der Bundestagswahl 2005* (Wiesbaden, 2008).
4. "CDU hat 800 Mitglieder mehr als SPD," *Spiegel online*; available at www.spiegel.de/politik/deutschland/0,1518,568510,00.html; accessed 6 March 2010.
5. Elmar Wiesendahl, *Mitgliederparteien am Ende? Eine Kritik der Niedergangsdiskussion* (Wiesbaden, 2006).
6. Statista 1. *Statistica*; available atwww.de.statista/statistic/daten/studie/12642/umfrage/unentschlossenheit-der-waehler-in-ihrer-wahlentscheidung/; accessed 10 October 2009.
7. ARD Deutschland-Trend. Juni 2009; available at www.infratest dimap.de/uploads/media/dt0906_bericht.pdf; accessed 6 March 2010.
8. Christian Junge, "Parteien ohne Eigenschaften? Zur Diffusion organisationaler Identität von CDU und SPD aus der Perspektive ihrer Mitglieder," in *Zukunft der Mitgliederpartei*, eds., Uwe Jun, Oskar Niedermeyer, and Elmar Wiesendahl (Opladen, 2009); Martin Bell, "Weichgespült, verfärbt, verwaschen. Als Politikmarken unterscheiden sich etablierte Parteien kaum noch," *Werben und Verlaufen* 16, no. 14 (2008): 10-13; Stefano Bartolini, "Electoral and Party Competition. Analytical Dimensions and Empirical Problems" in *Political Parties. Old Concepts and New Challenges*, eds., Jose R. Montero, Richard Gunther, and Juan J. Linz (Oxford, 2002), 84-112.

9. ARD Deutschland-Trend. Juni 2008; available at http://de.statista.com/statistik/daten/ studie/758/umfrage/vertrauen-zu-den-politischen parteien/#info; accessed 6 March 2010.
10. Susan Scarrow, "Party Decline in the Party State? The Changing Environment of German Politics" in *Political Parties in Advanced Industrial Democracies*, eds., Paul Webb, David Farrell, and Ian Holliday (Oxford, 2002), 77-106.
11. Richard S. Katz and Peter Mair, "The Ascendancy of the Party in Public Office: Party Organizational Change in Twentieth-Century Democracies," in Webb et al. (see note 10), 113-136, here 24.
12. ARD Wahlmonitor; available at http://wahlarchiv.tagesschau.de/flash/?wahl=2009 09-27-BT-DE; accessed 6 March 2010; Bundeswahlleiter. (2009) *Datensätze*, available at http://www.bundeswahlleiter.de/de/bundestagswahlen/downloads/bundestags wahlergebnisse/btw_ab49_wahlbeteiligung.pdf, accessed 6 October 2009.
13. Allensbacher Berufsprestige-Skala 2008, available at www.ifd-allensbach.de/news/ prd_0802.html; accessed 11 October 2009.
14. Bertelsmann Stiftung, *Politische Partizipation in Deutschland. Ergebnisse einer repräsentativen Umfrage* (Gütersloh, 2004).
15. Thomas Gensicke, Sybille Pikot Sybille, and Sabine Geiss, *Freiwilliges Engagement in Deutschland 1999-2004* (Wiesbaden, 2006), 23.
16. Stephen Coleman and Josephine Spiller, "Exploring New Media Effects on Representative Democracy," *Journal of Legislative Studies* 9 (2003): 1-16, here 11.
17. ARD/ZDF Online-Studie 2009; available at www.ard-zdf-onlinestudie.de/fileadmin/ Online09/Eimeren1_7_09.pdf; accessed 12 November 2009.
18. James Thurman and Urs Gasser, "Three Case Studies from Switzerland: Smartvote," *Berkman Center Research Publication*, No 2009/03.03, March 2009.
19. Georg Aichholzer and Rupert Schmutzer, "Organizational challenges to the Development of Electronic Government,", Proceedings from the 11th International Workshop on Database and Expert Systems Applications, New York, 2000, 379-383.
20. Rachel Silcock, "What is e-Government?" *Parliamentary Affairs* 54 (2001): 88-91, here 88.
21. Anthony G. Wilhelm, *Democracy in the Digital Age: Challenges to Political Life in Cyberspace* (New York, 2000).
22. Ken Hacker and Jan van Dijk, *Digital Democracy. Issues of Theory and Practice* (London, 2000), 14.
23. Rosa Tsagarousianou, Damian Tambini, and Cathy Bryan, eds., *Cyber-democracy: Technology, Cities and Civic Networks* (London, 1998).
24. Thomas Hart and Dirk-Christof Stüdemann, "E-Bürgerbeteiligung zwischen Online-Chat und Bürgernetz," in *Neue Medien und Bürgerorientierung*, eds., Thomas Hart and Dirk-Christof Stüdemann (Gütersloh, 2004), 6-17.
25. Scott Wright, "Electrifying Democracy? 10 Years of Policy and Practice," *Parliamentary Affairs* 59, no. 2 (2006): 236-249.
26. Richard Davies, *The Web of Politics. The Internet's Impact no the American Political System* (Oxford, 1999).
27. Yoneki Masuda, *Managing in the Information Society* (London, 1990), 83.
28. George Lawson, *Netstate: Creating Electronic Government* (London, 1998), 55.
29. Jinbaek Kim, "A Model and Case for Supporting Participatory Public Decision Making in E-Democracy," *Group Decis Negout* (2008): 179-193, here 179.
30. Alwin Toffler, *The Third Wave* (New York, 1980); David Rios Insua, Introduction to the special issue on E-Democracy," *Group Decis Negot*, 17,(2008): 175-177; Dick Morris, "Direct Democracy and the Internet," Symposium on Internet Voting and Democracy," Loyola Law School, October 2000, *Loyola of Los Angeles Law Review* 34 no. 3 (2001); Claus Leggewie and Christa Maar, *Internet und Politik. Von der Zuschauer- zur Beteiligungsdemokratie* (Cologne, 1998).

31. Benjamin Barber, *Strong Democracy: Participatory Democracy for a New Age* (Berkeley, 1984); Theodore Becker, "Teledemocracy: Bringing Power Back to the People," *Futurist* 15, no. 6 (1981): 6-20.
32. Jeroen van Hoven, "E-Democracy, E-Contestation and the Monitorial Citizen," *Ethics and Information Technology* 7 (2005): 51-59, here 53.
33. Geoffrey E. Kersten, "E-Democracy and Participatory Decision Processes: Lessons from E-Negotiation Experiments," *Journal of Multicriteria Decision Analysis* 12, nos. 2/3 (2003): 127-143.
34. Hacker and van Dijk (see note 22).
35. Kim (see note 29), 180; Ananda Mitra, "Marginal Voices in Cyberspace," *New Media and Society* 3 (2001): 29-48.
36. Jürgen Habermas, *Structural Transformation of the Public Sphere* (Cambridge, 1989).
37. Damian Tambini, "New Media and Democracy. The Civic Networking Movement," *New Media & Society* 1 (1999): 105-329.
38. Reima Suomi, "E-Democracy in Action: Websites of Finnish Members of Parliaments," *The Journal of Global Business Issues* (2008): 63-69, here 64.
39. van den Hoven (see note 32).
40. Michael Schudson, *The Good Citizen. A History of American Civil Life* (Cambridge, 1998).
41. van den Hoven (see note 32), 57.
42. Wright (see note 25), 237.
43. Coleman and Spiller (see note 16), 2.
44. AW 3. (2009) *Moderationskodex*; available at www.abgeordnetenwatch.de/moderations_codex-766-0.html; accessed 13 October 2009.
45. AW Interview 1, 29 October 2009.
46. "Politikportal sperrt Thüringer NPD-Bewerber," *Südthüringer Zeitung* 20 August 2009.
47. "Gregor Hackmack, einer der beiden Gründer von abgeordnetenwatch.de, im Gespräch;" available at www.politische-bildung-bayern.net/content/view/414/41; accessed 7 October 2009.
48. Ashoka, *About.* Online available from www.ashoka.org/about; accessed 11 October 2009.
49. Marc Winkelmann, "Animateur der Demokratie," *Handelsblatt* 16 January 2009, 2; AW 2. *Finanzierung*; available at www.abgeordnetenwatch.de/finanzierung-6320.html; accessed 12 October 2009; AW Interview 1.
50. Hackmack (see note 47).
51. AW Interview 2, 15 October 2009.
52. AW 1. *Wir über uns*; available ar www.abgeordnetenwatch.de/wir_ueber_uns-150 0.html; accessed 12 November 2009.
53. Eleni Klotsikas, "Stimmenfang im Netz. Die Rolle des Internets im Wahlkampf," *Deutschlandradio* (2009), available at www.dradio.de/dlf/sendungen/marktundmedien/1033121/; accessed 13 October 2009; AW 4. (2009) *Newsletter* 11/2009.
54. AW 2. Zahlen zur Bundestagswahl; available at www.abgeordnetenwatch.de/bundestagswahl-951-0.html; accessed 6 March 2010.
55. AW 3. Data from AW, obtained December 2009.
56. Christian Heise, "Beispiel für e-Partizipation in Deutschland: abgeordnetenwatch.de," (2008), available at www.e-demokratie.org/so-sollte-es-sein/beispiel-fur-e partizipation-in-deutschland-abgeordnetenwatchde; accessed 26 November 2009; AW 2 (see note 54).
57. Bruce Bimber and Richard Davis, *Campaigning Online: The Internet in U.S. Elections* (Oxford, 2003); Bruce Bimber, "The Internet and political Transformation: Populism, Community and Accelerated Pluralism," *Polity*, XXI, no. 1 (1998): 133-166.
58. Stefan Marschall, "Idee und Wirkung des Wahl-O-Mat," *Aus Politik und Zeitgeschichte* B 51-52 (2005) 41-46; Pippa Norris, *Digital Divide: Civic Engagement, Information Poverty, and the Internet Worldwide* (New York, 2001); Doris A. Graber, "The 'New' Media and Politics. What Does the Future Hold?" PS: *Political Science and Politics* 29 (1996): 33-36.
59. Bimber 1998 (see note 57), 3.

60. Ross Ferguson and G. Barry Griffiths, "Thin Democracy? Parliamentarians, Citizens and the Influence on Blogging on Political Engagement," *Parliamentary Affairs* 59, no. 2 (2006):,366-374; Lawrence Pratchett, Melvin Wingfield, and Rabia Karakaya Polat, "Barriers to E-Democracy: Local Government Experiences and Responses," *Local e-Democracy National Project* (2006), available at www.dmu.ac.uk/Images/dmu3_research percent20report percent204-3 percent20_formatted__tcm6-6306.pdf; accessed 12 October 2009; Michael Cross, "E-Democracy: Tied up in Red Tape," *The Guardian*, 22 February 2006, available at www.guardian.co.uk/technology/2006/feb/22/egovernment. epublic; accessed 19 November 2009; P. Evans, "How Local Authorities can Motivate Councillors to Update Their Websites and How They Can be Promoted to the Public," The Councillor Info project (2006), available at www.popteltechnology.coop/Shared_ ASP_Files/GFSR.asp?NodeID=89255&AttributeName=FileName; accessed 13 October 2009; Zahid Parvez, "Informatization of Local Democracy. A Structuration Perspective," *Information Polity* 11, no. 1 (2006): 67-83.
61. Coleman and Spiller (see note 16), 10.
62. Arthur Lupia and Matthew McCubbins, "The Institutional Foundations of Political Competence: How Citizens Learn What They Need to Know," in *Elements of Reason: cognition, choice, and the bounds of rationality*, eds., Arthur Lupia, Mathew D. McCubbins, Samuel L. Popkin (Cambridge, 2000), 47-66.
63. Georg Lutz, "The Unresolved Democratic Dilemma: Information, Cues and Ignorance," Paper presented at ECPR Conference Marburg, Germany 18-21 September 2003; Andreas Ladner, Gabriele Felder, and Jan Fivz, "Are Voting Advice Applications More Than Toys? First Findings on Impact and Accountability of VAAs," Paper presented at conference on "Voting Advice Applications between Charlatanism and Political Science," University of Antwerp, 16 May 2008.
64. Kate Kenski and Natalie Jomini Stroud, "Connections Between Internet Use and Political Efficacy, Knowledge, and Participation," *Journal of Broadcasting and Electronic Media*, 50, no. 2 (2006): 173-192; Caroline Tolbert and Ramona McNeal,"Unravelling the Effects of the Internet on Political Participation," *Political Research Quarterly* 56, no. 2 (2003): 175-185; Lori Weber, Alysha Loumakis, and James Bergman, "Who participates and Why? An Analysis of Citizens on the Internet and the Mass Public," *Social Science Computer Review* 21 (2003): 26-42.
65. Tolbert and McNeal (see note 64), 175.
66. Stefaan Walgrave, Michiel Nuytemans, and Koen Pepermans, "Selecting Statements for VAAs: the Need for Benchmarking. Paper at Voting Advice Applications (VAAs)," Paper presented at conference on "Voting Advice Applications between Charlatanism and Political Science," University of Antwerp, 16 May 2008; Marschall (see note 58).
67. Marschall (see note 58).
68. Bharat Mehra, Cecelia Merkel, and Ann P. Bishop,."The Internet for Empowerment of Minority and Marginalized Users," *New Media and Society* 6 (2004):, 781–802; Nicholas Jankowski and Martine van Selm,"The Promises and Practice of Public Debate in Cyberspace" in Hacker and van Dijk (see note 22), 149-165.
69. Corinna Di Gennaro and William Dutton, "The Internet and the Public: Online and Offline Political Participation in the United Kingdom," *Parliamentary Affairs*, 59, no. 2 (2006): 299-311; Sylvia Korupp and Marc Szydlik, "Causes and Trends of the Digital Divide," *European Sociological Review* 21, no. 4 (2005): 409-422; Rachel Gibson, Wainer Lusoli, and Stephen Ward, "Online Participation in the UK: Testing a Contextualised Model of Internet Effects," *British Journal for Politics and International Relations* 7, no. 4 (2005): 561-583.
70. European Commission, *Digital Divide Forum Report. Broadband Access and Public Support in under-served areas* (Brussels, 2005).
71. Steffen Albrecht, "Whose Voice is heard in the Virtual Public Sphere? A study of participation and representation in online deliberation," Paper at Research Symposium at Balliol College 17-20 September 2003.

72. Ibid., 4.

73. Zahid Parvez, "E-Democracy: From the Perspective of Local Elected Members," *International Journal of Electronic Government Research* 4, no. 3 (2008): 20-35.

74. Peter Lösche, "Parteienstaat in der Krise: Überlegungen nach 50 Jahren Bundesrepublik Deutschland," Vortrag und Diskussion einer Veranstaltung des Gesprächskreises Geschichte der Friedrich-Ebert-Stiftung, Bonn, 19 August 1999; Hans-Jürgen Puhle, "Still the Age of Catch-Allism? Volksparteien and Parteienstaat in Crisis and Re-equilibration," *Political Parties* 27 (2002): 58-84.

75. Claus Leggewie and Christoph Bieber, "Demokratie 2.0: Wie tragen elektronische Medien zur demokratischen Erneuerung bei?" in Demokratisierung der Demokratie: Diagnosen und Reformvorschläge , ed., Claus Offe (Frankfurt/Main, 2003), 124-151.

76. Constantin Binder, "Wo (fast) jeder Politiker ansprechbar ist," *Neue Osnabrücker Zeitung*, 21 September 2009, 6.

77. Thomas Zittel, "Political Representation in the Networked Society. The Amerciansiation of European Systems of Responsible Party Government," *The Journal of Legislative Studies* 9, no. 3 (2003): 32-53; Philip Norton, "Four Models of Political Representation: British MPs and the USE of ICET," *Journal of Legislative Studies* 13, no. 3 (2007): 354-369.

78. Hackmack (see note 47).

79. Congress Online, "Constituents and Your Web Site: What citizens want to see on congressional web sites," October 2001, available at www.cmfweb.org/storage/cmfweb/documents/CMF_Pubs/constituentsandwebsites.pdf/; accessed 6 March 2010, 5.

80. Parvez (see note 73), 26.

81. Norton (see note 32).

82. Coleman and Spiller (see note 16).

83. Ibid., 12.

84. Bimber 1998 (see note 57).

85. van den Hoven (see note 32), 52.

86. Andy Williamson, *MPs Online. Connecting with Constituents* (London, 2009), 2.

87. Christina Holtz-Bacha, "Fragmentierung der Gesellschaft durch das Internet?" in *Demokratie und Internet*, eds., Winand Gellner and Fritz von Korff (Nomos, 1998), 219-226.

88. Volker Leib, "Wissenschaftsnetze und Buergernetze. Vom selbstgesteuerten Internet zur elektronischen Demokratie?" in Gellner and von Korff (see note 90), 81-94.

89. Zittel (see note 77).

90. AW interview 2, 15 October 2009.

91. Paul Ronzheimer, "Das Wettrüsten der Parteien im Internet beginnt," *Bild Zeitung*, 27 April 2009; available at www.bild.de/BILD/politik/wahlen/04/27/internet-wahlkampf/parteien-wettruesten-bundestagswahl-wahlen.html; accessed 11 March 2010.

92. Manuela Glaab and Michael Weigel, "Die Bundestagswahl 2009," *Note du CERFA*, 29.

ᴛHE ROLE OF FOREIGN POLICY IN THE
2009 CAMPAIGN AND THE BLACK-YELLOW FUTURE

• • • • • • • • • • • • • •

Jan Techau

The General Backdrop

The 2009 general election campaign in Germany widely was perceived as having been one of the dullest and least controversial political contests in the history of the Federal Republic of Germany. Throughout the entire campaign, very little polarization was observed between the six major contending political parties or the two frontrunners for the office of chancellor, Angela Merkel (Christian Democratic Union, CDU) and Frank Walter Steinmeier (Social Democratic Party, SPD). Correspondingly, voter turnout was a mere 72.2 percent–an all-time low for national elections in Germany–reflecting the low mobilization power of this race. Before looking at the specific reasons for this phenomenon, it is pertinent to look at the more general forces that shaped this campaign.

First, there was a general lack of appetite for change (*Wechselstimmung*) in the electorate,[1] making it difficult for political parties to frame this election as truly decisive. This, to a large extent, explains the low turnout. Secondly, the main political opponents, the conservative Christian Democrats and the center-left Social Democrats were locked into a grand coalition between 2005 and 2009, which made it difficult, especially for the SPD as the coalition's junior partner, to undertake a full-fledged frontal attack on the very political partner with whom they had shared responsibility for government policies during the preceding parliamentary term. Finally, Chancellor Merkel made a strategic decision to adopt a markedly presidential campaign style, carefully avoiding controversy and staying above the political fray, thereby making herself all but immune to political attack.

Given these wider circumstances, political issues rarely took center stage in the campaign, leaving commentators, strategists, and analysts wondering where all the content had gone.[2] Against this backdrop, it was especially difficult for foreign policy issues to stand out as points of controversy. Add to this the long-standing German political tradition of giving low priority to foreign policy in national campaigns,[3] and it becomes abundantly clear why, from the outset, 2009 was not the year for foreign policy controversies to feature prominently in the campaign, let alone making them decisive for the outcome of the election. After this brief overview of the more general factors that shaped the election, it is now important to look at the specific factors that limited the role of foreign policy as a campaign issue in 2009.

Why Foreign Policy Did Not Play in 2009

Germany's Version of "Don't Ask, don't Tell"

Numerous studies of (West) Germany after 1949 have stated that the newly founded state—in a deliberate attempt to learn from Germany's responsibilities for two world wars and the Holocaust—was able to create a broad political consensus on foreign affairs, based on political self-restraint, skepticism vis-à-vis all things military, and a firm commitment to international multilateralism. Some scholars call this the "never again, never alone" mentality.[4] This consensus thoroughly permeated the emerging nation's psyche and remains intact to this day. In essence, this posture rests on a "three-plus-three" pillar consensus. The first three pillars represent Germany's multilateral embeddedness, i.e., the country's leading role in the European Union, its firm support for the United Nations, and its military integration into the North Atlantic Treaty Organization. The additional three pillars include the nation's key bilateral relationships, namely, close ties with the United States, reconciliation and real friendship with France, and a pragmatic, yet distanced relationship with the Soviet Union/Russia. By the mid 1970s, after the successful implementation of Willy Brandt's Ostpolitik and the accession of both German states to the United Nations, all elements of this posture were firmly in place and had been fully absorbed by the relevant, mainstream political forces and by the public in general.

Then, in the mid 1990s, the newly unified—and now fully sovereign—country was asked to develop a more proactive stance on international affairs, most notably in its approach to the deployment of military forces abroad.[5] Ever since then, successive governments, regardless of their ideological background, have changed Germany's foreign policy significantly, yet went to great lengths to keep these changes rhetorically within the "three-plus-three" pillar consensus. Germany has since become more assertive in the EU, thereby losing its reputation as the "good European" who would regularly forego on its own interests to further the greater good of the European project. Examples for a more unilateral pursuit of German national interests are the measures taken to protect the German car industry from EU environmental regulation (starting in the late 1990s and continued to this day), the country's undermining of a common European energy policy by pursuing strong bilateral relations in this sector with Russia, its reluctance to develop a meaningful Common Foreign and Security Policy (CFSP), its unilateral condemnation of the United States' war effort in Iraq 2003, and, more recently, Germany's reluctance and unilateral actions taken during the international financial and economic crisis 2008-2010. More generally, the country has also lost its erstwhile position as the leading member state to transfer EU legislation into national law.

Moreover, it has slowly but surely expanded its international military footprint, most notably in the 1999 Kosovo campaign and, starting in 2002, in Afghanistan. But despite some minor flare-ups of controversy, this process of change was largely accepted by the public, although it was never fully explained or justified by the political leadership. A widespread public debate on Germany's geostrategic interests, obligations, and capabilities was never held. Although, step-by-step, the concepts that framed the foreign policy consensus—Germany's guilty past, the Cold War, the allies' guardianship over the not fully sovereign states—either disappeared or became less relevant, the public kept embracing the old consensus as a sacrosanct truth that could and must not be challenged.

The public was still beholden to this mentality during the 2009 election season (as well as afterwards, as if to shield itself from unavoidable but inconvenient global developments). Consequently, voters never requested political parties to present any vision of Germany's foreign affairs, and, in turn, politicians were only too eager to avoid these issues altogether, especially regarding the escalating hostilities in Afghanistan. This silent agreement to not touch upon the post 1949 consensus was the German foreign policy equivalent of "don't ask don't tell," serving both the electorate and those running for office. Indeed, during the campaign of 2009, this tacit agreement did its part in keeping foreign policy issues from playing a significant role, despite the large number of pressing and imminent issues that require debate.

"I'm Against It, but It's Not Important"

If the public indeed had an inkling that the times were changing, they surely did not want to be reminded of it. Foreign policy issues were not important enough to register as a priority on the list of things about which voters were concerned. Various polls taken throughout the election year regularly and consistently indicated that the topics on voters' minds were the economy, jobs, and other issues directly related to their economic well-being and standard of living. To illustrate, a Politbarometer poll published on 3 July 2009 indicated that the most important issues on peoples' minds were unemployment (with 48 percent of all voters expressing concern), the financial crisis (25 percent), the general situation of the economy (25 percent), disillusionment with politics (8 percent), education (7 percent), inflation (6 percent), taxes (6 percent), healthcare (5 percent), and retirement entitlements (5 percent). Foreign policy issues did not at all feature on this list compiled from answers to an open question. So, while polls have regularly shown high levels of popular disillusionment with the Afghanistan mission of the German Bundeswehr,[6] the issue itself was not important enough to shape voters' opinions on what party or candidate to vote for in the Bundestag election.[7]

Similarly, in a popular annual poll focusing on what issues Germans are fearful of (conducted by a major insurance company and met with large media resonance each year), foreign policy related issues, once again, did not feature prominently. The highest ranking foreign policy issue was terrorism, ranking ninth on a list of sixteen issues, with 46 percent of Germans saying that they feared it.[8] Fear number one was economic meltdown, garnering 66 percent of the vote, with unemployment (65 percent) and inflation (63 percent) following closely behind. On this list, war–the only other foreign policy-related issue of notable relevance–was ranked thirteenth with 31 percent of those polled saying they were fearful of it, a comparatively low number. It is no exaggeration to state that low interest in foreign policy is a key part of, if not a pre-condition for, the national postwar consensus described above.[9]

With such low importance attached to foreign policy by voters, the parties' campaign strategists decided early on that issues in this field were not vote winners and could be treated as fringe issues at best. To turn a foreign policy issue into a vote producer against this backdrop, if not entirely impossible from the outset, would have required considerable effort, money, and political capital—all of which are perpetually in scarce supply. Of course, all party campaign platforms included numerous statements on foreign policy,[10] but in public—be it in speeches, on campaign posters, or in television advertisements—most parties made but rudimentary mention of foreign policy. The notable exception was the Left Party, which vigorously attempted to cash in on the unpopularity of the Afghanistan mission by demanding the immediate withdrawal of German troops from the Hindu Kush—without significant resonance or success.

They Were in It Together

Given the SPD's role as the junior partner in the grand coalition that had governed Germany since the 2005 Bundestag election, it should have been the Social Democrats' task to adopt an offensive strategy in order to make up for their weaker strategic political position. Nevertheless, the party never managed to pull it off. In the foreign policy field, a more aggressive strategy would never have had a chance in the first place. Psychologically, the situation was very difficult for Steinmeier because he and Merkel were deemed an efficient and harmonious foreign policy team with little or no real traceable policy differences between them. Most visibly, they had excelled in pulling off a hugely successful dual presidency of the European Union and the G8 in 2007. More importantly, however, was the fact that they both were stalwart supporters of Germany's engagement in Afghanistan. Steinmeier adamantly fended off all attempts from the sizeable pacifist wing of his party to change the SPD's position on the issue. In effect, on the only major foreign policy issue with the potential to generate a relevant debate during the campaign, the candidates stood firmly by each others' side. For the CDU, Steinmeier's unwavering support was hugely important because it effectively prevented the SPD from playing the "peace card" as it had done seven years earlier on the Iraq question. This old SPD strategy of exploiting the lingering pacifist preferences of the electorate by portraying the CDU as wobbly in its commitment to peace, had been the conservative's nightmare since the last-minute defeat of Edmund Stoiber by the masterful Gerhard Schröder in 2002.

In 2009 by contrast, Steinmeier did not waver, and his commitment held firm even after the much-criticized Bundeswehr-led airstrike on fuel trucks hijacked by the Taliban in the Northern Afghan town of Kunduz on 4 September 2009. After the news had broken about the Kunduz incident, observers held their breath: would Steinmeier pull a Schröder? But the special session of parliament, held a few days after the strikes, made clear that 2009 really was not 2002. The peace card was not played. Steinmeier, just as Chancellor Merkel (and all other speakers with the exception of those from the Left Party) defended the German involvement in Afghanistan and criticized all cries for immediate withdrawal as irresponsible. Raison d'état had prevailed over narrow party interest.

Or had it? It is very likely that Steinmeier acted according to his convictions. But even if he had been tempted to play the peace card, it would not have been a politically viable option—too strong was his and the party's established position on Afghanistan. A sudden change after the Kunduz incident most likely would have played out very badly for the SPD, being perceived as a blatantly populist case of flip-flopping, most certainly causing the party more harm than good. Not only would Steinmeier have lost all personal credibility, but his party also would have plunged immediately into nerve-wrecking, self-destructive turmoil. Had the SPD ever intended to play the peace card on Afghanistan, by the time Kunduz came along it was much too late. That strategy would have required a carefully managed change of position over a prolonged period of time. But the SPD was not tempted this time. SPD and CDU, Merkel and Steinmeier—were in it together and so the issue was muted.

Europe? Not Again, Please.

Another significant part of what could have been a foreign policy agenda during the 2009 campaign had already been used up earlier in the election year in another nation-wide poll. On 7 June 2009, Germany had held its part of the European Parliament (EP) elections. The preceding campaign had been short and not very substantial on the issues themselves, but it led to a general saturation of the electorate concerning international and especially European questions. Of course, by all reasonable standards, Europe should have remained a very relevant issue even after the June elections. The question of whether the new Lisbon Treaty would be ratified and could enter into force was far from clear by 27 September. Even more importantly, just a few weeks after the EP elections, the German Constitutional Court handed down a much-debated verdict on the Lisbon Treaty and its compatibility with the German Basic Law (*Grundgesetz*). The ruling, coming on top of a lingering sentiment that Germany people and elites had lost its appetite for further integration, raised a number of very substantial questions concerning Germany's commitment to the integration process, the limits of this process, and the nature of the EU as an institution.[11]

Yet, none of this reverberated in the election campaign. When Chancellor Merkel and Foreign Minister Steinmeier held their televised "duel"

(*Kanzlerduell*) on 13 September 2009, the term "Europe" was not mentioned once in the seventy-five minute debate. The earlier European election had drained all things European from the campaign–this after a relatively prolonged period of fatigue with the European project following the failed attempt to ratify a constitution in 2005 and wavering support for the traditional pro-Europe policy reflex–and it was certainly not the desire of the major parties to revive a debate that had already been held and had so visibly bored the electorate. It was as if the parties feared to associate themselves with an issue about which voters increasingly felt irritated and uncomfortable.

The World Kept Silent

In the run-up to the 2008 Presidential elections in the United States, many analysts (this author included), predicted that whatever new administration would take office in Washington, it would most certainly ask its European partners to share a larger part of the burden in the allies' joint global stabilizing efforts. This became largely true in the subsequent months, with one notable exception: the Obama administration did not publicly approach the German government for increased contributions (for example in Afghanistan) until some time after the election. Much speculation emerged about a possible deal that had been sealed between Merkel and Obama in order to keep the pressure off during the Bundestag campaign. It will probably never be known whether this kind of arrangement really existed, but the fact that no official request came from either the United States or NATO helped to keep foreign policy issues off the agenda, just as the major parties (again with the exception of the Left party) had intended it to be.

And then, of course, there was also sheer luck. The international scene, as it developed throughout the campaign weeks, remained largely uneventful and devoid of major international incidents. Throughout the campaign, no development outside Germany interfered with the already uneventful domestic campaign. Most certainly, the parties were quite happy about this, as it did not force them to create hastily fabricated ad hoc positions on unfolding events which could later haunt them. It certainly kept the contest calmer. But it also robbed the nation of a chance to embark on the much-needed debate about German interests and strategic outlook at a time when voters might actually bother to listen. For the development of a more mature German public discussion and a better understanding of its international role, the election campaign of 2009 was a squandered opportunity.

Accepting Westerwelle

Even though, as was discussed above, foreign policy is not a priority topic for German voters at any time, the issue of who would occupy the position of foreign minister traditionally has attracted significant public attention. In almost all German coalitions, the foreign minister also took over the largely ceremonial, yet symbolically important post of vice chancellor, i.e., the official first in line in case of absence or incapacity of the chancellor. Moreover, the job as Germany's first diplomat holds considerable prestige–especially given the stature of previous office holders such as Walter Scheel, Hans-Dietrich Genscher, and Joschka Fischer. As a consequence, the leader of the coalition's smaller party, regardless of where his policy credentials might lie, usually tends to opt for the glamorous job in the Foreign Office (*Auswärtiges Amt*). The decision of Free Democrat leader Guido Westerwelle to pick this post after the 2009 election is a case in point. The prominence of this position is clearly the most visible insignia of the importance and power of the government's junior element. Furthermore, foreign ministers tend to have very high popularity ratings. Theirs is not a law-making field of government with its permanent redefinition of taxes, entitlements, social transfers, and the like. Consequently, decisions by the foreign minister rarely intrude into peoples' lives in any direct, practical way and are not usually laden with painful consequences. Also, the position allows its occupant to develop a dignified, almost presidential aura by enabling him or (potentially) her to keep a distance from the daily grind of domestic political trench warfare, thus opening the door to a post-career career as elder statesmen–an option few other (more politicized and polarizing) cabinet ministers have. These are enough reasons, one might think, to make this important personnel question a relevant campaign issue.

In the 2009 campaign, the question of who would be Germany's next foreign minister boiled down to two options: either a re-appointed Steinmeier (as there was never really a chance that he could become chancellor himself), or a newly appointed Westerwelle (who subsequently did take the job). While Steinmeier's qualification for the job was beyond doubt, Westerwelle's persona and policy background led to some questions as to whether he would be the right candidate for the post. Speculation spread that he might be more interested in an economics related portfolio, possibly along the lines of those custom-made so-called super-ministries that Oskar Lafontaine had briefly run in the early days of the Schröder government after 1998, or the one that Edmund Stoiber had envisioned but then ultimately rejected after the formation of the Grand Coalition in 2005. Many observers thought that this would be a much more fitting portfolio for Westerwelle and his party with their well-established economic profile. But the doubts and speculations never led to a real debate, and ultimately, voters seemed to be able to live with the idea of Westerwelle as their foreign minister. Therefore, the minor, but not irrelevant, issue of who could best represent Germany did not stir up any kind of meaningful, behavior-shaping controversy in this campaign cycle.

What's ahead: Why 2009 Was the Last Inward-looking Campaign

As argued above, foreign policy did not play a significant role in the German election campaign of 2009. But that campaign was most certainly the last one in which the political parties could afford to repress the issues. Numerous external and internal forces will change the political landscape in ways that forcefully will put foreign policy on the agenda–and turn it into one of the handful of meaningful and divisive issues contested in future Bundestag elections.

First, both NATO and the EU (in its post Lisbon shape), the cornerstones of Germany's foreign policy posture, are currently undergoing substantial processes of change. This process will lead, on the one hand, to a more proactive role for the European Union as an international player, with all the internal frictions this will entail. By developing new capabilities, and by creating the internal competition of ideas over who will dominate Europe's new policies, the EU simply will force Germany to engage more actively both intellectually and politically. This import of competition from the EU will force the Germans to develop their own positions, thereby helping to create the kind of publicly accessible market-place of ideas which does currently exist in the country. The frantic attempts by the EU (and by Germany both inside and outside the EU) to manage the fallout from the financial and economic crisis overshadowed much of the German debate, but did not yet translate into larger foreign policy debates. It was, however, a not-so-subtle reminder of Germany's position as a strategic player in international affairs, a reminder which will most likely be issued more frequently in the coming months and years.

NATO's development, albeit markedly different from that of the European Union, will have a similar effect. The new strategic concept, to be presented in the fall of 2010, will, in one way or another, force Germans to ponder their foreign policy posture–regardless of whether NATO will adopt a more global agenda or return to its traditional, more confined tasks of regional territorial defense. Both German leaders and the public will have to adapt, partake in the new game, and cope with the controversies this will create at home. At the same time, both in NATO and the EU, Germany will be asked to provide more money, hardware and software (i.e., constructive and creative political thinking), thereby intensifying the newly emerging domestic debate even further.

Second, Germany's involvement in the Afghanistan campaign will continue to change the way the country thinks, speaks, and evaluates the importance of foreign policy. The debate over whether the country should be engaged in the Hindu Kush has already re-inserted the concept of the national interest into the public German debate, even though this is a fairly recent development. The Kunduz airstrike also has triggered a debate over what Germany wants to stand for, what risks military deployments entail, and how the discourse over these issues should be conducted. Also, the new German Defense Minister, Karl-Theodor zu Guttenberg, made it a point to change the vocabulary and the intensity of the conversation about the "war" in Afghanistan and Germany's role in it. It is only a matter of time until this new disposition will ripen into a full-fledged debate over German foreign policy and thus turn it into a relevant subject on the campaign trail.

Third, two major strategic questions with profound impact on the country most certainly will become virulent over the next few years. One of them is the question of Turkish accession to the European Union. Although this issue is a matter of highest geopolitical significance, Germany has not debated it as such. Instead, questions of the EU's internal functioning and the challenges to German identity posed by 77 million Turks inside the European Union have dominated the discourse. The closer the EU will get to decision time on the Turkey issue, the more potential will the issue have for German political parties to employ it during campaigns. The other issue is Israel, which, in its own way, will have a serious impact on the way Germany thinks about its international obligation. Chancellor Merkel effectively has given a firm bilateral security guarantee to Israel,[12] the only such guarantee ever issued by the Federal Republic. With the Iran nuclear standoff nearing decision time, and with the overall situation in the Middle East deteriorating, Germany could very well be reminded of this guarantee some day soon. Inevitably, a potential entanglement in the region will heat up the domestic debate—especially in light the historical responsibility for the Jewish state that Germany has made a *raison d'état* and which could easily get in conflict with the widespread sympathy to the Palestinian cause (especially, but not only, on the left).

Finally, the German party system is currently undergoing a major transition and will continue to do so for some time. In this changing process, the Social Democrats have so far turned out to suffer most heavily. In order to regain their structural ability to form governments under their leadership, the SPD will be forced carefully to alter some of its core policy positions. This might well lead to reconsideration of its foreign policy postures, especially given the powerful pacifist mainstream of its party base (and the continued pressure from the Left Party). Rather sooner than later, this could lead to a breaking-out of the current foreign policy consensus, thereby opening up the chances for debate where there was none before.

All of the political factors mentioned in this section will be hitting the German political market at roughly the same time. In all likelihood, this will turn foreign policy into a fruitful field to cultivate for party strategists and candidates. It might finally turn it into a subject on which parties could win–or lose–significant numbers of voters. Parties would then have to consider investing significant resources in their foreign policy apparatus. If so, the culture of political competition in Germany could change significantly. It remains to be seen, however, whether more debate will also mean better debate, and whether the country will be able to debate foreign policy in a way that is considered normal in other policy fields: lively, engaged, mature, heated and polemic at times, but always competitive and hopefully with a fair chance that the best idea might prevail.

Notes

1. For an in-depth analysis of the results and voters' motivations in the 2009 elections, see Matthias Jung, Yvone Schroth, and Andrea Wolf, "Regierungswechsel ohne Wechselstimmung," *Aus Politik und Zeitgeschichte* 51 (2009): 12-19.
2. See Renate Köcher, "Wahlkampf ohne Leidenschaft," *Frankfurter Allgemeine Zeitung*, 9 September 2009, 5. According to a pre-election poll by Forschungsgruppe Wahlen, only one third of German voters thought a more polarizing campaign was necessary. See Forschungsgruppe Wahlen, Politbarometer September I 2009, 4 September 2009.
3. There are two notable exceptions. In the 1972 election, Chancellor Willy Brandt's Ostpolitik, designed to initiate rapprochement with the Soviet Union, the German Democratic Republic, and West Germany's Eastern neighbors during the Cold War, was a major bone of contention; and in the 2002 election it was Chancellor Gerhard Schröder who used the looming Iraq War to mobilize voters in a cunningly orchestrated last-minute rally to beat narrowly his conservative contender Edmund Stoiber.

4. See: Hanns W. Maull, "Germany and the Use of Force: Still a Civilian Power?" Paper prepared for the Workshop on Force, Order and Global Governance–An Assessment of U.S., German and Japanese Approaches, The Brookings Institution, Washington, DC, 1-2 July 1999. The formula of "never again, never alone" is now so widely accepted that it is being used in official German government information on the nature of German foreign policy. See, for example, the website of Germany's diplomatic missions in the United States: http://www.germany.info/Vertretung/usa/en/05__Foreign__Policy__ State/02__Foreign__Policy/03/__Law.html; accessed on 25 May 2010.

5. No longer exempt from the demands of the international community and its allies in NATO and in the EU, Germany was forced to reconsider its niche-existence in international affairs. Military deployments in, for example, Cambodia, Somalia, Bosnia, Kosovo, and Afghanistan followed. Both Gulf Wars demanded a political positioning of unified Germany. Similarly, the drive towards a more cohesive EU foreign policy led to a–so far incomplete–learning process in terms of Germany's strategic interests and responsibilities. For a detailed analysis both of Germany's culture of restraint and the ongoing process of change, see: Anja Dalgaard-Nielsen, "The Test of Strategic Culture: Germany, Pacifism and Pre-emptive Strikes," *Security Dialogue* 3 (2005): 339-359; and Arthur Hoffmann and Kerry Longhurst, "German Strategic Culture in Action," *Contemporary Security Policy* 2 (1999): 31-49.

6. Two weeks before the election, a Politbarometer poll found that 53 percent of German voters thought the mission was not a good idea, with 44 percent supporting the deployment. See Politbarometer September II 2009, 11 September 2009.

7. In an opinion poll conducted by Forsa for *Stern* magazine, only 3 percent of voters stated that a political party's position on Afghanistan was a "very important" factor in their voting decision, while 12 percent said it was "important," 23 percent that it was "less important," and 57 percent claimed that it was "not important at all." The poll was published on 16 September 2009, i.e., eleven days before the elections. See: http://www.stern.de/wahl-2009/umfrage/stern-umfrage-zu-afghanistan-deutsche-fuer-abzug-und-fuer-jung-1509178.html; accessed 24 April 2010.

8. See "Die Ängste der Deutschen 2009," *R+V Versicherung*, 3 September 2009.

9. According to annual studies conducted by the German armed forces' Institute for Social Research, a solid majority of Germans (73 percent in 2006) regularly states they are either "interested," "very interested" or "exceptionally interested" in international security issues. This, however, does not translate into strong support for a more proactive German foreign policy. When asked whether they were in favor of a more active German role abroad, only about 48 percent say yes (the average number of those answering yes between 1996 and 2009). See: Sozialwissenschaftliches Institut der Bundeswehr, "Sicherheits- und verteidigungspolitisches Meinungsklima in Deutschland," January 2010; available at http://www.sowi.bundeswehr.de/portal/a/swinstbw/kcxml/04_ Sj9SPykssy0xPLMnMz0vM0Y_QjzKLNzSKNw4OMQZJgjnmLl76kQjhoJRUfV-P_ NxUfW_9AP2C3IhyR0dFRQDurZmv/delta/base64xml/L3dJdyEvd0ZNQUFz QUMvNElVRS82XzEyXzNTVDM!; accessed 24 May 2010.

10. A useful survey comparing the foreign policy positions of the major German parties can be found at http://aussenpolitik.net/themen/de_wahljahr/topthemen_deutscher_ aussenpolitik _im_bundestagswahlkampf/; accessed 12 April 2010.

11. In its ruling, the court, for the first time, established concrete limits of German participation in the EU integration process. It defined the core elements of German sovereignty, arguing that under the current Basic Law, further integration could not infringe upon this core. The court, however, did not bar completely the integration of Germany into a potential EU super state. It only stated that this was not possible under the current constitutional arrangements. It were not so much these technicalities that caused pro-Europeanists to speak of an "integration-averse" ruling, but rather the overall hostility of the ruling's tone and the court's far-reaching self-empowerment as future arbiter of

Germany's EU integration policy (thereby, according to some critical observers, over-stepping the boundary into the purely political realm of decision-making).

12. See the speeches Merkel gave before the Knesset on 18 March 2008, and before the joint session of the United States Congress on 3 November 2009. Both are available at www.bundeskanzlerin.de; accessed 24 May 2010.

$\mathcal{C}$ONTRIBUTORS

•••••••••••••••

CLAY CLEMENS teaches Government at the College of William and Mary. His work on the CDU/CSU has appeared in *German Politics and Society, German Politics*, and *West European Politics*. He wishes to thank the International Association for the Study of German Politics and the German Academic Exchange Service for the vital role both played in making it possible to conduct research for this article.

DAVID P. CONRADT is Professor of Political Science at East Carolina University. He has also held joint appointments at universities in Konstanz, Mannheim, Cologne and Dresden. Among his recent publications are *The German Polity* (New York, 2009), *Politics in Europe* (London, 2010), *A Precarious Victory: Schröder and the German elections of 2002* (New York, 2005), and *Power Shift in Germany: The 1998 Election and the End of the Kohl Era* (New York, 2000). He has also published a variety of articles and monographs on German political culture, parties and elections.

LOUISE K. DAVIDSON-SCHMICH is Associate Professor of Political Science at the University of Miami in Coral Gables, Florida. She is the author of *Becoming Party Politicians: Eastern German State Legislators in the Decade Following Unification* (Notre Dame, 2006) and numerous articles in this and other journals including *Party Politics, Democratization, The Journal of Legislative Studies, Communist and Post-Communist Studies*, and *German Politics*. Davidson-Schmich serves on the Executive Board of the German Studies Association and the Executive Committee of the International Political Science Association's Research Committee of Legislative Specialists. She has received grants from the Fulbright Program, the Council for European Studies, and the Alexander-von-Humboldt Foundation.

FRANK DECKER is a Professor in Comparative Government and Politics at the Institute for Political Science and Sociology of the University of Bonn, where he has been teaching and researching since November 2001. He studied Political Science, Economics, Journalism and Public Law at the

Universities of Mainz and Hamburg. After gaining his doctorate in 1993 on the failure of government in environmental protection (*Umweltschutz und Staatsversagen*), he completed his Habilitation in 1999 with the subsequent publication of a monograph on right-wing populism in Western democracies (*Parteien unter Druck*). Both were completed at the Helmut Schmidt University of Hamburg, where he was a research assistant from 1989 to 2001 at the Institute for Political Science. He has published numerous articles, chapters and several books on parties and party systems, institutional reforms, federalism, and democracy in the European Union.

CHARLES LEES is Senior Lecturer in Pol.itics at the Department of Politics, University of Sheffield. He is currently Managing Editor of the *Journal of Common Market Studies* and a member of the steering committee of the World Democratic Forum. He has written extensively on comparative politics, policy, and methodology as well as providing research and advice for organizations such as the Australian Labor Party, the Green Party of Aotearoa New Zealand, and the Scottish Executive.

ANDREA NÜSSER is a PhD student in Political Science at the University of British Columbia, Canada and completed her MA at Simon Fraser University. Her primary research interests are in comparative political behavior, with a concentration on public opinion, political identity and political participation in North America and Europe.

WILLIAM PATERSON is Honorary Professor for German and European Politics at the Aston Centre for Europe, Aston University, Birmingham (UK). Professor Paterson is Chairman of the German British Forum, a Fellow of the Royal Society of Edinburgh (1994), an Academician of the Academy of Social Sciences (2000), recipient of the lifetime achievement awards of the Association for the Study of German Politics (2004) and the University Association for Contemporary European Studies (2007). He was Director of the Institute for German Studies at the University of Birmingham from 1994 to 2008. To date, Professor Paterson has published, edited and co-edited twenty-eight books and over 140 articles and book chapters.

HARTWIG PAUTZ obtained his PhD from Glasgow Caledonian University in 2008, and is a currently a lecturer there. His research has discussed the role of think-tanks for policy-making in the UK and Germany and has followed the programmatic development of the German Social Democratic Party. Earlier, he published the first encompassing analysis of the 'Leitkultur debate' of 2000.

THOMAS SAALFELD is Professor of Political Science at the University of Bamberg. He is the Managing Editor of *German Politics*. His research interests include the comparative study of coalition duration in mature European democracies, coalition governance in Germany, political representation in the British and German parliaments, and the German party system. He has published articles in the *European Journal of Political Research*, *German Politics*, *International Studies Quarterly*, *The Journal of Legislative Studies*, *Parliamentary Affairs*, *Politics*, *Rivista Italiana di Scienza Politica*, *West European Politics* and *Zeitschrift für Parlamentsfragen*.

JAMES SLOAM is Senior Lecturer in Politics and Co-Director of the Centre for European Politics at Royal Holloway, University of London. His research focuses on German politics, political parties, and youth participation in democracy. Recent publications include (edited with Alister Miskimmon and William Paterson) *Germany's Gathering Crisis: the 2005 Federal Election and the Grand Coalition* (Basingstoke, 2008).

JARED SONNICKSEN is a Research and Teaching Assistant at the Institute for Political Science and Sociology of the University of Bonn. After completing his Bachelor of Arts in Political Science and German at Wabash College, he attended the University of Bonn as a Fulbright Scholar and completed his M.A. in Political Science there in 2003. He has been teaching at the University of Bonn since 2004 and is working on his doctoral thesis on EU reform and the limits and possibilities of democratization.

JAN TECHAU joined the NATO Defense College's Research Division in February 2010. He was the Director of the Alfred von Oppenheim Center for European Policy Studies at the German Council on Foreign Relations (DGAP) in Berlin from 2006 to 2010. From 2001 to 2006, he served at the German Ministry of Defence's Press and Information Department. Techau is an Associate Scholar at the Center for European Policy Analysis (CEPA) in Washington, D.C., and an Associate Fellow at both the German Council on Foreign Relations and at the American Institute for Contemporary German Studies (AICGS) in Washington, D.C.

STEVEN WELDON is Assistant Professor of Political Science at Simon Fraser University, Canada. His research focuses on comparative political behavior, political parties, and European integration. His recent articles have appeared in the *American Journal of Political Science*, *British Journal of Political Science*, *Party Politics*, and *West European Politics*.

$\mathcal{I}$NDEX

● ● ● ● ● ● ● ● ● ● ● ● ● ● ● ●

www.ingramcontent.com/pod-product-compliance
Lightning Source LLC
Chambersburg PA
CBHW072123020426
42334CB00018B/1694